A HISTORY OF THE 2nd LANCERS
(GARDNER'S HORSE)

A HISTORY OF THE 2ND LANCERS (GARDNER'S HORSE)

FROM 1809 TO 1922

COMPILED BY

CAPTAIN D. E. WHITWORTH

The Naval & Military Press Ltd

❖

Reproduced by kind permission of the Central Library,
Royal Military Academy, Sandhurst

Published by
The Naval & Military Press Ltd
Unit 10, Ridgewood Industrial Park,
Uckfield, East Sussex,
TN22 5QE England
Tel: +44 (0) 1825 749494
Fax: +44 (0) 1825 765701
www.naval-military-press.com

© The Naval & Military Press Ltd 2006

CONTENTS

PART I

1809 TO 1914

PART II

1914 to 1922

LIST OF MAPS

DESIGNATED IN

1809
LIEUT.-COL. GARDNER'S CORPS OF IRREGULAR
HORSE

1823
2ND REGIMENT OF LOCAL HORSE

1840
2ND BENGAL IRREGULAR CAVALRY

1861
2ND REGIMENT OF BENGAL CAVALRY

1890
2ND REGIMENT OF BENGAL LANCERS

1901
2ND BENGAL LANCERS

1903
2ND LANCERS (GARDNER'S HORSE)

1922
(*After amalgamation with the 4th Cavalry*)
2ND LANCERS (GARDNER'S HORSE)

PREFACE

In 1909, on the occasion of the Regimental Centenary, a history in extremely brief form of the Regiment since the date of its raising was produced. This is now reprinted as Part I of this history. It was felt at the time and always will be felt and regretted that the history was altogether an insufficient record of the hundred years of regimental service and of the many campaigns which the regimental battle honours show. It was, however, the best that could be put together from the meagre " Digest of Regimental Services " and a few other sources at the disposal of the compiler, Major-General (then Major) W. B. James, C.B., C.I.E., M.V.O. From 1909, however, it was resolved that a better record should be kept, and this was done until the Regiment left India in 1914 to join the army in France.

The record of the doings of the Regiment during its absence from India from 1914 to 1920, which forms Part II, was compiled from the Regimental War Diary, supplemented by personal reminiscences and recollections. The War Diary, after the first flush of enthusiasm of the beginning of the war, became a very bald and stilted epitome of events, compiled as it was by a succession of adjutants, overworked, and often bored. The first source of inspiration being thus of a somewhat sparing and telegraphic though accurate nature, and the second, the human memory, being necessarily vague, omissions and inaccuracies are inevitable and it is felt that no apology is due for them.

Records of this type must needs be written for two classes of readers, those who were there, and those who were not. Here it is intended to cater principally for the latter class, hoping that the former will find enough to refresh their memories of events, of which the earlier, even at the time of writing, are sufficiently distant to tax the memory in recounting them with any accuracy.

HAKONE,   D.E.W.
  JAPAN.
  1922.

PART I

1809 TO 1914

CHAPTER I

A Brief History of the 2nd Lancers (Gardner's Horse)

THE Regiment was raised by Major William Linnæus Gardner[1] for police and revenue duties in the ceded and conquered provinces between the Ganges and the Jamna.[2] *1809. 12th May. Raising of the Regiment.*

Lieutenant-Colonel Gardner's Corps of Irregular Horse, *Title.* soon abbreviated to " Gardner's Horse."

Almost exclusively Muhammadans of Hindustan with a *Composition.* few Brahmans, Rajputs and inferior Hindus.

Lances, shields, tulwars and long matchlocks. *Arms.*

Emerald green alkhalak with silver lace. Red pyjamas *Uniform.* (subsequently changed to " Multani Mutti ").

Original Head-dress, Persian " Kizil Bash," subsequently changed to a cloth cap and then to a red pagri.

Saddlery—Native " charjamas."

Pay Code of 1810.

					Rs.	
1	Commanding Officer	..	..	..	300	*Establishment and pay.*
1	Officer	..	..	..	150	
1	Adjutant	..	..	..	150	
6	Resaldars	..	..	each	70	
6	Naib-Resaldars	..	..	,,	40	
6	Jemadars	..	..	,,	35	
6	Kote-Dafadars	..	..	.,	30	
30	Dafadars	..	..	,,	25	
6	Standard Bearers	..	..	,,	25	
6	Drummers	..	..	,,	25	
6	Vakils	..	..	,,	17	
6	Bhistis	..	..	,,	4	
600	Troopers	..	..	,,	20	
1	Writer	..	..	..	20	
1	Nakib (Herald)	..	..	..	40	
	Allowance for ball, powder and matches, per Risala		..	..	100	
	Allowance for medicines, per Risala			..	100	

[1] See Appendix I.
[2] Resolution of the Governor-General in the Judicial Department, dated 12th May, 1809.

Risala.

A " Risala " subsequently consisted of 100 Native ranks. *viz.*, 1 Resaldar or Resaidar, 1 Naib-Resaldar, 1 Jemadar, 1 Kote-Dafadar, 9 Dafadars, 1 Standard Bearer, 1 Drummer or Trumpeter, 85 Sowars (Troopers).

First Stations. 1810.

Farukhabad.   Mainpuri.

Moved to Khasgunj, where Headquarters were established (Khasgunj being Colonel Gardner's own estate).

1814-1815. Nepal War.

A detachment, including several Native Officers, served in Kumaon during the Nepal War[1] in the column commanded by Colonel Gardner for the reduction of Almora, the Gurkha stronghold.

A detachment, 2 Risalas strong, served under Cornet John Bennet Hearsey (afterwards Sir John Hearsey, K.C.B.), with the Force on the Eastern Frontier under General Marley against the Gurkhas.

1814. 25th Novemb.

This detachment was present at the capture of Barhawa and then a small portion of it was left to form part of the garrison of Parsa-garhi (Goorpershad).

1815. 1st January.

The Gurkhas attacked Parsa-garhi, the garrison of which held out well, but after expending all its ammunition was overpowered and lost 121 killed, 134 wounded, and 3 missing.

Cornet Hearsey, on hearing of this disaster, obtained permission to try and bring in the wounded.   With 40 of his men he proceeded to Parsa-garhi and succeeded in bringing in the body of Major Sibley, the Commandant, and the severely wounded, and covered the retreat of the remainder.

19th Feby.

The detachment distinguished itself at the action of Pirari, under Cornet Hearsey who, after the capture of the place, collected 30 or 40 men and, gallantly followed by a Standard Bearer named Dilawar Khan, charged the retreating enemy and killed the Gurkha leader Bhagwant Singh Thappa.   Cornet Hearsey was slightly and Dilawar Khan severely wounded. Dilawar Khan was promoted to the rank of Dafadar; Cornet Hearsey and the detachment received the thanks of the Army Commander in Army Orders and the affair was mentioned by the Commander-in-Chief in General Orders.[2]

---

[1] Papers respecting the Nepal War.   Page 332.

[2] Papers respecting the Nepal War, pp. 567–586.
Supplement to London Gazette, 14th November, 1815.
"The Hearseys," by Colonel Hugh Pearse, D.S.O.

The Regiment was quartered at Khasgunj during these *1815-16-17.* years.

The Regiment joined the Army at Agra under Major- *1817-1818.* General Sir Rufane Donkin, and was posted to the right *Pindari-Mahratta* Division.[1] It took a conspicuous part in the rout of the Pindari *War.* force under Karim Khan at Kalana, besides making many long harassing marches in pursuit of the enemy and being present at several minor affairs.

For meritorious service the Regiment was placed on the *1817.* footing of a Corps of Irregular Horse. *20th June.*

The Regiment was quartered at Khasgunj and Bareilly. *1818-1824.*

Became 2nd Regiment of Local Horse. *1823.*

In the autumn of this year the Regiment marched, 621 *1824.* sabres strong, to join the force on the Eastern Frontier under General Morrison for the invasion of Arracan. The Regiment marched 2,000 miles without losing a single man by desertion, and during the campaign showed striking loyalty and gained much credit for serving cheerfully on foot after the loss of the greater part of its horses. *1825.*

The force left Chittagong. *1st January.*

Action of Padha Hills. *26th March.*

Action of Mahati. *27th March.*

Capture of Arracan. *1st April.*

For Extract from the Despatch of General Morrison, *vide* Appendix I.

The Regiment started on its return march to India and *1825.* was quartered at Bareilly. *November.*

G.G.O. 11th April 1826 authorised the Regiment to bear the *1826.* word " Arracan " on its standards and appointments.

Lances were abolished for sowars but retained for Non- *1827.* Commissioned Officers.

Colonel Gardner relinquished command of the Regiment on *1828.* retirement. *February.*

Lieutenant (afterwards Captain) R. F. Dougan, 10th Light *15th Feby.* Cavalry, appointed Commandant.

Captain Dougan died at Mussoorie while on leave on 30th July 1829.

---

[1] Mill and Wilson's *History,* Vol. III, p. 180, and Prinsep's *Transactions,* Vol. II, pp. 115–116.

6 A HISTORY OF THE 2ND LANCERS

1829. *March.*	Major J. B. Hearsey (afterwards Sir J. Hearsey, K.C.B.) appointed Commandant. At this time, owing to the enormous loss of horses during the Arracan Campaign, the Regiment was not very well mounted.
1829. *November.*	The Regiment left Bareilly by route march for Neemuch and arrived there in December.
1831–1832.	The Regiment was distributed in detachments in the provinces of Malwa, Kotah, Boondee and Meywar.
1833.	Marched to Saugor *via* Narsinghpur and Burseeah.
1835. *July 26th.*	Death of Colonel Gardner at Khasgunj.
1836.	Moved from Saugor to Bareilly.
1839. *12th August.*	Major Hearsey relinquished command on promotion to Lieutenant-Colonel.
3rd Septr.	Captain C. O'Hara, 4th Light Cavalry, appointed Commandant.
Autumn.	Moved from Bareilly to Saugor.
1840.	The Regiment became the 2nd Bengal Irregular Cavalry.
1840–42.	During these years the Regiment was almost continuously employed in suppressing disturbances in Bundelkhand.
1842. *12th Septr.*	Captain Joseph Leeson appointed Commandant in succession to Captain O'Hara.
1845. Sept.	The Regiment marched from Saugor to Amballa.
1846. *1st Sikh War.*	The Regiment originally formed part of the 3rd Cavalry Brigade.
10th Feby. *Sobraon.*	Headquarters and right wing present at the battle of Sobraon[1] as part of the 2nd Cavalry Brigade. Captain Leeson mentioned in Despatches. After the war the right wing was quartered at Lahore and the left wing at Tulwandi near Harighat. The Regiment was authorised to bear the word " Sobraon "[2] on its standards and appointments.
December.	Whole Regiment concentrated at Makhur. Percussion Carbines replaced matchlocks.
1847. Nov.	The Regiment moved to Hoshiarpur.

[1] Sir Hugh Gough's Despatches, dated 13th February 1846.
G.G.O. 14th February 1846.
G.O.C.C. 3rd March 1846.

[2] G.G.O. 12th August 1846.
G.O.C.C. 18th August 1846.

Death of Captain Leeson.

Captain George Jackson appointed Commandant.

October 14th.—The Regiment under Captain Jackson was present at the capture of Fort Rangar Nagal[1] and lost—killed, one man, one horse ; wounded, one man, two horses.

November 23rd.—Capture of Fort Kalalwala, Cavalry[2] covering the advance of the guns.

November 30th.—Action of Nerote.

Twenty men under Naib-Resaldar Mirza Haidar Beg pursued and routed a raiding party of 100 of the enemy,. killing eight and wounding several, with the loss of four men only wounded on our side.

Naib-Resaldar Mirza Haidar Beg and Sowar Karamat Ali greatly distinguished themselves in this affair.

Captain Jackson volunteered for dismounted service[3] and the Regiment acted thus in the action of the Heights of Dala against the Sikh leader Ram Singh.

The Regiment was authorised to bear the word " Punjab "[4] on its standards and appointments.

The Regiment returned to Hoshiarpur.

The Regiment moved to Peshawar.

October.—A detachment, 320 strong, took part in Sir Colin Campbell's operations against the Mohmands.[5]

The detachment posted at Shabkadr and Matta furnished strong patrols nightly on the frontier.

December 7th.—A patrol attacked and routed 500 of the enemy near Banda, losing two men killed and two men and two horses wounded.

December 8th.—The Regiment was attacked near Matta in great force by the enemy, but, with the assistance of a detach-

1848.
15th Feby.
24th Feby.
2nd Sikh War.
Operations in the Jullundur Doab.

1849.
January.

1849.
Spring.
1850.
January.
Operations against the Mohmands.

---

[1] Papers relating to the Punjab, pp. 417-418.

[2] Papers relating to the Punjab, p. 464.

[3] Papers relating to the Punjab, pp. 565-567.

[4] G.G.O. 2nd April 1849.
G.O.C.C. 5th April 1849.
Camp Ferozepore.
G.G.O. No. 803 of 7th October 1853.
G.O.C.C. 28th October 1853.

[5] Paget and Mason's Record of Expeditions against the N.-W. Frontier Tribes, pp. 232-238.

ment of Guides and some Artillery, drove off the enemy.[1] Captain Jackson was mentioned in despatches for his excellent management of this affair.

1852.
January 3rd.

A Troop, 43 strong, under Lieut. W. T. Hughes, charged and routed 50 Mohmands near Panjpao, killing 15, and losing one man killed and three wounded.

Operations
against the
Utman
Khels.
May 11th.

One squadron took part in the destruction of the Nawardan villages near Abazai, and in the action of Prangarh on May 13th.[2]

May 18th.
Operations
against the
Ranizais.

One squadron, 79 strong, under the personal command of Captain Jackson, was present at the storming and capture of the village of Shakot.[3]

1852.

The Regiment returned to Hoshiarpur.

1855.
1855–56.

The Regiment moved down country and took part in the suppression of the Sonthal revolt.[4]

1857.

Early in the year the Regiment marched back to the Punjab to Gurdaspur, in which district it was employed throughout the Mutiny, retaining its arms and remaining untainted and unaffected by the storm around it. It was attached to Major Patton's Moveable Column in the Gugaira district and took part in several small affairs.

Dafadar Mansabdar Khan, Sowars Moghal Beg, Bhup Singh and Ghulam Khan received the Order of Merit for gallantry in an action against the mutineers in the swamps of the Gurdaspur district on the 3rd August.[5]

Colonel Jackson, hearing that a party of mutineers were hiding near Gurdaspur, proceeded with a detachment of the Regiment to capture it. On approaching the village in which the mutineers had been located, Colonel Jackson's horse fell in a swamp and his detachment was much broken up owing to the difficult nature of the ground. The mutineers seeing this attacked Colonel Jackson with their swords as he lay on the ground. The above-mentioned men dashed to his assistance and Dafadar Mansabdar Khan and Sowar Moghal Beg threw

---

[1] Paget and Mason's Record of Expeditions against the N.-W. Frontier Tribes, pp. 235–236.

[2] Paget and Mason, pp. 215–219.

[3] Paget and Mason, pp. 198–201.

[4] Trotter's *History of the British Empire in India*, pp. 368–374.

[5] Punjab Mutiny Report.

themselves on Colonel Jackson's body and shielded him from the sword cuts, while the rest of the detachment drove the mutineers off. Moghal Beg was dangerously wounded, but eventually recovered. Dafadar Mansabdar Khan was promoted to be Jemadar and the other three men were promoted to be Dafadars.

The Regiment moved to Peshawar.

1859.
1st Novr.

The Regiment became the 2nd Bengal Cavalry[1] with an establishment of 499 all native ranks (13 Native Officers, 54 Dafadars, 6 Standard Bearers, 6 Trumpeters and 420 Sowars).

1861.

The Regiment left Peshawar by route march for Amritsar.

1862.
Feby. 11th.

Arrived Amritsar ; detachment at Gurdaspur.

March 13th.

The Regiment became a " General Mixture Regiment "[2] and was composed of equal parts of Muhammadans, Dogras, Sikhs, Jats, Rajputs, Brahmans and Mahrattas, and its strength was reduced to 463 all native ranks (Sowars 384).

1863.
January 8th.

The Regiment moved by forced marches to the Peshawar valley and was divided between the posts of Shabkadr, Abazai and Michni.

1863.
October.

An attack on Michni driven off without loss by the Regiment under Colonel Jackson.

7th Decr.

A large force of between 5,000 and 6,000 Mohmands attacked Shabkadr and was defeated and driven off, the Regiment losing 8 men wounded.

1864.
2nd Jany.

The late Resaldar Narain Singh, who was then awaiting enlistment in the Regiment, also displayed great gallantry by seizing a sword and running on foot with the mounted men when they charged the enemy.

The India Medal was granted for these operations but was not issued till 1876.

After the operations the Regiment returned to Amritsar and on November 22nd left by route march for Deoli arriving there on December 30th, detachments being quartered at Erinpura, Saugor and Jhansi.

1864.

Standard Bearers were abolished.[3]

1864.

---

[1] G.O.G.G. No. 494, 31st May 1861.

[2] Govt. Letter No. 671, 31st January 1863.

[3] Adjutant-General's Circular No. 62, 29th June.

1870. *16th Feby.*	The Regiment arrived at Bareilly and a detachment was stationed at Moradabad.
11th Feby.	Colonel Jackson resigned the command of the Regiment while on leave in England. Lieut.-Colonel Wilkinson, 14th European Light Cavalry, assumed command.
1873.	From November to February 1874 the Regiment was in camp at Lucknow acting as escort to the Viceroy and taking part in a Camp of Exercise.
1874. *24th March.*	The Regiment marched to Fyzabad, one squadron going on to Segowlie.
1875. *January.*	The Regiment marched from Fyzabad to Segowlie.
9th Feby.	Arrived Segowlie.

The medal to commemorate the Grand Durbar held at Delhi for the proclamation of Her Majesty Queen Victoria as Empress of India was presented to Dafadar (afterwards Resaldar) Ghulam Muhammad Khan as the most deserving Non-Commissioned Officer in the Regiment.

At the Assault-at-Arms at Delhi Dafadar (afterwards Resaldar-Major) Nizam Ali Khan won the tent-pegging for the Indian Cavalry after taking sixteen pegs consecutively.

1876. *8th January.*	One squadron arrived at Barrackpur.
1880. *31st March.*	Colonel Wilkinson relinquished command.
1st April.	Lieut.-Colonel Campbell assumed command.
7th Decr.	Left Segowlie.
1881. *January 6th.*	Arrived Lucknow.
12th March.	The squadron from Barrackpur rejoined.
1882. *3rd August,* *Egyptian* *Campaign.*	Orders having been received for the Regiment to proceed to Egypt to take part in the Egyptian campaign, the right wing, strength 5 British Officers (Lieut.-Colonel F. Knowles, Major C. T. M. Higginson, Captain M. K. Martin, Lieut. and Adjutant C. J. Robarts and Surgeon-Major F. Parsons), 7 Native Officers, 200 Non-Commissioned Officers and men, 182 Followers, 215 Horses and 117 Ponies left by train for Bombay.
4th August.	Left wing, strength 4 British Officers (Major H. C. Kemble, Major C. E. Salkeld, Lieut. St. G. L. Steele, Lieut. V. M. Stockley), 5 Native Officers, 219 Non-Commissioned Officers and Men, 179 Followers, 231 Horses and 117 Ponies by train to Bombay.

The Regiment embarked in Transports as follows :— *August 8th to 19th.*
Right Wing—Tenasserim, Iris, Dryburgh-Abbey.
Left Wing—Ethiopia, Hampshire, Norfolk.

The Regiment disembarked at Ismailia, being the first *August 24th to September 6th.* regiment of the Indian Contingent to do so.

The Tenasserim was the first Transport to arrive and Colonel Campbell came on board on rejoining from leave to England. The men and horses swam ashore and the 2nd Troop immediately formed two picquets to the west of Ismailia.

The Headquarters and 2nd Troop joined the camp of the *25th August.* Army near Kassasin, where the remainder of the Regiment joined as it disembarked.

The 2nd Squadron under Captain Martin took part in the *8th Septr.* reconnaissance in force under General Graham.

The battle of Kassasin—The Regiment formed the 2nd *9th Septr.* Cavalry Brigade with the 6th Bengal Cavalry and the 13th Bengal Lancers. The Regiment was employed dismounted during the action.

The Regiment was commended in Brigade Orders for *10th Septr.* coolness and gallantry.

Preparations for the advance on Tel-el-Kebir.—Colonel *September 11th, 12th.* Campbell, through ill-health, was obliged to return to England and the Command devolved upon Colonel Knowles.

The battle of Tel-el-Kebir. The 2nd Cavalry Brigade *13th Septr.* moved round the left of the enemy's position, the Regiment being on the extreme right of the Brigade, and converted the retreat of the Egyptians into a headlong rout, capturing a train full of fugitives.

Jemadar Fahme Khan was slightly wounded by the fragment of a shell.

The 2nd Cavalry Brigade continued the pursuit and reached Belbais, a distance of forty miles from the field, at 2 p.m.

The Regiment formed the advanced guard of the Brigade, the left flank patrol being commanded by Dafadar Ali Muhammad Khan (now Resaldar-Major and Sirdar Bahadur).

The baggage animals did not reach Belbais that night and the men and horses were without food or forage (except what they could gather from the fields).

The Brigade continued the advance and reached the out- *14th Septr.* skirts of Cairo, a distance of 30 miles at 3 p.m., the 3rd Squadron under Major Kemble having been detached from Belbais to Fehm-ul-Behr from which place it rejoined on the 4th of October.

17th Septr.   March past of the Army before the Khedive of Egypt.

6th October.   The Regiment left Cairo by route march for Suez—a distance of 131 miles—arriving there on the morning of the 12th, the embarkation on the Transports Duke of Argyll, Montreal, Hampshire, Norfolk and Sirdhana being completed by 1 p.m. The following proceeded to England from Suez as representatives of the Regiment and were decorated by Her Majesty Queen Victoria, Empress of India, with the medals for the Egyptian Campaign, and the two Native Officers received the 2nd Class of the Order of British India :—

Jemadar Narain Singh (who ran with the Regiment at Shabkadr).

Jemadar Muhammad Raza Khan.

Dafadar (now Resaldar-Major) Ali Muhammad Khan.

Sowar Ghulam Hazrat Khan.

Sowar Wariam Singh.

28th Octr.   The Regiment completed the disembarkation at Bombay and reached Lucknow on the 5th November.

The following Officers were mentioned in Despatches :—

Lt.-Colonel F. Knowles. .   Received 3rd class Order of Medjidieh.

Major H. C. Kemble   . .   Received 4th class Order of Osmanieh.

Capt. M. K. Martin   . .   . .

And Resaldar-Major Muhammad Yusuf Khan received the 5th Class Order of Medjidieh.

Establishment increased to 550 all native ranks.[1]

1883.
14th Decr.   H.R.H. The Duke of Connaught presented the Egyptian War Medal with clasp for Tel-el-Kebir and the Khedive's Bronze Star to the Native Officers and regretted that time did not admit of his doing so to the whole Regiment. H.R.H. also expressed his gratification at the smartness of the escorts on duty during his stay at Lucknow.

The Regiment was permitted to bear the words " Egypt 1882 " and " Tel-el-Kebir " on its standards, colours and appointments for distinguished and gallant conduct.[2]

[1] G.O. 210 of 1882.   [2] G.G.O. 341 of 15th June 1883.

The composition of the Regiment was changed to class troops. *1884. 1st October.*

The Regiment left Lucknow by route march for Saugor. *15th Octr.*

Arrived Saugor ; one troop being detached to Sutna and one troop to Jubbulpore. *20th Novr.*

A 4th Squadron (Jats) was added to the Regiment, the total strength of which was raised to 625 all native ranks.[1] *1885.*

Colonel Campbell relinquished command. *1886. 19th Feby.*

Lieut.-Colonel Clifford assumed command on appointment from the 9th Bengal Lancers. *20th Feby.*

This year the uniform of the Regiment was changed from the original green with red facings to dark blue with light blue facings. *1888.*

The Regiment left Saugor for Allahabad by route march. *15th Octr.*

Arrived Allahabad. *12th Novr.*

The 4th (Jat) Squadron in Calcutta for escort duty under Lieut. James. The Squadron did very well in the Calcutta Assault-at-Arms ; Lance-Dafadar Ram Kala being Best Man-at-Arms and Lieut. James winning the tent-pegging for Officers. *1889. October to April 1890*

Extract from the remarks on the inspection of the Regiment 1889-90 by H. E. Sir F. Roberts, V.C., C.-in-C. in India :— *18th June.*

" In consequence of the general all round efficiency of the 2nd Bengal Cavalry, I have obtained the sanction of the Government of India to its being armed with lances."

Directs that the Regiment be armed with lances and be in future designated " The 2nd Bengal Lancers."[2]

The Regiment attended the Cavalry Camps of Exercise at Aligarh and Meerut, during which a march of some 96 miles was performed in two days, the Regimental transport keeping up well. *1891. October to 1892. February.*

The following increases of pay were sanctioned by Government :—Sowars from Rs. 27 to Rs. 31 ; Dafadars from Rs. 38 to Rs. 42. *April.*

Colonel R. M. Clifford appointed Assistant Adjutant-General. *2nd May.*

Major Martin assumed command.

[1] Indian Army Circular 1885 clause 131.
[2] G.O. 67 of 1890.

12th May. Major Martin died from the effects of a fall from his horse while pigsticking.

2nd June. Lieut-Colonel F. C. Burton, 1st Bengal Cavalry, assumed command.

1893.
January 23rd. The Regiment left Allahabad for Bareilly by route march.

18th Feby. Arrived Bareilly.

April. Martini-Henry Carbines replaced Snider Carbines.

November The 3rd (Sikh) Squadron under Lieut. M. E. Willoughby
24th to was employed in aid of the Civil power against dacoits in the
December Budaon district, and after a march of 78 miles in 28 hours
2nd. surrounded and captured the dacoits. Lieut. Willoughby received the thanks of the Lieutenant-Governor of the North-West Provinces.

1895. At the B.P.R.A. Meeting, No. 757 Sowar Husain Bakhsh won the Viceroy's Silver Medal.

1896. The Magdala Gold Medal for the best shot in the Indian Army was won by Dafadar (now Resaidar) Bhajju Singh[1] with a score of 98 points out of a possible 105. Dafadar (now Jemadar) Abdul Samad Khan won the Viceroy's Silver Medal.

1897. Lieut.-Colonel C. H. V. Garbett appointed Commandant
11th July. in succession to Colonel Burton, appointed Assistant Adjutant-General, Rawalpindi District.

August. Resaldar-Major Ali Muhammad Khan proceeded to England to attend the Jubilee of Her Majesty Queen Victoria, Empress of India, and was decorated by Her Majesty at Buckingham Palace with the Jubilee Medal.

He received the 2nd Class of the Order of British India shortly after his return to India.

The Magdala Gold Medal for the best shot in the Indian Army was won by Kote-Dafadar Buta Singh with a score of 95 out of a possible 105.[2]

1898.
21st Jany. The Regiment left Bareilly by route march for Meerut.
3rd Feby. Arrived Meerut.

At the B.P.R.A. Meeting Dafadar (now Jemadar) Abdul Samad Khan won the Viceroy's Silver Medal and No. 757 Sowar Hussain Bakhsh won the Viceroy's Bronze Medal.

1899.
January The Regiment attended the Cavalry concentration at
2nd to 16th. Delhi forming part of the Northern Force.

---

[1] G.O.C.C. 49 of 25th January 1897.
[2] G.O.C.C. 218 of 30th March 1898.

The Regiment left Meerut by route march for Kohat.   *25th Jany.*

Arrived Jullundur, where the depôt was left.   *17th Feby.*

Arrived at Kohat.   Headquarters at Kohat, detachments *13th March.* at Ustarzai, Hangu, Thal and Parachinar.

Left Kohat.   By rail from Kushalgarh.   *19th Decr.*

Arrived Jullundur.   *22nd Decr.*

At the B.P.R.A. meeting at Meerut this year Jemadar Kirpa Ram won the Viceroy's Silver Medal and Dafadar Bhagwan Singh the Viceroy's Bronze Medal.

Resaldar-Major Ali Muhammad Khan received the 1st *1901.* Class Order of British India and Resaldar Kala Singh the *2nd Novr.* 2nd Class.

Lieut.-Colonel K. S. Davison appointed Commandant.   *17th Novr.*

Lee-Metford Carbines replaced Martini-Henri Carbines.

Left Jullundur by route march for Nowshera.

Arrived Nowshera.   Detachments at Dargai, Malakhand, *1902.* Chakdara and Khar and, for three months, at Peshawar.   *January 4th.*

Eusufzai Manoeuvres.   *January*

Lee-Enfield Carbines replaced Lee-Metford Carbines.   *22nd to 30th.*

Left Nowshera by route march for Fyzabad.

Arrived Fyzabad, having thus completed five moves, representing a distance of over 2,300 miles, in five years.

The following represented the Regiment at the Imperial *1903.* Durbar held at Delhi in honour of the Coronation of His *January.* Majesty King Edward VII, Emperor of India :—

Resaldar Kala Singh, Bahadur.

Kote-Dafadar Hasan Razza Khan.

Dafadar (now Jemadar) Suraj Singh.

Sowar Sarup Singh.

Thirty squares (750 acres) of land at Sargodha, Punjab, *November.* were allotted to the Regiment for horse breeding and rearing purposes.

The designation of the Regiment was changed to " 2nd *1903.* Lancers (Gardner's Horse) ".[1]

Resaldar-Major Ali Muhammad Khan proceeded to England as one of the Orderlies to H.M. the King-Emperor of India and was decorated by His Majesty with the 5th Class of the Royal Victorian Order.

[1] I.A.O. 181.

Lee-Enfield Rifles replaced Lee-Enfield Carbines, and are carried in the Paterson equipment : 90 rounds of ball ammunition are carried on the horses in bandoliers and 30 rounds on the men in bandoliers.

1904. Resaldar Kala Singh, Bahadur, proceeded to England as one of the Orderlies to H.M. the King-Emperor and was decorated with the 5th Class of the Royal Victorian Order.

1907.
November. A special train conveying a detachment of the Regiment from Calcutta to Fyzabad collided with a goods train near Ishapur and was derailed, four horse trucks being overturned. Sowar Bhagwan Singh, who was buried under horses and badly injured, was gallantly rescued by the following men from a truck which was balanced on the wheels on one side only and was in imminent danger of overturning.

Kote-Dafadar Nidhan Singh.
Dafadar Dasondha Singh.
Lance-Dafadar Ganda Singh.
Sowar Atar Singh.

Resaldar Kala Singh, Bahadur, was granted a Jagir, value Rs. 600 per annum.

1907.
January. A detachment at Calcutta under command of Captain Pritchard took part and did very well in the Minto Fête Assault-at-Arms, the trick riding being especially noticeable.

H. E. the C.-in-C. (Lord Kitchener) stated in a letter from his Military Secretary that it was the smartest and best mounted detachment he had ever seen in Calcutta.

1907. At the B.P.R.A. Meeting, No. 1482 Lance-Dafadar Muhammad Ghani Khan won the medal for the best aggregate score, cavalry and artillery.

1908.
1st May. Major F. H. B. Commeline appointed Commandant in succession to Colonel K. S. Davison, C.B., appointed to the command of a Brigade.

9th Novr. Left Fyzabad by route march for Saugor.

14th Decr. Arrived Saugor.

1909.
1st January. An increase of Rs. 3 pay was granted to the rank and file. The pay of Native Officers was raised to the highest of each rank, *viz.*, Resaldars Rs. 250, Resaidars Rs. 150, Jemadars Rs. 80.

1909.
May 12th. The 100th Anniversary of the raising of the Regiment.

At the present date the establishment and pay of the Regiment are :—

		Rs.	
1	Commandant	700	
1	2nd-in-Command and Squadron Commander	300	
3	Squadron Commanders	250	Exclusive of
1	Adjutant	250	pay of rank.
1	Quarter-Master	200	
5	Squadron Officers	150	
1	Medical Officer	600	
1	Resaldar-Major	300	
3	Resaldars	250	
4	Resaidars	150	
1	Woordie-Major	120	
8	Jemadars	80	
8	Kote-Dafadars	54	
38	Dafadars	45	
32	Lance-Dafadars	40	
58	Acting Lance-Dafadars	34	
1	Trumpet-Major (Dafadar)	50	
8	Trumpeters	41	
1	Farrier-Major (Dafadar)	45	
16	Farriers	34	
8	Camel Sowars	34	
419	Sowars	34	
25	Barghirs	16/6	
4	Ward Orderlies	16/6	
613	Horses.		
8	Camels.		
315	Mules.		

At present the Regiment is mounted on 488 Australian horses, 125 Country-bred horses and 8 camels.

Lee-Enfield Rifle replaced by Short Lee-Enfield Rifle.   *1911. Sept. 12th.*

c

APPENDIX I

BEING EXTRACTS FROM A SHORT ACCOUNT OF GARDNER OF
GARDNER'S HORSE

By COLONEL H. W. PEARSE, D.S.O.

Published in the Cavalry Journal of January 1908.

GARDNER was born in the year 1770. His grandfather, the
son of a Mr. Gardner of Coleraine, was Lieutenant-Colonel of
the 11th Dragoons. The Colonel's son, Valentine Gardner,
a Major in the 16th Regiment, married Alicia, daughter of
Colonel Livingstone, of Livingstone Manor, New York, and
their eldest son was William Linnæus Gardner. Major
Valentine Gardner's younger brother Alan earned distinction
in the Royal Navy, and was raised to the Peerage as Lord
Gardner.

William Linnæus Gardner was educated in France, and, as
was then usual, received an Ensign's commission at the age of
thirteen, his first regiment being the 89th Foot. In 1789 he
was an Ensign in the 74th Highlanders, but in October of that
year was promoted Lieutenant in the 52nd. Gardner first smelt
powder in France, for in December 1793 he took part in the
expedition to Brittany under Major-General Lord Moira, a
commander whom he was subsequently to serve in very
different circumstances.

In 1794 Gardner became a Captain in the 30th Regiment,
then stationed in India, and, exchanging at once to half
pay, embarked on his remarkable career as an adventurer.
Eminently fitted for success, he had no difficulty in obtaining
employment with Tukaji Holkar, one of the great Mahratta
tributary princes of the moribund Moghul Empire. Tukaji
died soon after his engagement of Gardner and the new chief,
Jaswant Rao, commissioned Gardner to raise and command a
brigade of regular infantry, at the head of which Gardner
took part in the battle of Ujain, in which Holkar defeated
Sindhia, a rival Mahratta prince. In October 1799, however,
he sustained a crushing defeat outside Indore, the chief city
of his dominions, which fell into the hands of Sindhia. Most

of Holkar's European officers now deserted his service and entered that of Sindhia, but Gardner and the others of English descent proved faithful.

Early in his career Gardner was sent by his master on a mission to Cambay, a Mahomedan state situated on the western coast of India, north of Bombay. The negotiations conducted by Gardner were, according to Eastern custom, inordinately protracted, and proved wearisome to the impetuous young Irishman. Alleviation came, for one day while sitting in Durbar with the Nawab, a curtain near Gardner was gently pulled aside, and, to use his own words, " I saw as I thought the most beautiful black eyes in the world. It was impossible to think of the treaty : those bright and piercing glances, those beautiful dark eyes completely bewildered me." Gardner demanded the princess in marriage (for the dark eyes belonged to the daughter of the Nawab), and after many difficulties and dangers won her hand. The begum was only thirteen years old but, in spite of the unconventional circumstances of her wooing, proved an ideal wife and lived with Gardner in complete happiness for over forty years, sharing the hardships of his earlier campaigns.

The strange story of Gardner's quarrel with Holkar has often been told. While the latter was hesitating whether or not to join the Mahratta confederation in war against the English, he sent Gardner to visit an English general (presumably Arthur Wellesley) to ascertain what terms would be offered him. The begum remained in Holkar's camp. Gardner's mission was fruitless, and on his return Holkar cross-examined him in Durbar as to what had transpired. Angry at the failure of his envoy, and always violent and suspicious, Holkar became more and more threatening and offensive in his language. At last he said to Gardner that he had been too long absent, and that, had he remained one more day with the English, the walls of his tents would have been cut down. Gardner had married his princess by Mahomedan rites, and had adopted the habits and prejudices of the followers of that religion. Holkar's words therefore conveyed an open and public insult which no self-respecting man could have endured. His action was prompt. " Drawing my sword," he used to say, " I attempted to cut Holkar down, but was prevented by those about him. Ere they had recovered from their amazement, I rushed from the tent, sprang upon my horse, and was soon out of reach of my pursuers." It is to Holkar's credit that Gardner's begum was permitted to join him.

Gardner now, for a short time, entered the service of Amrit Rao, brother of the Peshwa, but when, on the issue of Lord Wellesley's proclamation, Gardner handed in his resignation, Amrit Rao had him tied to a gun and threatened him with instant death if he refused to take the field. This threat was no empty one, for Holkar had just executed the three English born officers in his service on account of a similar refusal to bear arms against their countrymen. Gardner, however, defied all threats, and, in the hope of wearing out his endurance, Amrit Rao postponed his execution and placed him in charge of a guard who had orders never to leave him for a single moment. Walking one day along the edge of a steep cliff which overhung the river Tapti, Gardner was suddenly inspired to make a dash for liberty, and instantly flung himself down the cliff. Recovering his feet he plunged into the river, and though hotly pursued effected his escape to the British camp.

Gardner, who about this time was promoted Brevet-Major in the English army, presently joined General Lake's headquarters, and, considering the circumstances in which he had quitted Holkar's service, felt no reluctance to take up arms against him. Lake employed him in command of a body of Jaipur cavalry which formed part of the irregular horse accompanying Colonel Monson's detachment in its unfortunate operations in Central India during the rains of 1804. When Monson began his northward retreat, the irregular horse fought a rearguard action with disastrous results, and took no further part in the operations. Gardner escaped and in 1809 was employed to raise a body of horse, now the 2nd Lancers (Gardner's Horse), for police and revenue duties in the great tract of country between the rivers Jumna and Ganges, recently added to the British dominions. Gardner established his headquarters at his own property of Khasganj, about forty miles from Agra, which he held by " firman " from the Emperor of Delhi. The latter had adopted Gardner's begum as his daughter.

Gardner thoroughly liked and sympathised with his troopers and with his tenants, so that his corps of horse soon became famous throughout Hindustan and attracted many of the best riders and swordsmen of the scattered armies of the native states. Gardner's corps being irregular, he could administer its affairs as he thought best, and it is recorded that he would give a sowar of exceptional skill as a swordsman as much as a hundred and fifty rupees monthly pay. At the same time his estates had greatly increased in value since they came into his hands, and he lived at Khasganj in great state and comfort. He was a keen sportsman, and was in the habit of making yearly expeditions after tiger to the Oudh terai in company with his brother-in-law, Major Hyder Hearsey, who owned a large property on the eastern borders of Oudh.

Gardner subsequently travelled with Hyder Hearsey in Kumaon, and shot elephants by the beautiful lake Naini Tal, then unknown, but now surrounded by a large hill station. The brothers-in-law also established friendly relations with some of the leading Gurkha officials in Kumaon, and, being soldiers as well as sportsmen, made a number of useful observations on the military possibilities of the country.

So it was that when the continued inroads of the Gurkhas into territory under British protection compelled the Marquis of Hastings to embark on the Gurkha War of 1814–15, Gardner and Hearsey were called into consultation as to the most desirable line of invasion of the mountain kingdom of Nepal.

When war had broken out, Lord Hastings employed Gardner and Hearsey to make an advance against the Gurkha garrisons in Kumaon with the object of weakening the force opposing Ochterlony in the north. This bold enterprise, for Gardner and Hearsey were to act with irregular infantry only, without artillery, was the suggestion of Gardner himself, and the conception of so sound though daring a military undertaking stamps him as a soldier of a high class.

As Gardner had the brain to conceive, so had he the bold hand to execute. His reputation, and that of Hearsey, stood so high in Oudh, that in a very short time Gardner advanced into Kumaon by way of the Kosi·valley at the head of 3,000 irregular troops of good quality, while Hearsey, with 1,500

Rohillas, advanced from Philibhit, a frontier town.   Gardner's plan was a converging movement on Almora, the chief fortress of the Gurkhas in Kumaon.   The advance was one of extreme difficulties, for the portion of the Himalayas in which Kumaon lies was at the time densely wooded and unprovided with roads, beyond the narrow footpaths leading from village to village.   Neither food nor ammunition could be carried save on the backs of the soldiers, for no coolies dared to face the Gurkhas, and the tracks were too rough even for pack animals. Gardner and Hearsey must have been men of the most daring character to march against the victorious Gurkhas under such conditions.

The fate of Hearsey's column was soon decided.   It was surprised at an unfavourable moment and defeated with heavy loss, Hearsey himself being severely wounded and carried as a prisoner to Almora.   Gardner with his stronger column advanced successfully through the mountains, passing by the tracks discovered by him during his shooting expeditions, over the range where the station of Ranikhet now stands, and avoiding all the defensive positions held by the Gurkhas, Gardner arrived before Almora about March 20th, 1815, and on the 22nd received a reinforcement of 850 men from India.   With this force he sat down before the fort, but was unable, from the insufficiency of his means, to capture it, until, in April, he was joined by a column of regular troops under Colonel Jasper Nicolls, afterwards a Field Marshal and Commander-in-Chief in India.   On April 27th Almora surrendered to Colonel Nicolls, and Hyder Hearsey was released. Gardner's services in the Gurkha War were not liberally recognised.   He received the rank of Lieutenant-Colonel.

Colonel Gardner saw service at the head of his corps in the Pindari War of 1817–19, serving in the division under Sir Rufane Donkin, and his last campaign was that in Arakan in 1825, when the corps took the field with a strength of 621 sabres.   Gardner's Horse on this occasion showed striking loyalty.   The Burmese war was very unpopular with the Bengal Army and the feeling against it led to widespread disaffection.   In a book called *A Rough Sketch of the Bengal Irregular Horse* it is stated that Gardner's Horse " gained much credit when having lost the greater part of their horses they served on foot with the infantry—a duty which native horsemen consider degrading. This regiment marched from Khasganj in the Doab to Arakan a distance of about two thousand miles without losing a man by desertion at a time when our native infantry were deserting by hundreds."

There was a well-known native officer in Gardner's Horse named Bhim Singh who conveyed an immense bell all the way from a temple in Arakan to his own village near Khasganj ; and there he built another temple to place it in, as a memorial of the services of his regiment and himself. This bell doubtless still exists.

When Gardner engaged in this his last campaign he was sixty years old, and long years of service in the fiery plains of India had exhausted his strength, but not his martial spirit. In the despatches of Brigadier-General Morrison, under whom he served, there appears this paragraph, written in the pompous official language of the period : " If ever instances of mental energy triumphing over bodily infirmity were exemplified, they have been displayed by Colonel Gardner of the 2nd Local Horse, who on each occasion when there was a probability of the cavalry being engaged, caused himself to be removed from his palanquin, to be placed on his horse, though so weakened by long sickness as to be unable for any length of time to prolong the exertion."

Gardner survived his last campaign some ten years. He resigned the service in February 1828, and died at Khasganj on July 29th, 1835, his faithful princess following him to the grave one month later.

The property of Khasganj still belongs to the descendants of Gardner and the princess of Cambay, who to-day form a small Christian community in that secluded portion of the United Provinces of Agra and Oudh. Gardner's descendants are also interesting in that his son married into the royal house of Delhi, so that the present zamindar of Khasganj is not only descended from a country gentleman of Ireland, but also from the Emperors of Delhi—the " Great Moghuls " of our forefathers. From the marriage of a daughter of Gardner and his princess with a cousin, who was in remainder to the peerage conferred on Admiral Alan Gardner, is descended the Indian claimant to that title.

APPENDIX II

List of Officers who have served with the 2nd Lancers (Gardner's Horse) from 12th May 1809, the date on which the Regiment was raised, to the present date (12th May 1909) :—

Rank and Names.	Dates.	Remarks.
Colonel W. L. Gardner	1809–28.	Commandant.
Cornet J. B. Hearsey	1814–15.	With detachment in Nepal War.
Major ,,	1829–35.	Commandant.
Lieut. James Manson ..	1815–18.	
Captain Borlace	1819.	2nd-in-Command.
Asst. Surgeon Peter Sutar	1819.	
Dr. James Johnstone	1823.	
Captain Henry Monke ..	1824–26.	
Surgeon D. Knight	1824–25.	
Lieut. James Maclean	1825.	Adjutant.
Captain J. D. Douglas	1826.	
Lieut. W. Anderson	1826–39.	Adjutant.
Asst. Surgeon Stevenson	1826–28.	
Captain Robert F. Dougan	1829–30.	Commandant.
Captain Charles O'Hara	⎰ 1829–39. ⎱ 1839–44.	2nd-in-Command. Commandant.
Asst. Surgeon Foley	1832–39.	
Lieut. W. B. Lumley ..	1840–42.	2nd-in-Command.
Lieut. George Jackson	1840–41.	Adjutant.
Captain ,,	1843–47.	2nd-in-Command.
Major ,,	1847–71.	Commandant—24 years.
Colonel ,,	,,	,,
Asst. Surgeon Mark Richardson	1841–46.	
Lieut. A. Carrington	1842.	Adjutant.
Lieut. H. Ternan	1843.	Adjutant.
Captain Archibald McKean	1844.	Offg. Commandant.
Captain Joseph Leeson	1842–47.	Commandant.
Lieut. W. C. Alexander	1844–46.	Adjutant.
Lieut. W. T. Hughes ..	⎰ 1847–50. ⎱ 1851–52.	Adjutant. 2nd in Command.
Asst. Surgeon G. C. Wallich ..	1847–50.	
Lieut. T. Waston	1848.	2nd-in-Command.
Lieut. S. C. A. Swinton	1849–50.	2nd-in-Command.
Lieut. A. H. Alexander	1851–56.	Adjutant.
Asst. Surgeon D. McDonald, M.D.	1851–55.	
Lieut. C. Cureton	1853–59.	2nd-in-Command.
Lieut. H. P. W. Wynch	1857–59.	Adjutant.
Asst. Surgeon J. A. C. Hutchinson.	1856.	

Rank and Names.	Dates.	Remarks.
Asst. Surgeon Picthall	1857–58.	
Asst. Surgeon S. C. Townsend	1859.	
Lieut. C. Shaw	1860.	
Lieut. Gregory	1860–61.	Adjutant.
Asst. Surgeon T. Atchinson ..	1860.	
Lieut. G. L. K. Hewett. ..	1862.	Adjutant.
Captain A. K. J. C. Mackenzie..	1864.	
Colonel C. W. Campbell ..	1864–86.	Commandant.
Lt.-Colonel F. Knowles ..	1864–86.	Adjutant, 2nd-in-Command.
Colonel H. C. Kemble	1864–88.	2nd-in-Command.
Lt.-Colonel C. T. M. Higginson	1864–88.	
Major W. R. E. Alexander ..	1865.	Offg. Commandant.
Captain H. Melvill	1865.	Offg. 2nd-in-Command.
Major H. G. Jenkins	1866–71.	Offg. and 2nd-in-Command.
Colonel C. E. Salkeld	1867–91.	Adjutant and 2nd-in-Command.
Surgeon T. D. Crawfurd ..	1864–70.	
Colonel O. Wilkinson	1871–80.	Commandant.
Lieut. T. R. B. Bennett, 7th Hussars.	1871.	
Asst. Surgeon T. D. Skardon	1871.	
Captain W. B. Craigie	1872–82.	
Surgeon F. Parsons	1872–85.	
Major T. C. Graham	1873–76.	Offg. 2nd-in-Command.
Surgeon-Major A. S. Reid, M.B.	1875 & 1886.	
Major M. K. Martin	1876–92.	Adjutant. 2nd-in-Command. Commandant.
Surgeon T. R. Swaine, M.B. ..	1876.	
Lt.-Colonel C. W. Fletcher ..	1877.	Offg. 2nd-in-Command.
Lieut. J. F. D. Fordyce ..	1877.	Adjutant.
Lieut. R. F. Gartside Tipping..	1877–79.	
Lieut. C. J. Robarts	1879–85.	Adjutant.
Surgeon C. J. Bamber	1880.	
Surgeon F. F. Perry	1881.	
Colonel St. G. L. Steele ..	1881–1906.	Adjutant. 2nd-in-Command.
Lieut. P. B. Lindsell	1882–83.	
Lieut. V. M. Stockley	1882–83.	
Lieut. T. S. M. Woolley ..	1884–86.	Adjutant.
Lt.-Colonel F. H. B. Commeline	1885 to date.	Commandant. Adjutant. 2nd-in-Command.
Major-General R. M. Clifford ...	1886–92.	Commandant.
Lt.-Colonel J. A. Douglas ..	1886 to date.	2nd-in-Command.
Major M. E. Willoughby, p.s.c.	1887 to date.	Adjutant.
Lieut. H. G. Stainforth ..	1887.	
Surgeon-Major J. Young ..	1887–92.	

Rank and Names.	Dates.	Remarks.
Lieut. A. MacConaghey	1888–91.	
Lieut. S. F. Crocker	1888.	
Surgeon E. A. W. Hall..	1888–89.	
Major W. B. James	1888 to date.	Adjutant.
Lieut. J. L. W. ffrench-Mullen..	1889–91.	
Major H. H. F. Turner, p.s.c.	1889 to date.	Adjutant.
Lieut. A. R. Saunders	1890.	
Lt.-Colonel A. W. Dawson, I.M.S.	1891–96.	
Brig.-General K. S. Davison, C.B.	1890–1908.	2nd-in-Command and Commandant.
Colonel J. G. Turner	1892–1902.	
Major L. L. Maxwell	1891 to date.	Adjutant.
Lieut. R. L. Morris	1891–92.	
Colonel F. C. Burton	1892–97.	Commandant.
Colonel C. H. V. Garbett	1892–1901.	2nd-in-Command and Commandant.
Major A. G. Pritchard ..	1892 to date.	Adjutant.
Major F. O'Kinealy, I.M.S.	1892.	
Lieut. F. T. Moore	1893–96.	
Lieut. E. A. Swinhoe ..	1894–95.	
Captain P. B. Sangster	1896 to date.	Adjutant.
Lieut. C. Thomson, M.B., I.M.S.	1896.	
Major G. Thomas, p.s.c.	1897 to date.	
Lieut. R. C. Harbottle	1896–98.	
Captain W. K. Bourne, p.s.c.	1897 to date.	
Captain J. F. Bennett ..	1899 ,,	
Captain G. Knowles, D.S.O. ..	1899 ,,	
Lieut. M. R. H. Webber	1899–1900.	
Captain J. A. Black, I.M.S. ..	1901.	
Captain H. C. S. Ward..	1901 to date.	Adjutant.
Lieut. H. R. MacNee, I.M.S. ..	1902.	
Captain A. N. DeV. Scott	1902 to date.	
Lieut. K. Robertson	1906 ,,	
Captain H. Y. Salkeld ..	1906 ,,	
Lieut. G. Gould	1906 ,,	
Lieut. G. E. Dunsterville	1908 ,,	
Lieut. D. S. Davison ..	1908 ,,	
Captain Emslie Smith, I.M.S.		
Captain L. Lloyd, I.M.S.		
Captain Melville, I.M.S.		
Captain Meakin, I.M.S.		
Captain Hulbert, I.M.S.		
Captain W. L. Trafford, I.M.S.	1907 to date.	
Captain W. Carr, I.M.S. ..	1898–99.	
Captain A. E. Walter, I.M.S. ..	1899–1900.	
Captain J. Irwin, I.M.S. ..	1900.	
Captain Weinman, I.M.S. ..	1902.	

APPENDIX III

LIST of British and Native Officers serving with, or borne on the rolls of, the Regiment on the 12th of May 1909, with their services. Also a statement of the war services of Non-Commissioned Officers and men since the Egyptian Campaign of 1882 :—

Lt.-Colonel F. H. B. Commeline.	South African War, 1899–1900. Medal with three clasps.
Lt.-Colonel J. A. Douglas..	N.-W. Frontier of India, Waziristan, 1894–95. Medal with clasp. China, 1900. Relief of Pekin. Despatches. Medal with clasp.
Major M. E. Willoughby, P.S.C.	N.-E. Frontier of India, Chin Lushai, 1889–90. Medal with clasp. China, 1900. Despatches. Medal.
Major W. B. James ..	South African War, 1902. Medal with two clasps.
Major H. H. F. Turner, P.S.C.	South African War, 1900. Medal with clasp. East Africa, 1903–04. Despatches. Medal with two clasps.
Major L. L. Maxwell ..	N.-W. Frontier of India, Waziristan, 1894–95. Medal with clasp. Tirah, 1897–98. Medal with two clasps. South African War, 1900. Severely wounded. Despatches. Medal with three clasps. Brevet of Major.
Major A. G. Pritchard.	
Major G. Thomas, P.S.C.	
Captain J. F. Bennett.	
Captain G. Knowles, D.S.O.	West Africa, 1901. Ishan Ulia Expedition. Medal with clasp. West Africa 1901–02. Aro Expedition. Severely wounded. Despatches. Clasp. D.S.O. East Africa, 1903–04. Clasp.
Captain P. B. Sangster ..	Tirah, 1897–98. Medal with two clasps.
Captain W. K. Bourne, P.S.C.	
Captain H. C. S. Ward.	
Captain A. N. DeV. Scott.	
Captain H. Y. Salkeld.	
Lieut. K. Robertson.	
Lieut. G. Gould.	
Lieut. G. E. Dunsterville.	

Lieut. D. S. Davison.

Captain W. L. Trafford, M.B. N.-W. Frontier of India, 1908.

BIKANER, His Highness
  Sir Ganga Singh, Baha-
  dur, G.C.I.E., K.C.S.I.,
  Maharaja of —— Hon.
  Lt.-Colonel, Hon. A.D.C.
  to H.R.H. The Prince of
  Wales.

Resaldar-Major Ali Muham-   Egyptian Campaign, 1882. Medal with clasp.
  mad Khan, Sirdar Baha-   Khedive's Bronze Star.
  dur.

Resaldar Wazir Chand.

  ,, Nabi Jang Khan. Egyptian Campaign, 1882. Medal with
          clasp. Khedive's Bronze Star.

  ,, Mukand Singh.

Resaidar Ganga Dat.

  ,, Wurriam Singh.

  ,, Bhola Nath.

  ,, Bhajju Singh .. East Africa, 1903–04. Medal.

Jemadar Abas Ali Khan.

  ,, Muhammad Raza Wurdi-Major.
      Khan.

  ,. Sohan Singh .. Egyptian Campaign, 1882. Medal with clasp.
          Khedive's Bronze Star.

  ,, Mokham Chand.. Chitral, 1895. Medal with clasp. Tirah,
          1897–98. Two clasps.

  ,, Ghulam Nabi Egyptian Campaign, 1882. Medal with clasp.
      Khan.   Khedive's Bronze Star.

  ,, Suraj Singh .. East Africa, 1903–04. Medal with clasp.
          Officially mentioned for good work in the
          field. D.G.S. and T. 6144T, 23-6-04.

  ,, Mukh Ram.

  ,, Sirdar Singh.

  ., Abdul Samad Khan.

Egyptian Campaign, 1882.

Dafadar Muhammad Kasim
  Khan.

Sowar Ahmad Wali Khan.

  ,, Saadat Ali Khan. .. Still serving.

  ,, Bakshish Singh. ..

  ,, Karim Ullah Khan.

  ,, Abdul Rahman Khan.

N.-E. Frontier of India, Manipur, 1891.

Kote-Dafadar Kaku Singh.

Chitral, 1895.

Kote-Dafadar Nand Lal .. Sowar Bhima.

N.-W. Frontier of India, Waziristan, 1894–95.
841 Dafadar Fateh Singh.

Soudan, 1896.
Sowar (Salutri) Muhammad
  Ibrahim.

Tirah, 1897–98.

994 Dafadar Molar.	626 Dafadar Harnam Singh.
841 Dafadar Fateh Singh.	1678 Sowar Kala Singh.
918 Sowar Nanu Singh.	Sowar Bhima.

South Africa, 1899–1902.

411 Kote-Dafadar Hasan Raza Khan.	1017 Dafadar Kanwal Singh.
629 Lance-Dafadar Dhian Singh.	1068 Lce.-Dafadar Wahid Ali.
1357 Sowar Jora Singh.	1424 Sowar Molar.
1277 Lce.-Dafadar Munshi Ram.	1225 Sowar Atar Singh.
Farrier Bhup Singh.	

China, 1900.
1008 Sowar Lal Chand.   1586 Dafadar Neki Ram.

East Africa, Somaliland, 1903–04.

1069 Sowar Mangat Ram.	966 Sowar Gul Hasan.
1131 Farrier Rahmat Ullah.	1038 Sowar Surmukh Singh.
1332 Sowar Naurung Singh.	1212 Sowar Neki Ram.
1112 Dafadar Anokh Singh.	

Tibet, 1903.

901 Dafadar Ahmed Yar Khan.   1117 Sowar Pullah Khan.
1313 Sowar Ahmed Ullah.

Burmah Survey, 1895–96.
Kote-Dafadar Nidhan Singh.

APPENDIX IV

Records of Assaults-at-Arms, Sports, etc.

1891 Connell Cup, Polo Tournament, Allahabad.. Won by 2nd Lancers.

TEAM
1. Lieut. A. McConaghey.
2. Capt. St. G. L. Steele.
3. Lieut. F. H. B. Commeline.
4. Lieut. W. B. James.

1896 Hog Hunter's Cup, Lt. A. G. Pritchard's " Midnight " Owner up 3rd
1896 Pony   do.   Do.   " Kendall "   do.   2nd
1897 Kadir Cup.   Final   Do.   " Midnight "   do.
      Heat.
1898 Pony Hog Hunter's   Do.   " Connaught Ranger " late
      Cup.   " Kendall "   1st
1898 Delhi Cavalry Concentration Assault-at-Arms : 2nd Lancers   1st
      Tentpegging by 8's.
1899 Hog Hunter's Cup. Lt. A. G. Pritchard's " Black Jess " Owner up. 2nd
1899 Bengal Cavalry Chase.   Do.   do.   do.   1st
1900 Hog Hunter's Cup.   Do.   do.   do.   2nd
1900 Bengal Cavalry Chase   Do.   " Midnight " do.   W.O.
1901 Kadir Cup. Final Heat. Capt. A. G. Pritchard's " Toffee " do.
1901 Bengal Cavalry Chase   Do.   " Dick " do.   2nd
1901 Lahore District Assault-at-Arms. Capt. A. G. Pritchard's " Dick "
      Jumping Competition.   Owner up   ..   1st
1901 Lahore District Assault-at-Arms. Lce.-Dafadar Molar   1st
      Lance v. Sword.
1901 Lahore District Assault-at-Arms. Lce.-Dafadar Molar   1st
      Bayonet v. Sword.
1901 Lahore Horse Show. Native Res. Major Ali Muhammad Khan
      Officers' Chargers.   " Nowsha " 1st
1901 Lahore Horse Show. Best   Res. Major Ali Muhammad Khan's
      Horse in the Show.   " Nowsha " 1st
1902 Lahore District Assault-at- Capt. A. G. Pritchard's " Dick " 1st
      Arms. Jumping Competi-
      tion.
1902 Lahore Horse Show. Native R. M. Ali Muhammad Khan's
      Officers' Chargers.   " Nowsha " 1st
                                  Res. Nabi Jang Khan   ..   2nd
1902 Peshawar District Assault-at-Arms :—
      Tent-pegging with sword .. Sowar Umrao Singh   ..   2nd
      Jumping by sections   .. C Squadron 2nd
      Jumping, British Officers .. Major Douglas 1st
1903 Kadir Cup. Final Heat   .. Major L. L. Maxwell's " Poppet "
                                  Owner up.

30

1903 Kadir Cup. Final Heat .. Major L. L. Maxwell's " Jo Hukm "
    Capt. Pritchard.

1904 Lucknow District Assault-at- Capt. A. G. Pritchard's " Dick "
    Arms. Jumping Competi- Owner up 1st
    tion.
    Native Officers, Tent-Pegging. Res. Kirpa Ram 1st

1904 Lucknow District Assault-at-Arms :—
    Native Officers, Jumping .. Res. Mukand Singh 1st
    Tent-pegging Rank and File Dafadar Maluk Singh .. 1st
    Lance v. Sword .. .. Dafadar Molar 1st

1905 Kadir Cup. Final Heat .. Capt. A. G. Pritchard's " Toffee "
    Owner up.

1905 Pony Hog Hunter's Cup .. Major L. L. Maxwell's " Jo Hukm "
    Owner up 1st

1905 Hog Hunter's Cup .. .. Capt. G. Knowles' " St. Crispin "
    Owner up 3rd

1905 Lucknow District Assault-at-Arms :—
    British Officers, Tentpegging. Major L. L. Maxwell 1st
    Native do. do. Res. Mukand Singh. ⎫ Best Nat- 1st
    Do. do. Jumping Do. ⎬ ive Officer 1st
    Do. do. Heads and Posts Do. ⎭ at Arms 2nd
    Do. do. do. W. M. Muhammad Raza Khan 1st
    Do. do. Lime-cutting Do. do. 2nd
    Do. do. Mounted Combat Res. Wariam Singh .. 1st
    Do. do. do. Res. Kirpa Ram 2nd
    Section Tent pegging .. 2nd Lancers 1st
    Heads and Posts .. .. Dafadar Suraj Singh .. 1st
        „ Jiwan Singh .. 2nd

1906 Lucknow District Assault-at-Arms :—
    British Officers, Sword v. Sword. Captain Sangster 1st
        Major Maxwell 2nd
    Tent-pegging by sections .. 2nd Lancers 1st
    Native Officers, Sword v. Sword. Res. Kirpa Ram 1st
        „ Wariam Singh 2nd
    Do. Tent-pegging, Lance. „ Mukand Singh 1st
    Do. Tent-pegging, Sword „ Kirpa Ram 2nd
    Do. Heads and Posts W. M. Muhammad Raza Khan 2nd
    Do. Jumping .. Do. do. .. 1st
    Rank and File. Sword v Sword L. D. Dhanna Singh .. 2nd
    Do. Lance v. Lance Do. .. 1st
    Do. do. Juniors Sowar Basti 1st
    Do. Tent-Pegging Dafadar Udey Singh .. 3rd
    Do. do. Juniors. L. D. Abdul Wahid Khan 2nd
        ⎧ Sowar Basti 3rd
    Rank and File. Lime-cutting ⎨ Dafadar Ahmed Beg.. .. 2nd
        ⎩ „ Bishnath Singh .. 3rd
    Best Man at-Arms .. .. Lance-Dafadar Dhanna Singh.

1906	Tollygunge Horse Show, Jumping.	Capt. A. G. Pritchard's " Young Poetess "	2nd
1906	Native Cavalry Pony Chase ..	Capt. F. Bennett's " Pinfire " Owner up	1st
1906	Native Cavalry Grand Annual Chase.	Lt. K. Robertson's " Ryong " Owner up	2nd

1907 Lucknow District Assault-at-Arms :—

Native Officers, Sword v. Sword	Jemadar Mokham Chand	..	1st
Do. Lime-cutting	W. M. Muhammad Raza Khan		1st
Do. Tent-pegging	Jemadar Bholanath	.. ..	2nd
Rank and File, Sword v Sword	Sowar Basti	.. ..	1st
Do. Tent-pegging by sections	2nd Lancers ..	.. ..	1st
Best Man-at-Arms	Sowar Basti.		

1908	Hog Hunter's Cup	Major L. L. Maxwell's " Upstart " Owner up	1st

1908 Lucknow District Assault-at-Arms :—

British Officers, Sword v. Sword	Capt. G. Knowles, D.S.O.	..	1st
Do. Tent-pegging	Do.	.. ..	1st
Native Officers, Lime-cutting	{ Jemadar Sohan Singh	..	1st
	{ W. M. Muhammad Raza Khan		2nd
Do. Sword v. Sword	Jemadar Suraj Singh	..	2nd

1908 Lucknow District Assault-at-Arms :—

Rank and File, Lance v. Lance	Dafadar Ali Raza Khan	..	2nd
Do. Sword v. Sword	L. D. Dhanna Singh	..	1st
Do. Lime-cutting	K. D. Kehri Singh ..	..	2nd
	Dafadar Ali Raza Khan	..	1st
Do. Jumping by sec-tions	2nd Lancers	.. ...	1st
Do. Tent-pegging	L. D. Dhanna Singh	..	2nd
Best Man-at-Arms	Lce.-Dafadar Dhanna Singh.		

1909 Jubbulpore Brigade Assault-at-Arms :—

Native Officers, Jumping ..	{ W. M. Muhammad Raza Khan		1st
	{ Res. Mukand Singh	..	2nd
Do. Sword v. Sword	W. M. Muhammad Raza Khan		2nd
Rank and File, Lance v. Sword	K. D. Kehri Singh ..	..	1st
Do. Lance v. Bayonet	Do.	.. ..	3rd
Do. Tent-pegging by sections	B. Squadron 2nd Lancers	..	2nd

1909	Jubbulpore Polo Tournament	Won by 2nd Lancers.

TEAM .. {
1. Lieut. G. Gould.
2. Lieut. K. Robertson.
3. Capt. H. C. S. Ward.
4. Capt. W. K. Bourne.

THE EGYPTIAN CAMPAIGN OF 1882

BY COLONEL ST. G. L. STEELE

WHEN it was first decided to send an Indian contingent to Egypt in 1882, to assist in quelling the revolt of Araby Pacha, one cavalry regiment, the 13th B.L., and five Infantry battalions were selected; but owing to the nature of the terrain over which the operations were to take place, a change was made in the composition of the force and it eventually consisted of the 2nd and 6th B.C., the 13th B.L., 7th Bengal Infantry, 20th Punjab Infantry, and the 29th Bombay Infantry (2nd Baluch.). The Cavalry brigade was under the command of General Wilkinson, 16th Lancers, and the Infantry of General Sir Herbert Macpherson. The 72nd Highlanders, an Indian Mountain battery and the necessary complement of the Indian Commissariat Department, completed the force.

When mobilization orders were received, the regiment was stationed at Lucknow, and great satisfaction was felt by everyone on receipt of the news as the regiment had not had the luck to share in either of the Afghan campaigns of '79 or '80. It was in the middle of the hot weather and the journey to Bombay was accomplished satisfactorily, halts being made at rest camps at Allahabad and Deolali, the men and horses being detrained and rested during the heat of the day. The officers actually with the regiment at the time were Major Fred Knowles (Officiating Commandant), Major H. C. Kemble, Major G. E. Salkeld, Captain M. K. Martin, Lieut. C. J. Robarts (Adjutant), Lieut. V. M. Stockley, Lieut. St. G. L. Steele (Attached), and Surgeon Major F. Parsons. Lieut. P. B. Lindsell (Attached) was detailed for duty with the Depôt, and Colonel C. W. Campbell and Major C. M. Higginson, who were on leave in England, joined the regiment in Egypt. Unfortunately Colonel Campbell was never fit enough to get into the saddle and consequently had to return to England. The transports encountered a strong monsoon in the Indian Ocean, necessitating the closing of portholes and even hatches.

The intense heat and the sickness of the men, who had, of course, never been to sea before, led to less efficient stable management and the consequent loss of some horses.

According to the original plan of campaign the Indian contingent was to have disembarked at Suez, but en route these orders were changed, consequent on Sir Garnet Wolseley moving his base from Alexandria to Ismailia, and they were ordered to disembark at Ismailia. As might have been expected, the landing facilities in such a backwater were exceedingly poor and the depth of water did not admit of transports coming alongside. The R.E. were kept busy erecting small piers and landing stages, and all men and stores had to be brought on shore on lighters and barges, manned by the R.N., but as these were few and time was precious, the horses, mules, ponies, etc., had to be slung over and made to swim ashore. This was a severe strain on those which were still feeling the effects of a rough and hot sea voyage, and there were consequently a few more casualties amongst them, although several men did excellent service swimming with the weaker horses, for which they gained their lance stripe.

During the landing the booming of guns from the direction of Tel el Kebir told us that a big fight was taking place. That evening we received news that the Household Cavalry had made their great charge on the Egyptian batteries, and although successful it was considered advisable to reinforce them with all the mounted troops available. We had settled down for the night and hoped for an opportunity of shaking off the effects of the cramped life on board ship, but orders were received to strike camp, saddle up, and march to Camp Quassassin, which was reached by midday the following day. This camp was on the north bank of the Sweet Water Canal, and the Indian Cavalry Brigade was camped alongside the Household Cavalry Brigade. It was amusing to see the big troopers straight from London coming into our lines to have their swords sharpened by the sikhligars, and gladly exchanging clasp knives, etc., for the Indian chupatti to supplement their rations which had been rather short. While at Camp Quassassin the regiment suffered the sad loss in the death of their fine old Thakur Risaldar Major, a Mutiny veteran, who had been unwell before leaving Lucknow but who refused to remain behind.

The Indian Cavalry furnished the line of observation during the day, sending out patrols in the direction of Tel el Kebir and reconnoitring the country round. The British Cavalry, consisting of the Household Cavalry, the 7th Dragoon Guards, relieved them at night on a line closer withdrawn to the camp. The syces were kept pretty busy, as, after going out with the regimental transport to cut green forage on the cultivated land bordering the canal, they had to make a second daily journey to cut and bring in stuff for the British cavalry. In this connection it may be mentioned that the Household Cavalry were carefully located near a field of jowar. Their officers came to us asking what they were to do for forage, and were astounded when told that it was growing at their doors. Our men turned out and cut the field down for them. The heat was excessive ; there was no shade and the flies were very troublesome, and with all this there was sickness amongst all the troops as a result of the pollution of the fresh water canal by the Egyptians, who threw dead animals into it at Tel el Kebir.

On the 9th September the Egyptians made a reconnaissance in force, and the whole camp turned out to meet them, and the resulting action is known as the battle of Quassassin. The regiment was that day split up, squadrons and troops acting independently to horse and field artillery. Although subjected at times to a hot fire, we were fortunate in suffering few casualties as the majority of the shells from the Krupp guns failed to burst on impact with the sand. On the evening of the 12th September, secret orders were issued that the whole force was to be ready to move off at midnight with man and horse rationed for 48 hours. The Indian brigade led the advance and halted as near as possible to the enemy's advanced posts, which consisted of a series of open lunette works where the gun crews were afterwards found chained to the guns.

The force was disposed as follows :—

The cavalry in two lines on the extreme right at a point outflanking the works, with the Indian cavalry in front ; the British infantry, three brigades, in line in the centre, and the Guards Brigade, under H.R.H. the Duke of Connaught, in reserve ; the Indian Infantry Brigade across the fresh water canal on the left.

As dawn appeared, the infantry advanced under a heavy artillery and rifle fire, and, gallantly assaulting the strongly fortified camp, took it at the point of the bayonet. Directly the first gun flash lit up the sky the cavalry mounted and rode round the works, outflanking them. They passed through masses of armed Egyptians fleeing in disorder ; these were at first speared or cut down, as rumour had it that they would otherwise lie down and hamstring the horses passing over them or rise up and shoot our troops in the back. However a staff officer rode up with an order that all Egyptians throwing down their arms were to be spared. The two lines of Cavalry continued their outflanking movement up to the railway passing through the camp, which they reached just as a train full of armed men was steaming off. This they were unable to stop, but they effectually stopped three more trains which were getting up steam by shooting the engine driver and stoker of the leading train and blocking the line with a dead camel. The large number of armed men in these trains inflicted some casualties on us here. After the action the British Cavalry remained at Tel el Kebir, but the Indian Cavalry Brigade and some other mounted troops were ordered to push on to Bilbeis without delay. They arrived the same afternoon, overtaking streams of fugitives en route, and taking possession of many horses. They nearly succeeded in capturing Araby Pacha and his staff, but these on their fresher horses were able to escape. The Indian Cavalry Brigade bivouacked that night at Bilbeis, and early next morning, following the line of the fresh water canal, advanced on Cairo and reached it in the late afternoon (September 14th). By this time the men and horses, who had been fighting and marching over very heavy going and under a hot sun for two days, were very tired. Fortunately when in sight of the citadel the force was met by a mounted flag of truce, and, after some parleying, the British troops accompanied the flag bearers into the citadel and held Araby a prisoner. The Indian troops, after watering their horses in the Egyptian cavalry barracks, bivouacked on the racecourse. Early next morning Cairo was occupied and thus saved from being burnt. All approaches were patrolled and movements at railway stations and points of exit stopped. The 2nd took their share in this work, and our troops on duty at a station, hearing that a horse train was expected, arranged for all the horses to be escorted into the regimental lines in Cairo, and promptly branded them 2 B.C. These horses and those seized on the march to Cairo helped to make good the many casualties the regiment had suffered. The barbs and Egyptian mules which we took were all splendid animals. Most of our trumpeters rode the flea-bitten grey barbs, and the last of them must have died out in the regiment about 1900 or soon after, although one was playing polo in 1899. A general parade of the troops in Cairo was ordered, and the column passed through the town and proceeded to the fort of the Abdin Palace, where Sir Garnet Wolseley took the salute.

While in Cairo parties of troops were sent by rail to Alexandria to see the effect of the bombardment of that town by the British Navy, and a hundred rank and file under Lieut. Steele represented the regiment.

After a few days stay at Cairo, the Indian contingent received orders to return to India. They therefore marched through Tel el Kebir to Suez, and from there had a fine voyage to Bombay, with no further casualties.

Bombay was gaily decorated for the arrival of the troops and a triumphant march was arranged through the crowded streets of the town to the open space near the esplanade, where sports with prizes were held and all ranks hospitably entertained.

The regiment proceeded on to Lucknow, which it reached after an absence of exactly three months, and was met at the station by several officers of the 10th Royal Hussars, who kindly brought their fine band to play the regiment back to its lines.

ST. G. L. STEELE, Colonel.
Late 2.B.C.

HYTHE.
December 2nd, 1922.

CHAPTER II

1909 TO 1914

THE Regiment completed its Centenary on May 12th, 1909. The Centenary Celebrations were held between November 29th and December 4th, 1909, at Saugor, C.P. These were attended by 181 pensioned Native and N.-C. officers and men, who were the guests of the Regiment. Owing to the refusal of certain railways to grant any concessions, it was at first feared that the expense of bringing so many guests from their homes to Saugor would fall too heavily on the Regiment ; but the Native officers volunteered to bear any of the extra expense, and requested that the number of invitations should on no account be cut down. Eventually, H.H. Sir Gunga Singh, Bahadur, A.D.C., G.C.I.E., K.C.S.I., Maharajah of Bikaner, Hon. Major in the 2nd Lancers, most generously offered to pay all railway fares. The amount of these was 2677/-. Amongst the guests were Pensioned Rissaldar Majors Mohammed Yusuf Khan, Nizam Ali Khan ; Rissaldars Ghulam Mahommed Khan, Hira Singh, Man Singh, Bahram Singh, Kala Singh (Bahadur) ; Ressaidars Mohammed Razza Khan, Dal Singh, Ram Singh, Sawan Singh, Kirpa Ram, Bhura Singh, Tara Singh, Bahadur Ali, and other Native officers.

The oldest pensioner present was Farrier Major Nur Khan, who served in the Regiment from 1833–1880, enlisting at the age of 16. Periods of his service were performed by substitute (Ewazi ki naukri). Nur Khan's father, Farrier Major Rahmat Khan, served in the Regiment under Colonel Gardner, and took pension in 1845. Of Nur Khan's three sons, one was also Farrier Major in the Regiment, one a trumpeter, and one a Farrier. A fourth generation is now represented by Farrier Nizamuddin.

Owing to the season of the year, many European guests who had been invited were unable to come. Amongst those present were the four Misses Hearsey, granddaughters of Sir John Hearsey, K.C.B., who served in the Regiment from 1814, and who commanded it from 1829 to 1839. Brigadier-General K. S. Davison was unable to come, but Mrs. and Miss Davison were present. Brigadier-General A. Wallace, C.B., and Staff

commanding Jubbulpore Brigade, Major H. Lawrence (E.
Surrey Regiment) and Mrs. Lawrence, and others also came.
The Maharajah of Bikaner, owing to the illness of his mother,
was unable to come.

The best native Officer-at-Arms was Ressaidar Mukand
Singh. The best Man-at-Arms was 1507 Duffadar Abdul
Latif Khan, L.A.S. ; and 1608 Sowar Sarjit Singh, L.B.S.
To defray the expenses of the Centenary Celebrations, the
Mess had some two years previously, by Colonel St. G. L.
Steele's suggestion, started a Centenary Fund which
amounted to 3645/-. The actual expenses incurred by the
Mess amounted to 6876/- ; by the Regiment 1841/-.

Major James, 2nd Lancers, compiled, with much labour,
a brief history of the Regiment, since its raising ; this was
published in English, Urdu and Hindi. Of the British Officers
then in the Regiment, Captains Knowles, Salkeld and Lieut.
Davison had fathers in the Regiment.

Here a few remarks on the mounting of the Regiment, and
particularly about the Regimental Farm at Mitalak, may not
be out of place. In 1909 there were in the ranks :—

Australian Horses   487 .. Average price 389/-
[1]Mitalak Horses   27 ..   ,,   ,, 300/-
Countrybred Horses   98   ,,   ,, 304/-

The Regimental Transport was entirely mules—average
price 176/4/0. The average price of cast horses sold in 1909
was 225/-. The balance credit in the following Regimental
Funds was :—

Horse Fund 67,693/11/0
Mule Fund 10,903/10/2
Miscellaneous Fund 13,909/2/4

The Regimental Farm at Mitalak was started by Col. K. S.
Davison, Commanding 2nd Lancers, in November, 1903.
It was placed under the charge of Rissaldar Wazir Chand and
a Staff of 1 Duffadar, 1 Lce. Duffadar, 1 Salutri, 6 Regimental
Syces and 3 extra Syces. Its area was 750 acres, all, except
100 acres, canal irrigated. The 650 acres were let out on the
half-produce System. The remaining 100 acres were par-
titioned into paddocks for the stock. The sale of half produce
from the YTP acres (irrigated free for the first two years)

---

[1] Reared, but not bred at the Regimental Farm.

amounted at first to 15,000/-, and later, when water rates
were charged, and the land required deeper ploughing and
more manuring, the half produce averaged 8000/- to 9000/-
yearly.   In 1903, 30 branded Regimental mares were drafted
on to the Farm, but these were within a year all disposed of
as unfit for breeding purposes.   In 1904, 20 more Regimental
mares were sent, and these were covered by local (Govt.)
English, Australian and Arab stallions.   A few C.B. year-
lings were bought that year, at Sargodha Fair, for the farm.
In 1905, Colonel Davison and Major Commeline, 2nd Lancers,
bought about 20 2-3-year-old C.B.'s, at Amritsar, for the
Farm, and some of the barren mares were disposed of.
Total stock now amounted to about 40.   During the subsequent few years the total stock, now including some two year
old purchased mules, rose to between 50 and 60 head.   The
B.A. Entire " Curate " was purchased by Major A. G.
Pritchard as regimental stallion.

In 1909, the experiment was made of putting the " Curate "
to three and four-year-old Australian remounts, and thereby
getting a foal out of them while too young for training.   The
produce was sent to the Farm.   In 1911 the first purely bred
farm horses were bought by the regiment at 300/-.   Rissaldar
Wazir Chand was replaced on the Farm by Jemadars Mokham
Chand and Wariam Singh in succession.   The latter was
succeeded in 1908 by Duffadar Fateh Chand who did exceedingly well.

The annual income of horses from Farm to Regiment was
now about 20.   Purchases of two and three-year-old C.B.'s
and mules at Amritsar were still made, but these, as a rule,
were not as good as the Farm-bred ones.

The stock of the Farm now totalled 100 horses and 10 cows.
The buildings, Keekur tree hedge, orchard etc., were all
initiated by Rissaldar Wazir Chand.   He also started a brick
kiln, planted 4000 Sheeshum trees, and the policy of annual
planting was henceforth carried out.

NOVEMBER 1909 TO MARCH 1911.

The regiment took part in Divisional Manoeuvres, N. of
Saugor, January 28th to February 8th, 1910.
In March 1910, Lieut. G. Dunsterville left the Regiment in

exchange with Lieut. O. Wilkin, Devon Regiment. The latter joined in September.

Squadron training by wings was carried out in November and December at Chitora.

The following team attended the B.P.R.A. and were beaten in the " Meerut Cup " competition by one point only, by the 30th Lancers :—Lieut. O. Wilkin, Ressaidar and W. M. Abdul Sammad Khan, Jemadar Jiwan Singh, Duffadars Abdul Wahid Khan, and A. L. D. Mohammed Ghanni Khan. Duffadar Abdul Wahid Khan for firing in the winning team of " Native Officers and other ranks " won a bronze medal.

The polo team (Gould, Robertson, Scott, Salkeld), won the Bechtler Cup at Jubbulpore in November, 1910, beating, in the finals, the 22nd Punjabis by 3 goals to 2. In January 1911, Ward, Gould, Knowles, Robertson, were beaten in the Allahabad Exhibition Junior Tournament, by the 39th C.I.H. In February, the same team, in the Native Cavalry Tournament, at Amballa, were beaten 5—3, by the 39th C.I.H., who won the tournament.

Captain G. Knowles ran a good fourth, in the Hog Hunters' Cup on his B.W.M. " Rabies."

In March 1911, 2nd Lieut. D. E. Whitworth joined from the Royal Warwicks. In the Spring of 1911, Capt. H. C. S. Ward joined the Staff College, Quetta.

MARCH 1911 TO NOVEMBER 1911.

At the Cavalry School Horse Show in 1911, Capt. K. Robertson won (1) Light weight polo ponies (Arabs), with his Ch. A. G. " March Past."

(2) Best horse in the show, with his E.T.B.B.G. "Damboob."

(3) Light weight Australian ponies, with his Ch. W. M. " Lolo."

In April, Ram Krishen Chanda received a direct commission as Jemadar. The latter is grandson of the late Ressaldar Major Hira Singh, of the regiment.

In 1911, Lieut. Colonel J. A. Douglas was appointed Commandant of the 39th C.I.H. and left the 2nd Lancers, after 25 years' service in it.

On May 25th, Lieut. O. Wilkin died of enteric, at Simla.

In September 1911 the short rifle with bucket was issued to the regiment.

Owing to scarcity, the regiment received orders that it would not attend the Coronation Durbar concentration.

The polo team (Knowles, Scott, Robertson, Davison) were beaten in the Bhopal Cup Tournament at Jubbulpore, in October, by the Cavalry School team, 5 to 3.

Squadron training by wings tóok place at Dhana, in November 1911. Regimental training at the same place in January 1912.

Lieut. D. E. Whitworth won the Cavalry School Heavy Weight Pony point-to-point on " Belinda II."

DECEMBER 12TH 1911 TO MARCH 1ST 1912.

The Coronation Durbar was celebrated at Saugor by a parade of the troops in the garrison, a durbar, fireworks, etc. Ressaidar Suraj Singh, representing the Cavalry School Staff at Delhi, had the honour of being presented to H.M. the King Emperor.

Major A. G. Pritchard commanded the detachment of trick riders (32) sent to Calcutta for the military tournament there. Ressaidar Mohammed Razza and Jemadar Abdul Latif Khan were presented to His Majesty at Calcutta. His Majesty inspected the Detachment Camp at Calcutta.

The following pensioned and serving Indian officers were present at the Delhi Durbar :—Rissaldar Ganga Dat, Ressaidars Bhajju Singh, Sohan Singh : Pensioned Rissaldars Bahram Singh, Man Singh, Mohammed Razza, Kala Singh, Bahadur (A.D.C. to M. of Patiala), Hira Singh, Rissaldar Major Ali Mohammed Khan, Bahadur, and Ressaidar Sawan Singh.

In the "Queen Empress' Light Weight point-to-point," Major F. Bennett's B.E.M. " Reinforcement " ran fourth (17 starters).

The polo team (Knowles, Gould, Robertson, Davison), played in the Calcutta Tournament in December 1911. They beat the 4th Cavalry 7—4, and were beaten by the 10th Hussars 9—5.

In the 1912–1913 Reliefs, the regiment was ordered to Meerut. The I.G. of Cavalry, Major-General M. F. Rimmington, C.B., inspected the Regiment, January 25th to 27th.

1912.—FEBRUARY 6TH TO DECEMBER 5TH.

Rissaldar Major Wazir Chand died on February 6th after a long illness. He had served for 25 years in the regiment. To him is largely owing the success of the Regimental Horse Farm at Mitalak, and he had made a particularly good Rissaldar Major.

The funeral was attended by all ranks of the regiment, and by British officers and Indian officers, and Indian officers from the Cavalry School. A tablet was erected to his memory in the Regimental Quarter Guard.

The Mess received, during February, a very handsome silver cup, presented on the occasion of the Regimental Centenary, by the Maharajah of Bikaner.

Captain K. Robertson was appointed extra A.D.C. to H.H. the Governor of Bengal, September 1st, 1912.

A regimental team competed at the B.P.R.A. in October 1912, and won second prize in the " Long aggregate " competition.

Lieut.-Colonel M. E. Willoughby rejoined the regiment on November 5th. In 1909, he had been appointed Military Attaché at Peking, till July 1st, 1912, including two extensions, owing to the revolution. His services in China were acknowledged by both the British Minister and H.M.'s Secretary of State for Foreign Affairs.

Previous to rejoining he had, on August 27th, 1912, on the occasion of the Chino-Thibetian agreement, been deputed by the Foreign Office, to take charge of the Chinese Repatriation Mission, to meet the surrendered Chinese troops on the Sikkim-Thibet frontier, and arrange for their repatriation via India. Some 3,000 troops passed through Colonel Willoughby's hands at Gnatong, and were embarked under his arrangements at Calcutta for Shanghai on October 17th and 31st, 1912.

1912–1913

Squadron training was carried out at Camp Dhana, by wings, in November and December, 1912, and regimental training in January, 1913.

On December 28th, 1912, Major H. H. F. Turner and Captain H. S. Ward rejoined the regiment, the former on completion of his term as D.A.Q.M.G. on Army Headquarters Staff, and the latter after completing the Staff College Course at Quetta. On January 22nd, 1913, Colonel M. E. Willoughby was again deputed for repatriation duty to the Sikkim-Thibet frontier. In recognition of his services in connection with the Coronation Durbar at Delhi, December, 1911, Lieut.-Colonel W. B. James received the M.V.O. and in a later Gazette the C.I.E. A tablet let into the wall of the verandah of the Quarter Guard at Saugor, bears the following inscription :—

" IN MEMORY

OF

RISSALDAR MAJOR DIWAN WAZIR CHAND

2ND LANCERS

Who died at Saugor—February 6th, 1912.

This memorial has been erected by all ranks and followers of the 2nd Lancers, as a mark of esteem."

In November, 48 Australian remounts arrived from Hurly, Calcutta ; average price 400/-.

1913

In January, 1913, the polo team (Knowles, Ward, Gould, Davison, with Salkeld 5th man) won the Cooper Allen Challenge Cup at Cawnpore, beating first, the Inniskilling Dragoons and in the final the R.W. Fusiliers. Owing to Davison being ill, Salkeld played in the final.

On January 27th, 1913, at Rampur, died Rissaldar Major Mahommed Yussuf Khan, who served in the regiment for over 32 years, accompanying it to Egypt in 1882 (Medal, Khedive's Bronze Star and 5th Class order of Mejidieh), and taking pension in 1886.

In February 1913, the regiment appeared in the 1913–14 reliefs as moving to Meerut.

In February, 1913, the polo team, as above, but with Robertson as 5th man, played in the Native Cavalry Tournament at Delhi. They beat the 4th Cavalry 6—2, and were beaten by the 18th Lancers (winners) by 6—1.

At the Cavalry School races, held at Saugor on February 22nd, and 24th, the following wins are recorded :—

Pony Hurdles, Major Knowles. 1st B.W.G. Upstart.

Arab Selling Plate, Major Bennett. 1st B.A.G. Pagoda.

Horse Hurdles, Major Bennett, 1st, B.E.M. Pearl.

Handicap Horse Hurdles, Major Bennett, 2nd, B.W.G.
Jongleur.

Stonewall Chase, Major Thomas's Ch. C.B.M., 2nd.

At the Cavalry School Horse Show, held at Saugor on February 25th, and 26th, Major Knowles won four firsts on his B.W.M. " Rabies " and two firsts and one second on his B.W.M. " M.M."

Jemadar Abdul Latif Khan was first in the single jumping for Indian officers of the Cavalry School.

The regiment was ordered to move in relief of the 11th (K.E.O.) Lancers to Delhi, in the relief programme for 1913–14, instead of to Lucknow.

Owing to shortage of rain and scarcity, the interchange of the 2nd and 11th Lancers between Saugor and Delhi was first held in abeyance, and finally postponed till the cold weather of 1914–15 (February).

Lieut.-Colonel F. H. B. Commeline vacated command of the regiment on April 30th, 1913, and Lieut.-Colonel M. E. Willoughby was appointed commandant, and Major H. H. F. Turner 2nd in Command.

Squadron training was, as usual, carried out by wings at Dhana in November and December 1913, and the regiment went into camp there for a fortnight's training in January 1914.

The detachment of the regiment (one Duffadar and five Sowars of " C " Squadron) which had been furnishing the escort for H.B.M.'s Minister at Addis Ababa since 1911, returned in December 1913.

The regiment furnished a skeleton force for a Cavalry Staff tour in combination with the Cavalry School, Saugor, on February 25th to 27th, 1914, under the direction of Major-General M. Rimmington, C.B., Inspector of Cavalry in India, who expressed himself as well pleased with the regiment.

Lieut. Colonel M. E. Willoughby received a C.M.G. in the New Year's Honours List for 1914.

The Regimental Sports were held on February 9th and 10th, 1914.

The regiment competed in the Championship tournament at Calcutta in December 1913 ; the N.C. Tournament at Delhi in February, 1914 ; and the Cooper Allen Tournament at Cawnpore in February 1914.

PART II
1914 TO 1922

INTRODUCTION TO PART II

By Brigadier General L. L. Maxwell, C.M.G.

When the regiment sailed from Bombay in November 1914, it little realized through what vicissitudes it would pass before it again reached India.

The regiment passed four winters in France. Long before it left that country it had become acclimatized to the utmost rigours of wet and cold that Flanders and Piccardy could offer to those most exposed to the elements. It had become habituated to the life, on the most intimate terms, of the French peasant, and had acquired his language. It had arrived in France trained in the use of the lance, rifle, and sabre. It left that country trained, in addition, to the bayonet, bomb, automatic rifle, catapult, and trench mortar. And it was very intimate with pick and shovel.

During that long period in France, from day to day, sometimes from hour to hour, the regiment scarcely knew whether it was a cavalry regiment or an infantry company. In the twinkling of an eye, squadrons became platoons, regiments became companies, and a cavalry brigade would become a battalion, far separated from its horses and entirely engaged in infantry warfare of the most static nature. On one occasion, so sudden was this transition from infantry back to cavalry, that man and horse were only reunited a few hours before a mounted attack, and lances were still being thrown to men of rear squadrons as the regiment actually moved forward to the galloping of enemy trenches at Villers Guislain. Three-quarters of the regiment exchanged the lungi for the steel helmet. Many representatives became acquainted with London and Paris. And the sight of a sowar seated by the fire-side of some French peasant's home was so common as to be thought no longer remarkable.

When in the fifth year of its absence from India, the regiment left the shores of Europe to form the Egyptian Expeditionary Force, part of it passed through Italy and sailed from Taranto, and part (with all the horses) sailed from Marseilles.

49

E

It reassembled within those very entrenchments at the storming of which it had been present, and past which it had ridden, on its dash to Cairo 36 years previously. From these entrenchments it now rode out en route for Philistia. Later it climbed the Judaean Heights, knew Jerusalem, and the City of Palms, and descended to the valley of the Jordan. Here in one of the lowest parts of the earth, hitherto considered uninhabitable during the hot months, it passed a great part of summer occupied sometimes with fighting, and always with flies, scorpions, and sickness. From time to time the regiment passed across Judaea and refreshed itself on the coast of the Mediterranean. From Jordan it passed almost at a stride to the rivers Abana and Pharpar, and learnt that the preference expressed for them by the leprous Syrian captain was a well-founded one. On the way thither, during the great cavalry ride which began in September 1918, it passed through the long defile of Musmus, which had rung to the tramp of armed hosts through past ages. It emerged from that pass to add to the many fights already fought in the Plain of Megiddo and at the crossings of the Jordan. It saw Damascus and tasted of the grapes thereof. It crossed the Lebanon, and when the " cease-fire " went, it lay at Beirut.

But neither its marchings nor its fighting were yet ended. Again it traversed Lebanon, saw Homs, again crossed the Lebanons, and became acquainted with Sidon, Tyre, the Sea of Galilee, the Hills of Samaria, the crossings of Jordan, and was now engaged in defending from raiding Arabs the country so recently over-run by their aid.

On December 12th, 1920, the regiment was once more at Suez and there re-embarked for India as it had done in 1882. On December 25th, it brought its long period of six years' absence from India, in journeyings often, in perils in the wilderness, in perils in the sea, to an end.

1922.   L. L. MAXWELL.

CHAPTER I

FROM 1909 to 1914 the 2nd Lancers had been greatly envied by others for its long stay at Saugor, where the good climate, the low cost of living, and the magnificent sporting country surrounding made a station which could hardly be equalled in India.

Such names as Dhana, Udipura Tiwaree, Chitora, Rechawar, or Dilchaori will always conjure up happy memories for some of us of soldiering, shooting, and pigsticking carried out under very pleasant conditions.

That the cavalry regiment at Saugor was marked for internal security duties in case of war seemed to be a matter of no great importance when the British Empire appeared in every continent to be at peace within itself and with its neighbours.

The sudden gathering of war clouds in August 1914 therefore brought up our appreciation of our good fortune in station with a decisive jerk, and we had to view with dismay the mobilization and departure for France of the 1st Indian Cavalry Division. There followed rumours of a second cavalry division to be mobilized but there seemed little hope of the 2nd Lancers being included, for many regiments in possession of mobilization equipment still remained in India.

On the night of October 23rd, such subjects were being discussed at dinner in the Mess, when a telegram was brought to Colonel Willoughby. It contained orders to take over mobilization equipment, which was as good as telling us that we had been picked for active service, and should be shortly sailing for France.

The regiment suffered from one disadvantage, the preponderance of senior officers among the British officers. Many of these, in the rapid expansion of the British Army in the war, found employment more suited to their seniority than that of second-in-command of a squadron. As a result, throughout the war there was a dearth of officers proper of the regiment to serve with it, and so one or two officers of other regiments were drafted in. These were followed by officers of the India Army Reserve of Officers (I.A.R.O.), and later on by young officers of the Unattached List, fresh from training at Wellington and Quetta.

The Indian ranks were reinforced throughout the war by drafts of officers and men of other regiments, as well as by drafts from the regimental depot in India. The equal treatment which the former met soon reconciled them to service in a strange regiment, and it was difficult at times to realize how many men from other regiments wore the badges of the 2nd Lancers. The regiments to whom we were principally indebted for reinforcements were the 4th, 5th, 8th, 22nd, 28th Cavalry and the 32nd Lancers.

It is worth noting how much importance was attached to the machine gun at this time. Only a few favoured " mobilized " regiments of the Indian Cavalry had machine guns. Those sent to the 2nd Lancers on mobilization by the 32nd Lancers were 23 and 24 years old respectively, and were mounted on tripods which, even when clamped with a spanner, were seldom able to stand the strain of a burst of more than twenty rounds without collapsing. The regiment was armed with the Short Lee Enfield rifle, firing Mark VI ammunition ; hence it was necessary to entirely rearm it on arrival in France, where the use of Mark VII ammunition was universal. The Indian other ranks were armed with curved tulwars, and the officers with straight cutting swords : these were subsequently replaced, in 1916, for all ranks by the the British cavalry pattern pointing sword. It is not possible to compare the efficiency of the old and new pattern swords, as only a few officers, who had no acquaintance with the tulwar in battle, used swords, as the lance was found sufficient for the needs of the regiment on the occasion when the arme blanche was used. It may be noted that the first enemy to die at the hands of the 2nd Lancers by cold steel in this war was killed with a hogspear (see page 107).

The war diary between October 24th and December 14th sufficiently describes the mobilization of the regiment, its move by rail to Bombay, and the voyage from Bombay to Marseilles.

W.D. 1.30 p.m. Saugor, 24 Oct. 1914.

Telegraphic mobilization orders received from Jubbulpore Brigade Headquarters.

Saugor, 25th Oct. 1914.

Summonses recalling men on leave issued.

Saugor 27th to 31st Oct. 1914.

Mobilization proceeding. On 30th October orders received to take over mobilization equipment from 16th Cavalry at LUCKNOW, whither accordingly a party under Major G. KNOWLES proceeded on 31st October. On 30th October, also, intimation received from 5th Mhow Division H.Q. that a complete machine gun section (under Lieut. V. H. S. SMITH) would be supplied by the 32nd Lancers.

Saugor, 1st November 1914.

Major KNOWLES telegraphed from LUCKNOW that the mobilization equipment of the 16th Cavalry already handed over to the 17th Cavalry. Matter referred to Brigade H.Q. whence orders received following day that mobilization equipment would be supplied us by 32nd Lancers (JUBBULPORE). Major KNOWLES directed to proceed thither accordingly.

Saugor, 4th November 1914.

Telegraphic orders received from SIMLA for the regiment to proceed, at once, to JUBBULPORE to concentrate in brigade.

Saugor, 5th to 10th November 1914.

Mobilization measures proceeding.

Saugor, 10th November 1914.

The regiment proceeded by rail to JUBBULPORE in three trains. . . . On arrival at Jubbulpore, the regiment went into camp on the new polo ground. (The British regiment of the brigade, the 6th Inniskilling Dragoons, from MUTTRA, also arrived at Jubbulpore by rail this day and encamped.)

Jubbulpore, 11th November 1914.

Major-General FANSHAWE, C.B., commanding 5th Cavalry Brigade, and staff informally visited the camp. The remaining regiment of the brigade, the 38th Central India Horse, arrived by rail from GOONA and encamped alongside us.

Jubbulpore, 12th November 1914.

An advance party (2nd Lieut. BLOMFIELD, Jem. JIWAN SINGH and one N.C.O.) left by mail train for BOMBAY to take over sea rations and make preliminary arrangements for embarkation.

Jubbulpore 13th November, 11 a.m.

G.O.C. 5th Cavalry Brigade inspected the horses in the lines. Orders received for movement to BOMBAY by rail leaving JUBBULPORE on 15th November. Rail timings received.

Jubbulpore, 15th November, 1914.

The regiment entrained at Jubbulpore in three trains.

Bombay, 17th November 1914.

Regiment arrived at Bombay Docks at 6.30 a.m. and received orders to go into camp at the MARINE LINES and to embark next day. Officers were accommodated at the Taj Mahal hotel.

54   A HISTORY OF THE 2ND LANCERS

Bombay, 18th November 1914.

The regiment embarked at ALEXANDRA DOCK :—

Regtl. H.Q., B Squadron and D Squadron, and M.G. Section in the Transport " CITY OF LAHORE," with following British officers :—

Colonel M. E. WILLOUGHBY, C.M.G. (Commandant).

Major J. F. BENNETT.

Capt. G. GOULD (Offg. Adjutant).

Lieut. V. H. S. SMITH (32nd Lancers) (M.G.O.).

2nd Lieut. P. V. BLOMFIELD.

2nd Lieut. E. W. D. VAUGHAN (Offg. Qr. Mr.).

A and C Squadrons embarked in the Transport " MANORA " with the following British officers :—

Major L. L. MAXWELL.

Major G. KNOWLES, D.S.O.

Lieut. H. BANISTER, I.A.R.O. (Attd.).

Captain GOULD WILLIAMS, I.M.S. (M.O.).

At sea, 20th November 1914.

Owing to inefficiency of engine room crew on " CITY OF LAHORE," this ship steadily fell behind during the night and by 10 a.m. had come to a standstill, the engine room crew giving trouble. Escorting cruiser asked by wireless reason for delay and gave orders that unless ship could steam over. 5 knots she was to return to Bombay. Fatigue parties from the troops were employed to hoist cinders, the engine room hands having allowed same to accumulate. These fatigues lasted all afternoon and night. The ship started to return at 12.40 p.m.

Bombay, 21st November 1914.

Ship arrived and anchored 11.30 a.m. The insubordinate Arab firemen sent ashore in arrest under military escort with police.

Bombay, 22nd November 1914.

Ship left anchorage to overtake convoy with a new engine-room crew. One charger died this evening.

At sea, 23rd November to 30th November 1914.

Passed ADEN 11.15 p.m., 28th November, and PERIM 8.30 a.m. 29th. The weather was favourable and sea smooth across the Arabian Sea and the horses exercised daily on Manj mattings. Ordinary board ship routine carried out. Owing to the following wind the 'tween decks were very trying to the horses, several of which suffered from fever during the first few days. Each morning, in addition to stables routine, the men were daily exercised on the upper deck at physical drill and musketry exercises. Theoretical instruction each afternoon.

Suez, 3rd December 1914.

Arrived at anchorage and caught up convoy again.

Suez, 4th December 1914.

Remained at anchorage. Leading ships of the convoy filing into the SUEZ CANAL.

Suez Canal, 5th December 1914.

Weighed anchor 8.53 a.m. and entered canal shortly after 9 a.m. Arrived

ISMAILIA 4.30 p.m. and anchored for the night with several other ships of the convoy in LAKE TIMSAH. Between SUEZ and ISMAILIA passed many regiments guarding the canal, and at work at entrenchments on the east bank (among others 24th Punjabis, 126th Baluchis, 7th Gurkhas, and 2nd Rajputs).

Suez Canal, 6th December 1914.

Weighed anchor 8 a.m., arrived Port Said 2.50 p.m., passed Bikanir Camel Corps where canal leaves lake Timsah. Again various other corps along east bank, and a considerable encampment, including cavalry at EL KANTARA, where old Pelusium caravan route from Cairo to Syria crosses the canal. Allowed Indian officers, Kot Dafadars and batmen to go ashore at Port Said. The men here saw aeroplanes for the first time.

Port Said, 7th December 1914.

Weighed anchor and formed convoy outside breakwater. Convoy started at 1.15 p.m., escorted by the French cruiser FOUDRE, in three lines, 25 ships in all.

At sea, 12th December 1914.

Passed MALTA 4.15 a.m., GOZO at 7 a.m., and PANTELLARIA at 6 p.m. 10.30 p.m. off CAPE BON, where convoy allowed to disperse and proceed independently.

At sea, 13th December 1914.

Off SARDINIA 10 a.m. Considerable westerly swell.

Marseilles, 14th December 1914.

S.S. MANORA docked by 1 p.m. After veterinary inspection horses came off by 7 p.m. and tied up to rope on docks. S.S. CITY OF LAHORE arrived but did not come alongside.

Marseilles, 15th December 1914.

A and C squadrons, after drawing new rifles, bayonets, ammunition, and extra warm clothing, marched to CAMP BORELLY.

The regiment disembarked at Marseilles under a leaden sky and in a biting wind, conditions very strange to the Indian ranks. The enthusiasm of the Marseillais for the Indian troops had passed the first vociferous stage in which it greeted General Sir James Wilcocks and his Corps, but an occasional shout of " Vivent les Hindous ! " from onlookers, as the men led their horses through the cobbled streets, testified to its continued existence.

Marseilles, 15th December 1914.

A and C Squadrons encamped at BORELLY racecourse on eastern outskirts of the city. Ground very wet and no iron picketting peg would hold. Tents for the regiment were ready pitched. Water arrangements were good. Supplies 1,000 yards distant, all had to be carried. H.Q., B and D squadrons and M.G. Sect. disembarked and remained in dock all night.

Marseilles, 16th December 1914.

H.Q. and remainder of the regiment marched into camp BORELLY 1 p.m. Col. M. E. Willoughby, C.M.G., commands the Brigade vice Maj. Gen. Fanshawe. Major Maxwell officiates in command of the regiment. Regiment continues to draw warm clothes and other equipment. All leaders learning bayonet work. Frost at night.

Marseilles, 19th December 1914.

In camp BORELLY. The regiment received five interpreters (Sous Officiers of French cavalry regiments).

These interpreters were employed principally in assisting in billeting work, and occasionally in the purchase of extra forage and mess stores. Their command of English varied, the interpreting of one of them being limited to rendering the Flanders patois into French more comprehensible to the British officer. As a matter of fact we found in certain parts of Flanders that it was easier to converse with the inhabitants in English mixed with a few words of German than in French.

The regiment left its mess tent and all camp equipment in the skating rink at Marseilles. For the latter some compensation was paid later.

Marseilles, 21 December 1914.

At 8 a.m., H.Q., A Squadron, and 5 A.T. carts (1st line transport) marched to ARENC railway station, followed during the day by (1) C squadron, and (2) B and D Squadrons and entrained for ORLEANS in three trains. Arrangements good. Troops travelled in covered trucks. Officers in 1st Class compartments. Rations and forage till 25th inclusive were taken. We were received everywhere with much kindness. Guards of honour were paraded at many stations. Hot coffee and water provided at all stops. Each day there was a three-hour halt for cooking ("*Halte répas*"). Fuel, water, and bricks were provided; but officers were taken to nearest hotel.

Orleans, 23rd December 1914.

The first train (H.Q. and A squadron) arrived at LES AUBRES (an outlying station at ORLEANS), 7.30 p.m., detrained at once and marched 7 miles to CAMP LA SOURCE. Last mile heavy mud. Motor lorries had to shift loads to A.T. carts provided for the purpose. Arrived in camp at midnight. It was found with some difficulty. No guide was provided. It was a very dark night. The only directions we received on marching off were to be very careful not to leave the road, for a man and horse who had done so on the previous day had been swallowed up in the mud. We passed the statue of Joan of Arc as the clocks struck 10 p.m. As we proceeded, the sky seemed to come down on us, and it was impossible to see one's hand in front of one's face. After marching for about two hours, we judged that we should be nearing camp. Large white flakes of snow were falling. We saw a light and found it was in the tent of an officer who knew where camp was, and he supplied us with a guide. This man conducted us across about a mile of liquid mud and we found two rows of empty, flapping and sodden tents. This was camp. The snow, the first which our men had ever experienced, was now falling steadily. A trumpeter was told off to blow the regimental call and after about two hours, the transport was summoned up out of the darkness. We turned in just as dawn was breaking. At that time the regiment was still in drill uniform.

Orleans, 24th December, 1914.

It snowed heavily on arrival in camp : transport was delayed by mud. A Squadron was settled down (camp already pitched) by 4 a.m. C squadron arrived by 5 am., and B and D Squadrons by midday. Arrangements here as follows : B.H.Q. at ORLEANS six miles away. Ordnance and Veterinary hospital nine miles away at LA CHAPELLE. Water 1½ miles distant. Forage one mile. The motor transport necessary to draw warm kurtas and frost shoes from ordnance very limited. A water cart has been supplied us as part of our transport.

Orleans, Christmas Day, 1914.

A very hard frost during night froze all the mud. Their Majesties' Christmas cards to all officers and Indian troops arrived at 9 a.m. and were distributed.

Orleans, 26th December to 30th December 1914.

Busy equipping and reclothing. Only five combatant B.O.'s with the regiment. Much rain and mud. The Queen's body belts with autograph letter and Princess Mary's pipes and tobacco for all ranks were received and issued.

At Orleans the regiment had perhaps the most uncomfortable time of its stay in France. Had it not been for the issue of warm serge clothing, it is doubtful whether the majority of men could have withstood the conditions of snow, rain, and deep mud. The efficiency of the Ordnance Department in equipping the regiment at Orleans was the first example it met with of the organization of the rearward services of the B.E.F.

Orleans, 1st January 1915.

Regiment began its move from CAMP LA SOURCE at midnight 31st December/1st January, and entrained by squadrons at LES MURLINS station and PORT SEC station.

The French troop trains were all made up of a fixed number of covered and flat trucks, with a passenger coach for officers. Each covered truck held eight horses, four at each end, heads towards the centre. In the centre was room for two men and rations for the complete journey. Rings were fixed in the

roof above the heads of the horses, but they were not tied to
them, as it was found the horses were liable to break their
necks if they came down.   Breast ropes tied across from the
side rings were used to tether the horses.   The O.C. train
held a paper called the " Bon de transport," which showed
what stops were laid down for watering and as " haltes
répas."   All watering had to be done at these stops, and during
the time laid down for the " halte."   Any watering at any
other stops, or after the limit of the " halte," made men
liable to be left behind, as the French staff started the train at
the advertised time regardless of what the troops were doing.
Troop trains in France ran to the minute, and the retarding
of any train owing to slowness in entraining or detraining was
regarded as a serious offence.   To troops newly arrived from
India this strictness in the matter of trains was strange.

CHAPTER II

Marthes, 3rd January, 1915.

Detrained at BLENDECQUES (near ST. OMER) whence it was a 10 mile march to the regiment's billets at MARTHES. The last squadron was in billets by 3 p.m. Steady rain. Capt. K. ROBERTSON (who had been attached to the 2nd Lifeguards) rejoined and was posted to A Squadron.

On leaving India, the regimental mess was split up into five, one for headquarters and four squadron messes. Where two squadrons found themselves in one village they usually amalgamated if a house could be found large enough for this purpose. Here headquarters and A Squadron were billeted in Marthes, which was situated on a ridge and so moderately dry. C Squadron and the M.G. Section in the straggling village of Ham, however, experienced the full discomfort of living in a waterlogged Flanders marsh. Blessy, in which B and D found themselves, was almost as low as Ham.

This march to Marthes was the first of very many night marches in France. Dawn came with drizzling rain, and soon after the regiment reached Marthes, a dingy village of sixty or eighty houses. As it is typical of hundreds of other villages in that country, it is worth describing. The majority of the houses are small labourers' cottages, some detached in tiny gardens, others built in long rows, all fronting on the village street. These cottages are of little value for billeting purposes, at least from the cavalry point of view. The larger houses, which are mostly situated on the outer edges of the village, are for the greater part small farms all built on the same plan. The living house and outhouses are built round a square courtyard, in the centre of which is always a malodorous midden heap. A cobbled pavement runs round the edge of the courtyard. The outhouses consist of spacious barns, made with a frame-work of beams filled in with mud, or bricked low cowhouses and stables. The barns make excellent airy stables or billets for men ; as a rule they were dry but very draughty, and the men soon became acclimatised to an amazing degree to conditions of wet and cold. They quickly became as hardened to the weather conditions of northern France as any British troops in the country. At the back of the farm buildings are usually pent houses intended for the shelter of waggons and agricultural instruments but, according to the French billeting regulations, all unpainted waggons must be put out into the open and army horses put in their place, and so these waggon shelters were the chief source of accommodation for our horses.

British and Indian officers were willingly given rooms by the inhabitants, partly for the honour of entertaining an officer, thus proving their house of a status above that of a vulgar cottage, and partly because an allowance of a franc a day was paid for each officer.

It was always difficult to find rooms for messes and kitchens, as no government allowance was given for them, and the inhabitants found it very inconvenient to have strange servants sharing their kitchens and freely borrowing their pots and pans. The regiment had been authorized to buy a two wheeled cart at Orleans as a mess cart. This was a yellow and black hooded cart capable of carrying a good quantity of stores, and invariably forced to carry an excess. It is almost incredible that it lasted for the whole of the regiment's time in France, but its frequent breakdowns furnished a constant source of employment for that most ingenious artificer Armourer Dafadar Bishen Singh.

The cafés of Flanders are known as estaminets, and cannot be compared for magnificence with the public houses of England. As a rule they are ordinary cottages, one room of which is set apart for the " débit de boissons." They dispense at low rates thin French beer, which British troops found very disappointing, amazingly bad cognac, poor coffee, and a variety of sweet sticky syrups, beloved of the French.

The winter of Flanders is too well known now to need any description, and by the beginning of spring 1915, the men resigned themselves to an indefinite continuance of such conditions. The advent of a European spring therefore came as a welcome surprise to them. During the regiment's stay at Marthes, including the variable excursions and returns, the weather was vile. There was little or no frost and the rain was never ceasing. The men at that time piled on as many clothes as they could get hold of, and but for the strictest orders, would have worn Bálaclava caps under their lungis on all parades. In this condition they were very like " the adder which stoppeth her ears " and the consequent shouting and repeating of orders was very trying. At first some of them slept with their boots on ; but they soon found that the price of this was swollen feet, and that a dry pair of socks without boots kept the feet much warmer.

Issues from ordnance at this time were most profuse, and without any check, and so the Indian ranks, fresh from the thrift-enforcing conditions of the silladar system, were some-what exuberant in their demands. As a result the men's kits developed gigantic proportions, resulting in the overload-ing and consequent breakdown of the transport in the first move to Lozinghem. After that the strictest supervision of the loading of transport and constant kit inspections were found to be necessary to check this evil. Some of the men, finding that their transport kits were so rigorously inspected and reduced, went to the most ingenious lengths in loading up their horses, such as wearing a double amount of under-clothing, folding extra articles in their great coats or even in their saddle blankets, and filling their canvas water buckets with all sorts of miscellaneous gear. Pack horses especially were liable to be loaded with unauthorised kit. Squadron commanders' inspections of their squadrons on the morning of a march were therefore not as a rule uneventful.

EXTRACT FROM REGIMENTAL ORDERS. BY MAJOR L. L. MAXWELL,

COMMANDING 2ND LANCERS

No. 233 Field Service Order. Dated, Marthes, Tuesday, January 5th, 1915.

In default of any special orders, the following will be carried in F.S. Order.

(A). *On the horse.*
  (1) Rest of day's feed.
  (2) Hay net (empty).
  (3) One blanket for horse (under saddle).

(4) One blanket for man (under saddle if possible, otherwise
    behind saddle).

Behind saddle.

(1) Corn Sack (underneath).

(2) Warm coat or Kurta (on top of (1a)).

In front of saddle.

Mackintosh (if not on man).

No cape, no picketing peg.   The " agari " will be carried
    in the feed bag.

Two canvas buckets per section will be taken, to be carried
    on the rifle bucket.

Feed bags on near side.

Thirty rounds ammunition in horse bandolier.

Spare fore-shoe and nails as heretofore.   Arms as heretofore.

(B) On the man :—

(1) Under-clothing as required, a dry change always to be
    left in field kit.

(2) A " coat warm " or kurta, not both.

(3) A dry pair of socks when available, in pocket.

(4) Water bottle and haversack and filled bandolier as
    usual.   To be worn over the coat but under the water-
    proof.   The waterproof to be worn when possible over
    everything.

(5) Wire-cutters to be worn at back of belt.

(6) Field glasses to be worn as found most convenient.

NOTE (1)—The " iron " ration must at all time be kept ready
    in the ration tin, ready in case of a sudden move when
    preparation of cooked food would not be possible.

    The " iron " ration is never to be consumed without
    orders.

(2) The ammunition carriers and ration bags to be retained
    ready for use when ordered.

To this marching order were added successively at later
periods mackintoshes, steel helmets, and gas masks.   Lungis
were worn by all officers on regimental parades until the issue
of steel helmets in 1916.   When these were withdrawn in
Palestine the practice was not resumed ; this was perhaps a
mistake, as it was more than probable that the enemy,
unaccustomed as they were to the constant sight of Indian

troops at close quarters, could not distinguish British officers in lungis from the Indian ranks.

The attractions of the French towns behind the line increased with the progress of the war. Aire-sur-la-Lys was the local town for Marthes. It is a sleepy old town, full of ancient buildings reminiscent of the period when the citizens of Flemish towns were such a thorn in the side of the Duchy of Burgundy. A fine church will be remembered by some who were there, while others will retain a clearer impression of the shop of M. Abel Delbond hard by it, where one could buy excellent brandy at three francs a bottle, and red or white wine at equally moderate rates. In 1915, there were two or three third-class hotels, two tea shops of modest pretentions, and a well stocked branch of Félix Potin, the great French grocery firm. By 1917 the town could boast several excellent restaurants and a host of tea rooms.

Marthes, 4th January, 1915.

Regiment ordered to furnish one picquet, and take other precautions against spies. Capt. H. Y. SALKELD (who had come from India with the Secunderabad Brigade as interpreter) rejoined and took over command of B squadron.

Marthes, 5th January 1915.

Inspection by Brigade Commander. Lieut. D. E. WHITWORTH rejoined from duty as Railway Transport Officer, and was posted to A Squadron. The following were attached to the Regiment :—

One Acting Corporal and 10 men (drivers) of the A.S.C. ; 5 G.S. and 1 cook's waggon, 2 water carts (horsed with shire horses).

Five A.T. mule carts, 8 ditto for jhools, 46 mules and 23 Indian drivers.

The constitution of the transport went through many changes during the war. In its first form it lasted for only very few months. The British personnel were somewhat hastily made soldiers, and were difficult to look after, as there was no old regular N.C.O. to drive them. They were soon replaced by Indians. A.T. carts were found to take up too much road space, and to be unable to contain the loads which were required to be carried in France. They were replaced in the following summer by limbered G.S. waggons manned by Indian drivers from the Royal Horse Artillery.

Marthes, 9th January 1915.

Inspection of the brigade in marching order at CRECQUES by Major-Gen. COOKSON, C.B., Commanding 2nd Indian Cavalry Division. A pouring wet

day. Orders received for the brigade to do a tour of duty in the trenches
from the 11th to the 13th January.

Marthes, 10th January 1915.

An advance party under Major Knowles proceeded by motor-lorry to
BETHUNE.   Major A. G. PRITCHARD (from City of London Yeomanry)
rejoined and took over command of A squadron.

Marthes, 11th January 1915.

Fine all day. The regiment, 300 strong, assembled dismounted at
CRECQUES at 9.45 a.m. and left in 13 motor buses (converted London omni-
buses) at 10.15 a.m., followed by the Inniskilling Dragoons and the 38th
C.I.H., arrived at BETHUNE 12.50 p.m. and halted at the Marché aux Che-
vaux until 2.15 for mid-day meal, and proceeded thence on foot for LES
PLANTINS (between GIVENCHY and FESTUBERT), and took over our section
of trenches after dark from the 29th Lancers. The advanced fire trench at
this point being generally over waist-deep in water, orders had been issued
to the support trench, which closely skirts the east edge of the village, to
merely hold the forward trench by night with a few men, to prevent the
enemy from occupying it in the dark.

On the first night, Jemadar Abdul Latif took out his
patrol. On the second night 2nd Lieut. Vaughan took out
some men of C Squadron. His recollections of this patrol
are of standing in waist-deep water from about 8 p.m. to
4 a.m., very cold, very frightened (this being his first patrol),
and with three men who were so cold that he and Jemadar
Jiwan Singh had to rub their hands for a considerable period
before they could work their bolts.

A small standing patrol at some haystacks about 150 yards in
advance of the support trench acted as a link with this advance party.
Connection was maintained with the 38th C.I.H. on our right. 2nd Lancers
regimental H.Q. was at the northern end of the village immediately opposite
regimental H.Q. of the Inniskilling Dragoons, whence telephonic communication was established with B.H.Q. at the hamlet of RUE DE BETHUNE,
1 mile in rear.

Our dispositions were :—1 squadron in the trench, 1 squadron in close
support of it, and 2 squadrons in reserve in the village. The M.G. section
was in the trench with the advanced squadron. It was thus possible to
relieve the men in the water every twelve hours, and the reliefs were carried
out before dawn and after dusk. Except for desultory firing from the
enemy's trenches and occasional close shots from snipers, who appeared to
have managed to creep up to the outskirts of the village, we were unmolested
during the night.

Les Plantins, 12th January 1915.

Weather showery. The south end of LES PLANTINS was shelled for about
an hour. No casualties. Major G. THOMAS (from 7th Reserve Regiment of
Cavalry, TIDWORTH) rejoined and took over command of B Squadron. An

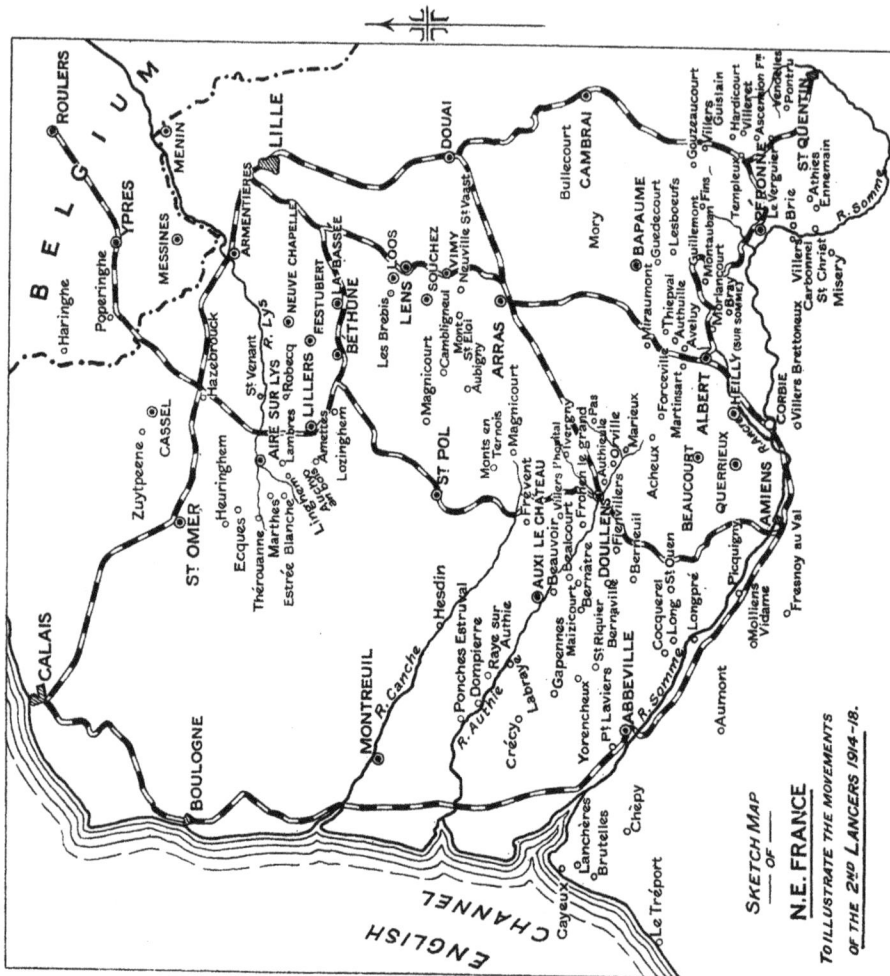

SKETCH MAP
— OF —
N.E. FRANCE

To ILLUSTRATE THE MOVEMENTS
OF THE 2ND LANCERS 1914–18.

advance party of the 3rd Skinners Horse, who are to relieve us, arrived in the evening.

Les Plantins, 13th January 1915.

In accordance with orders from the brigade, the men were withdrawn from the water and the edge of the village was held. The construction of breastworks was started last night by the R.E., and these were registered on by the German artillery during the day. After dusk we were relieved by the 3rd Skinners Horse and marched back to BETHUNE, which was reached by midnight, and where the S. and T. had made arrangements for hot food and rum for the men.

Marthes, 14th January 1915.

The Brigade left BETHUNE in motor buses at 1.30 a.m. and arrived at CRECQUES at 4 a.m.

Marthes, 15th January 1915.

In billets resting the men.

The first march up to the trenches was a most impressive one to troops new to war. As we left Bethune the sound of our guns became louder and louder until we passed through them and the men began to hear German shells coming over and to see Very lights and star shell for the first time. The sound of the guns was varied occasionally by a rattle of musketry, which seemed to run up and down the line, then die away in the distance. By the time we were nearing the trenches it was pitch dark and one kept running into the man in front if there was a check. The trenches in front of Les Plantins were swamped out and the section of trench which we held was five hundred yards behind the front line proper. Fifty yards behind the trench was a building, then in tolerable repair, afterwards to become famous as " Smelly Farm." The trench itself was about three feet across and two feet deep, and had about two feet of extremely dirty water in it. The parapet was about two feet high and in very few places bullet proof. The machine guns were in the trench and sited for frontal fire. It is doubtful whether these old Maxims with their rain-soaked belts would have given much of an account of themselves if we had been attacked. Dawn broke to show a waterlogged plain in front of us, and on our right a road lined with willow trees running out towards the enemy. A fog obscured the distance and nothing could be seen of the German trenches. On our right we were in touch with the C.I.H. ; but on our left no contact was obtained with the Inniskillings until the evening. Reconnaissance in that

F

direction involved either walking along the top, to the great
pleasure of the German snipers, or going along the trench,
which, within a few yards of our left flank, involved actual
swimming ; and be it here remembered that it was January
in Flanders.

A regimental mess was formed at H.Q. in Festubert in
a small cottage where a single shell might have knocked out
the lot of us ; but in those days we were green. A cottage
near Smelly Farm had been converted into a hospital, where
the men on coming out of the trench had their feet rubbed
with whale oil, and were given hot tea, rum, and a pair of dry
socks each. That no men were evacuated with trench feet
was a triumph for the doctor (Capt. W. P. Gould Williams),
especially as other units evacuated up to sixty or eighty from
exposure to cold under the same conditions.

During the morning of the 12th, the Hun gave us an
instructive exhibition of the harmless nature of his 77 m.m.
gun when firing shrapnel.

When relieved by the 3rd Skinners Horse on the evening
of the 13th, all the men were very much exhausted, and the
march back to Bethune was a slow and painful affair, only
relieved by the drabi of an A.T. cart, which was taking back
the machine guns, driving into the La Bassée canal, where the
mules were drowned and the machine guns only retrieved with
difficulty. A halt was made at Bethune before embussing,
during which the battalion officers had a supper of bread and
cheese and beer at the Café de L'Univers. During the meal,
one officer who was asked why he did not take his gloves off,
replied laconically, " Not gloves, only mud." This sufficiently
indicates the condition of all of us.

Billets at Marthes were reached in the early hours of the
morning of the 14th, and the following day was devoted to
resting and getting clean again. This was a red letter day
from the British officers' point of view, for short leave to
the United Kingdom was opened for the first time (at first
three days, then five days, and later extended to eight days).
It was generally closed before and during any general action,
such as Neuve Chapelle or Loos. Notwithstanding these
interruptions, it is probable that most officers got home on the
average at least three times a year.

Entries in the war diary from January 15th to March 11th show a succession of inspections, route marches, and tactical exercises, varied by a few expeditions towards the front to dig rear line trenches.

On January 10th, H.R.H. the Prince of Wales visited the regiment.

Sir John French inspected the corps on January 18th. Those who were there will not forget the long wait in the snow, the mud, the bitter cold and the spectacle of the Brigadier's horse rolling in the slush in front of the brigade. Another diversion was afforded by a patrol of the C.I.H., who galloped in with the news that a force of enemy cavalry were approaching. This force turned out to be the Commander-in-Chief and his staff.

On the 21st, Colonel Commeline, who had come out to France as a Field Cashier, visited the regiment ; also Colonel James and Major Trafford. A local photographer was therefore engaged to take a group of 2nd Lancer officers. An A.S.C. officer who happened to be in the vicinity joined the group uninvited, and his presence was not discovered until after the group had been taken. The group included the French interpreters. A copy of it may be seen in the regimental war album.

Lieut. D. S. Davison, who had been wounded when serving with the 4th Dragoon Guards in the neighbourhood of Messines, rejoined and resumed his duties as adjutant.

The life of the regiment during this period developed into a routine of stables, exercise, and foot parades, punctuated by corps and divisional outings, which, as the ubiquitous crops confined all movements to roads, were neither very interesting nor instructive to the troops, and involved much sitting about on the sides of roads and coffee-housing. On such days as squadron parades were ordered, they consisted usually in exercise and stables in the morning and foot parades in the afternoon. At first, before the horses became muscled up again after their long voyage, there was a little foot-lameness and a good deal of brushing. Cracked heels, now made their appearance. One of the most effective checks to this was a regimental order forbidding horses to be ridden into ponds to water. It was astonishing to see the eagerness with which the horses drank from these village ponds. The water was always brown and discoloured, and often malodorous. Yet the horses invariably drank better from them than from the clear and more inviting-looking streams which abounded in the Pas de Calais. The prevention of thrush was an ever present worry. While in billets the horses often stood on a thick layer of decaying straw, the removal of which was impossible owing to the swampy nature of the ground beneath. As time went on, and the horses became acclimatized, there was very little lameness, a fact almost entirely due to the strictness with which all trotting was restrained to the hound jog of eight miles an hour, although perhaps over ninety per cent. of the horses' work at this time was done on metalled roads. Horses which came to France unsound in a great many cases improved considerably under the slow, steady work, coupled with the effect of the excellent rations of English oats and hay. A good example of this was " Reinforcement," an old thoroughbred mare of Major Bennett's, which had no sound leg in 1914, and which by 1916 was being galloped across country day after day without a thought of dicky tendons.

Mention may be made here of the extraordinary devotion of the silladar to his horse throughout the war, especially in stress of very cold weather, when British troops deprived their horses of their rugs, but never the silladar. The story is told of an astounded French farmer who found that his cow, although she was carefully tethered each night on a new patch of clover and ate the whole of her allotment every night, grew thinner and yielded less milk daily. One night he kept watch and saw a sowar with his sword carefully reap the clover to the exact limits of the cow's tether, and bear away the proceeds to his horse.

Most of the officers of the regiment who had been temporarily employed elsewhere had now rejoined. The following were present with the regiment :—

Commandant	..	Col. M. E. Willoughby, C.M.G.
2nd-in-Command	..	Major L. L. Maxwell.
Adjutant	..	Lieut. D. S. Davison.
Quarter Master	..	Lieut. H. Banister.
M.O.	..	Capt. W. P. Gould Williams.
A Squadron ..	..	Major A. G. Pritchard

		Capt. K. Robertson.
B Squadron ..	..	Major G. Gwyn-Thomas.
		Capt. H. Y. Salkeld.
C Squadron ..	..	Major G. Knowles, D.S.O.
		2nd Lieut. E. W. D. Vaughan.
D Squadron ..	..	Major J. F. Bennett.
		Capt. G. Gould.
		2nd Lieut. P. V. Blomfield.
M.G. Section	..	Lieut. D. E. Whitworth.

Davison, Pritchard, Robertson, Gwyn-Thomas, and Whitworth were all on furlough when war broke out, and rejoined the regiment from appointments in England or France.

CHAPTER III

MARCH 11TH, 1915 TO JULY 22ND, 1915.

LOZINGHEM—THE MARCH TO BELGIUM—AUCHY AU BOIS.

THE battle of Neuve Chapelle, as far as the Indian Cavalry Corps was concerned, ushered in a period of feverish marching, counter-marching, standing to, and standing down, which continued until the middle of May, when the corps, as if hopeless of ever coming into contact with the Hun, settled down to a state of lethargy which ended with the move down to the Somme in the following August. As a direct result of Neuve Chapelle occurred what was popularly known in the corps as the " first battle of Lozinghem."

Marthes, 11th March 1915.

Orders received by motor cyclist from Brigade H.Q. a little before midnight 10th/11th that, the 1st Army having driven the enemy from NEUVE CHAPELLE and now attacking the AUBERS ridge, the division is to move to a position of readiness by daylight in the wood LEMARQUET, and that the MHOW Brigade accordingly is to march to LOZINGHEM. The regiment assembled at MARTHES at 3.15 a.m. and joined the brigade at BASSE BOULOGNE at 4 a.m. Night very dark. We were the rear regiment of the brigade, the 38th C.I.H. in front of us. At ESTRÉE BLANCHE the MEERUT Brigade (13th Hussars, 3rd Skinners Horse, and 18th Lancers) joined the column. We arrived at LOZINGHEM about 9.30 a.m. and the whole brigade picketed in the woods about Château MONT EVENTÉ. Towards dusk, the men were allowed to go into billets in the village of LOZINGHEM, the horses and 100 men remaining bivouacked in the woods. Throughout the day the brigade was held in readiness to move at an hour's notice. News received to-day that attack on AUBERS RIDGE was checked, but German counter attack was repulsed and 1,000 German prisoners taken.

Lozinghem, 12th March 1915.

Just before daybreak a heavy and continuous cannonade N.E. of us. Regiment out of billets and concentrated at MONT EVENTÉ Château woods at 5.30 a.m. in readiness to move at one hour. During the forenoon news received that our 2nd Army had captured LEPINETTE, and that all German counter attacks at NEUVE CHAPELLE had been repulsed. Went into billets at night as for yesterday.

Lozinghem, 13th March 1915.

Still standing to ; but one squadron at a time allowed to exercise for one hour each. Notice of readiness extended to two hours. News received that the attacks of 4th and Indian Corps yesterday were very successful, the line having been moved forward about three-quarters of a mile over a front of some 3,000 yards.

Lozinghem, 14th March 1915.

Standing to at 1 hour 20 minutes notice. Orders received at 4 p.m. to move to new billets in rear, the 2nd Lancers being sent to the villages of LIETTRES and LINGHEM. The brigade marched at 5 p.m. and the regiment reached its billets at 9 p.m.

These extracts from the war diary give a very good idea of the usual experiences of cavalry in France during the next three years, when the British contemplated breaking through the German line. The procedure was known colloquially as " assembling before the *G* in *G*ap." It invariably terminated in sudden and urgent orders to return to billets in some back area. The march back from Lozinghem was a particularly gloomy affair. It was wet and dark, and behind us the horizon was continually lit up by gun flashes, as if that were needed to remind us that the longed-for opportunity of closing with the Hun had not materialized.

Heuringhem, 18th March 1915.

. . . " left LIETTRES at 7.45 a.m. . . . arrived HEURINGHEM 10.45 a.m."

Heuringhem, which is just south of St. Omer (then G.H.Q.), was a very good billet. Stabling was plentiful and the inhabitants friendly. An amusing incident occurred when Pardessus, one of our four interpreters, went into a farm, wearing a lungi. The patronne of the house, imagining him to be a Hindu, refused to understand a word he said, and to his reiterated shouts of " mais je suis français comme vous," would only answer " anglais non compris " in the new Franco-British language, then in its infancy.

During our stay in this village we used to send digging parties to Robecq to construct a chain of breastworks and strong points. It would be interesting to discover whether these were used in the big German push of 1918.

Lieut. J. Nethersole, 25th Cavalry, arrived here and remained attached to the regiment until the end of April.

Lambres, 6th April 1915.

Regiment moved to LAMBRES (2 miles S. of AIRE).

72 A HISTORY OF THE 2ND LANCERS

From this village digging parties were sent in 'buses for work round St. Venant. The following officers of yeomanry regiments were attached to the regiment here :—

Major J. H. Beer, Sussex Yeomanry.

2nd Lieut. L. A. Downey, Sussex Yeomanry.

2nd Lieut. M. C. Hayter, County of London Yeomanry.

It was about this time that British batmen were supplied for British officers of Indian cavalry regiments. Those attached to us were mostly recruits of the Inniskillings. Batmen continued to be attached until they were withdrawn at Beirut in 1919. Among the more prominent of these were Ahearne, Morgan, Tester, Nagington, and Bartington.

On April 12th, we marched back to Heuringhem ; but on arrival there were ordered to return to Lambres the next day. This afforded the troops a grand opportunity for grousing at the staff, and they took full advantage of it.

Lambres, 24th April 1915.
Orders for regiment to be ready to move at two hours' notice received at noon. Orders received to turn out at 4 p.m. Brigade marched at 5.15 p.m., from LAMBRES *via* AIRE, WITTES, WARDRECQUES, to ZUYTPEENE, three miles W. of CASSEL. While trotting through AIRE, Major THOMAS' horse slipped and he broke his leg. Arrived ZUYTPEENE 11.45 p.m. and moved into close billets.

Zuytpeene, 25th April 1915.
At half-an-hour's notice, 2nd Lieut. R. G. Seymour, Royal N. Devon Hussars, joined the regiment. Heavy cannonade from the direction of YPRES.

Zuytpeene, 26th April 1915.
Standing to as yesterday. Expedients for the pack carriage of 2 days' rations for men on one troop horse per troop were devised.

Zuytpeene, 27th April 1915.
Orders received to turn out at 12 noon. Marched to HAANDEKAT near HARINGHE in Belgium.

Haandekat, 28th April to 1st May 1915.
Standing to. Reconnoitring patrols sent towards LIZERNE.

Haandekat, 2nd May 1915.
Orders received at 1.30 a.m. to return to ZUYTPEENE. Marched 5.50 a.m. Three hundred mufflers received to be used as respirators to combat effect of poisonous gases.

Zuytpeene, 4th May 1915.
Marched 4 p.m. *via* STAPLE—WALLON—CAPPEL—SEROUS—BOESEGHEM —LAMBRES—LINGHEM to new billets at AUCHY AU BOIS.

Spring had now definitely arrived and the night march should have been a more comfortable affair than previous ones. As a matter of fact it will probably be remembered still by many as one of the worst marches of their recollection. It was very dark and the orders which were passed down the column were most confusing. Such orders as " dismount," probably given by some disgruntled squadron commander after a quarter of an hour's unexplained halt, were immediately followed by a shout of " trot," possibly emanating from a troop leader half-a-mile in front. Short bursts of trotting were usually followed by two or three minutes of halt. Further difficulties in keeping touch were caused by squadron commanders forgetting to leave a man at any turn or fork of roads to see that the next squadron did not go astray. Added to the then defective march discipline and " march cunning " of the brigade, was the fact that the head of the column was continually losing its way. On the whole, therefore, it was an unhappy night ; but it had good effect in drawing attention to the necessity for the strictest march discipline at night. Later it became the custom to announce in march orders that the head of the column would not proceed out of a walk, and to lay down the times and durations of all intended halts. Squadron commanders were then not taken in by cries of " trot " from in front of them, but contented themselves with pushing out a string of connecting files, sometimes until they had used up nearly the whole squadron, rather than give the order to dismount when a halt occurred, unless it happened at one of the hours notified for a halt in march orders.

Since our arrival in Flanders, the regiment had worn a distinguishing badge in the form of a light blue ribbon with dark blue edges tied round the left shoulder strap. This was now changed to a badge which remained in use up to the end of the war. It consisted of a square patch of braid with sides 1½ inches long, which was sewn on to the left sleeve about two inches below the numeral. The colours were in three equal horizontal stripes, dark blue above and below, and light blue in the centre.

The long winter and widely isolated billets and messes had had rather a disintegrating effect on the British officers of the regiment. At Auchy au Bois, where all messes were in or round about the same village, every effort was made to remedy this state of affairs.

About this time the 2nd Lancers called on a regiment of Chasseurs à Cheval, and their Colonel at first said he would return the call at an early date. A little later he said he would bring all his officers with him, and later still, when he had warmed towards his visitors, he announced his intention of returning the call accompanied by his whole regiment. Perhaps it was as well that these chasseurs were suddenly moved away and so were unable to return the call.

The long spell at Auchy au Bois was broken only by minor alarums and excursions. Among these was the " second battle of Lozinghem " where, as before, we did nothing. The corps marched to Lozinghem on May 17th, and returned to billets on the 19th.

About this time there was a call for Mahommedan volunteers to serve as machine gunners with the Shereefian army : Dafadar Mahomed Ali and some others of the 32nd Lancers went in response to the call. Mahomed Ali rejoined the regiment again at Homs after distinguishing himself by good service with the Arab forces.

The following are some events of importance :—

May 8th.—Col. Willoughby appointed Liaison Officer, Indian Cavalry Corps ; command taken over by Lieut.-Col. L. L. Maxwell.

May 20th.—Gas respirators issued to all ranks.

May 21st.—Five L.G.S. waggons, 20 draught mules, 1 N.C.O., and 10 men A.S.C., replaced S. and T.A.T. carts of A Echelon.

May 23rd.—6th Inniskilling Dragoons Horse Show at Febvin Palfart.

   2nd Lancers won :—

Waler Troop Horse Indian Cavalry	1st and 3rd.
C.B.	1st, 2nd, 3rd.
Jumping	1st and 2nd.

May 30th.—Mhow Cavalry Brigade Sports near Amettes.

   The 2nd Lancers won :—

 I.O.'s Tentpegging   1st Ris. Mikand Singh.

Section tentpegging   1st A Squadron (K.D. Ali Raza
                       Khan, K. D. Abdul Wahid,
                       A.L.D. Abdul Razaq, Sr. Mir
                       Mahomed).

½ Sect. Jumping
    N.C.O.'s   ..   1st D Squadron (Daf. Dalla Ram,
                      A. L. D. Nihalu).

The regimental trick-riders gave a display. It created an extremely good impression on the spectators, the larger proportion of whom were French, Moroccan, and Algerian cavalry-men. A regiment of Moroccan cavalry was billeted near Amettes. It was interesting to see them on parade and to see how similar their drill was to our own, and as far as one could see, their regimental drill was exactly the same. In squadron drill there were a few minor differences.

June 3rd.—M. Bellicourt, of the French Academy, and M. Jonas of *L'Illustration*, visited the regiment, and made sketches of various people. Some of these were afterwards published in Paris.

June 13th.—The 18th Lancers gave tentpegging and the 2nd Lancers trick-riding displays before the King and Queen of the Belgians at Linghem. The latter was most successful, and greatly interested their Majesties, who afterwards presented the regiment with 17,000 cigarettes and 26 lbs. of sugar candy.

June 15th.—The transport was completely reorganized. and consisted of :—

    A Echelon.—5 L.G.S. Waggons (4 mules each).
                1 (G.S.) Cooks' Waggon (4 L.D. horses).
                1 Water cart (4 mules).
                   (2 spare mules.)
    B Echelon.—5 G.S. Waggons (4 mules each).
                   (2 mules and 2 L.D. horses spare.)

June 23rd.—Indian Cavalry Corps Horse Show.

The British officers went to this in a rubber-tyred ambulance, which was attached to the regimental transport. Three subalterns—Vaughan, Blomfield and Whitworth—drove it " ride and drive," mounted on mules whose training had only begun a fortnight before. Except for carrying away a small tree on the way home. the experiment was a complete success.

It was decided that this regimental brake should be a permanent institution, but this happy decision was reversed by some highly placed medico who had happened to see its arrival at the horse show, and who invoked thunder and lightnings upon our heads for what he alleged to be a breach of the Hague Convention's rules. Our reply that the red crosses had been carefully painted out brought him no comfort. The ambulance was shortly afterwards withdrawn from our care.

At the horse show, the regiment won the 2nd prize for Indian Cavalry troop horses jumping (Daf. Ganda Singh).

Polo was now being played regularly both at Amettes and Linghem. It was about this time that the regiment played the 17th Lancers, and won a game which was quite fast, considering the conditions.

July 1st.—A party of 200 were sent to Vermelles to dig trenches, returning on July 6th without casualties.

July 8th.—Lord Kitchener inspected the Indian Cavalry Corps.

July 15th.—Brig.-Gen. G. de S. Barrow relinquished command of the brigade on appointment to B.G.G.S. 10th Corps.

July 20th.—A party of 70 went by bus to Les Brébis. The village was heavily shelled the next day by a naval gun. It was a small mining village and the houses were rather jerry built. One of the big shells sufficed to completely demolish a house. There were many casualties among the inhabitants, but we only had one man wounded.

CHAPTER IV

JULY 23RD, 1915 TO SEPTEMBER 10TH, 1916.

THE MARCH TO THE SOMME—TRENCHES AT AUTHUILLE—
TRANSFERRED TO THE 1ST INDIAN CAVALRY DIVISION—
VILLERS L'HÔPITAL—WINTER BILLETS AT AUMONT AND CHÈPY
—IVERGNY

JULY 23RD.—Lieut. Col. Neil Haig, 6th Inniskilling Dragoons appointed to command the Mhow Cavalry Brigade.

July 24th.—Capt. O. A. Duke, 22nd Cavalry, joined the Regiment. He remained with the Regiment until it left France and commanded D Squadron from September onwards.

Auchy au Bois, 1st August 1915.

The Mhow Brigade marched to AUBIN ST. VAAST (25 miles). The 2nd Lancers billeted at CONTES on the banks of LA CONCHE.

Contes, 2nd August 1915.

The brigade marched at 9.30 a.m. for the neighbourhood of BERNAVILLE (30 miles). The 2nd Lancers billeted at SURCAMPS.

Surcamps, 3rd August 1915.

Brigade marched at 9.30 a.m. for PICQUIGNY (10 miles), about 8 miles W. of AMIENS, on the banks of the SOMME. Very heavy rain during the march making the roads difficult for the transport. The transport went through the above marches without any casualties, B Echelon being on the road from 7.30 a.m. to 8.30 p.m. on the second day, and A Echelon arriving 45 minutes after the regiment.

In Picquigny, historical as the scene of the Field of the Cloth of Gold, we found for the first time the sort of French country town which popular stories of France might lead one to expect. The red roofed, and green shuttered houses cluster below a huge ruined castle, and there are big woods on the hill behind ; there is a little " place " with cafés and a row of lime trees, in fact, the country town described in any French novel. The Somme here, as elsewhere, is canalized, and runs through a maze of reedy marshes, crossed by poplar lined roads raised on causeways. Here and there one sees small loopholed cabins, from which the local sportsmen murder the

77

wild duck, using decoy duck to help them.   There are a good
many bream and perch in the marshes, and bottom fishing is
a very popular amusement.

The horses had been picketted out of doors since our arrival
at Auchy au Bois.   At Picquigny they were between the
river and a swamp, on very shaky ground, and the men were
bivouacked with the horses.   Later a disused factory was found
where some of the horses were taken, and the crowding relieved.

At Picquigny we were given our first practice in gas helmets
with real gas.   At this time the gas helmet consisted of a
flannel hood, which came right over the head and was tucked
inside the collar.   It had two eye pieces of mica, and a rubber
mouthpiece which only allowed of exhalation.   You had to
inhale through the nose, breathing the air which found its
way through the interstices of the flannel, which was soaked
in chemicals.   Needless to say this performance was most
uncomfortable.   The form of gas mask which was eventually
evolved was luxurious in comparison; in fact, after sufficient
practice it was possible to sleep in it.

Picquigny, 11th August 1915.

A party of 319 of all ranks left for a tour of duty in the trenches at AUTH-
UILLE.   This party went by bus to FRANVILLERS, and slept the night in an
uncarried field of barley, marching the next night through MARTINSART to
AUTHUILLE.

We found ourselves in a sector recently taken over from the
French.   When we first arrived it had a remarkable reputation
for tranquillity, which the neat and gardened dugouts handed
over by the French seemed to endorse.   We were immediately
opposite Thiépval Château, which was afterwards to become
famous in the battle of the Somme, and the equally famous
Leipzig Redoubt was a little to our right.   As always happened,
the advent of the British soon roused the neighbourhood to
activity, as it was our policy to wear out the enemy.   Consequently machine guns and the newly-invented "Minen-
werfers" quickly combined to destroy the rural peace of the
neighbourhood.   Our H.Q. was located in a steep bank,
honeycombed with dugouts, which overlooked the inundated
valley of the Ancre.   One or two of the dugouts connected
with the cellars of some of the houses on the northern outskirts of Authuille village.   From these dugouts the rats

came in thousands, and it became a regular pastime at night
to hunt them with sticks and electric torches ; the rats would
face the light and let you come right up to them.

We had just been issued with a mixed assortment of new-
fangled bombs, and it seemed a good idea to bomb the Ancre
for fish.   Unfortunately we found that the idea had occurred
to the French some time before, and that no fish remained.
During this tour our party was in support, and was principally
engaged in digging support trenches in front of the village.
When relieved on August 22nd, the trench party marched to
Forceville, where a party with led horses met them.   They then
marched to Beaucourt, a pleasant village full of fruit gardens,
in which the greengages were just ripe.   It was at Beaucourt
that we first tried to ride partridges.   We went in heats of
four or five.   It was essential that the horses should be fit, for
the galloping was severe.   The idea was to break up a covey
and to follow up any bird which took a solitary line, marking
him down, and trying to put him up again.   After about four
flights, each usually shorter than the one preceding it, the
bird would become too exhausted to fly further, and if he were
carefully marked down it was an easy matter to catch him.
Three partridges in a morning was reckoned a good bag.

Picquigny, 30th August 1915.
    Lieut. Wilson, and 2nd Lieut. Buck (both I.A.R.O.) with a draft of 1
Indian officer and 99 men, joined the regiment.

These were intended as a dismounted reinforcement to help
to look after the horses when the regiment went into the
trenches.   During the remainder of our time in France we
generally had a party of dismounted men.   At both the
Somme and Cambrai they were employed in making the
" cavalry track."

Picquigny, 31st August 1915.
    A conducting party was despatched to bring back led horses of trench party
from BEAUCOURT on the latter returning to the trenches at AUTHUILLE.

Beaucourt, 2nd September 1915.
    The Mhow Brigade trench party took over the sector immediately oppo-
site Thiepval from the Ambala Brigade, who relieved them on the 13th.

The relief of the 2nd Cavalry Division by the 1st Cavalry
Division, and later the reverse process, entailed the movements

of very large bodies of mounted men and of led horses to and
fro.   Billets were situated 25 to 30 miles distant, and all such
movements were carried out by dark.   During the actual
hours of relief, *i.e.* about 8 p.m. to 2 a.m., there were assembled
close in rear of Martinsart, and well within enemy shell fire,
approximately 5,500 led horses, and 2,000 mounted men to
lead them.   It was a very dark night.   This was repeated
ten days later during the relief by the 1st of the 2nd Cavalry
Division.   The regiment began to move out of trenches about
10 p.m., had reached their horses and ridden off by 2.30 a.m.
without confusion or delay.   The orderly march and forming
up in the dark, the four to five hour wait of such masses of
led horses, the discipline which ensured silence and the showing of no lights (with consequent immunity from shell fire),
the quiet and orderly arrival of the relieved troops, each man
to his horse in the dark, and the quiet departure, struck one
as a wonderfully fine performance.   Our losses were caused
chiefly by rifle grenades.   They were—1 died of wounds, and
9 wounded.   The German trenches were from 75 yards to
300 yards from our own.   Our patrols were out most nights,
examining and repairing our own wire, and reconnoitring the
enemy's works.   During this tour Major Pritchard commanded the trench party.   After this tour, the following
decorations were awarded to the 2nd Lancers :

I.O.M. (2nd Class), A. L. D. Udey Singh.

I.D.S.M., Res. Abdul Latif Khan.

,,   K.D. Ram Pershad Singh.

Picquigny, 15th September 1915.

The Mhow Cavalry Brigade was transferred from the 2nd Indian Cavalry
Division to the 1st Indian Cavalry Division, in exchange for the Ambala
Cavalry Brigade, and marched to a new billeting area.   The 2nd Lancers
were billeted in LONG and COQUEREL.

Long, 21st September 1915.

Indian Cavalry Corps inspected by Lord KITCHENER.

Long, 22nd September 1915.

Marched to new billets at BERNAVILLE.

From this village Major A. G. Pritchard left to take over
a mobile column which was being organized especially for the
battle of Loos.   After the second day of the attack he was

offered, and accepted, the command of the 2nd Battalion
Royal Warwickshire Regiment, which had been ordered to
attack through un-cut wire that day and was practically
annihilated in the process. From this command he was
appointed to the command of a brigade, and did not again
return to the regiment.

Major Gwynn-Thomas had left the regiment shortly before
to be Brigade Major to an infantry brigade. He also rose
subsequently to the command of a brigade, and did not rejoin
the regiment, although he was appointed commandant in
succession to Colonel Turner. These were but two of the
Indian cavalry officers who from this time forward went to
the infantry. Many were killed, few rejoined their regiments,
and all were a credit to the silladar cavalry. Gen. Maxwell
visited the Somme front shortly before the battle opened and
found four battalions, on a front held by about six, commanded
by native cavalry officers.

In preparation for our anticipated share in the battle of
Loos, we dumped at Bernaville our field kits, and 20 men
with 40 horses were detached to form a pack supply train.
On September 26th, two Vickers machine guns were issued to
the regiment with complete pack equipment. This at once
doubled the Machine Gun Section. Fortunately there was a
sufficiently large trained reserve of machine gunners to meet
this demand ; but they were, of course, trained in the old
Maxim, and it was only by strenuous effort on the part of the
M.G.O. that they were even moderately acquainted with
their new weapon when the battle of Loos began, although
their services were not actually called for. On October 20th,
two more Vickers guns were sent to replace the old Maxims,
making a total of four Vickers. At this time the Machine
Gun Section used only pack transport ; for each gun there
were six pack horses, one for the gun, four carrying 1,000
rounds of ammunition each, and one spare pack horse. The
personnel comprised two British officers (Lieuts. Whitworth
and Blomfield), two Indian officers (Jemadars Dhara Singh,
and Devi Chand), and 66 I.O.R. There were about 90 horses
in all. For his conspicuous good work on all occasions,
Jemadar (afterwards W.M.) Dhara Singh was awarded the
I.D.S.M.

G

Bernaville, 1st October 1915.

The brigade marched to close billets in VILLERS L'HÔPITAL. The corps was now concentrated for the operations at Loos.

Lieut. W. M. Dorling joined the regiment on September 28th, Lieut. H. G. Monks, I.A.R.O., on 3rd October, and Major J. H. Beer, Sussex Yeomanry, left to take over command of his own unit.

After a fortnight's fruitless waiting at Villers l'Hôpital, the division moved back again, the 2nd Lancers going to Berneuil and Fienvillers, the squadrons at the latter place closing in to Berneuil on the 17th.

Berneuil, 22nd October 1915.

1st Indian Cavalry Division marched to new billeting area. 2nd Lancers were billeted as follows :—H.Q., D Squadron, and transport at AUMONT, A and B Squadrons at DROMESNIL, C Squadron and M.G. section at MERI-COURT.

We now settled down to winter billets. It is beautiful country round Aumont, with big woods and rolling hills. We once beat a wood out for pig, but saw none. A few roedeer came out and were ridden unsuccessfully, but one was killed by a stick thrown by a beater who was trying to stop it from re-entering the wood. This we ate, and very good it was.

We made several attempts in France to spear pig, but never had the luck to have big enough woods round us. The 18th Lancers killed two or three very big boars near the Forest of Crécy in 1915 or 1916. Gen Maxwell was present at one meet, and killed a boar, one of the feet being now in the mess.

During this winter, a dismounted regiment was formed for purposes of trench warfare. Its organization varied from week to week and was never found to be entirely satisfactory until the whole idea of a dismounted cavalry regiment was dropped, and it became a battalion, pure and simple. This battalion was composed of three companies, each of which was furnished by one regiment of the brigade. Battalion H.Q. Staff was found by the various regimental staffs in turn. With this organization it was simple to take over a subsector of trenches from infantry.

November 6th.—2nd Lieut. L. J. Peck, I.A.R.O., joined the regiment.

November 8th.—Kote Dafadar Sant Singh, C Squadron, was decorated with the French Médaille Militaire,

November 11th.—Gen. Allenby, commanding 3rd Army, inspected the Indian Cavalry Corps. (A very big parade and a correspondingly heavy bill for damaged crops.)

December 2nd.—Lieut.-Col. H. H. F. Turner rejoined from staff employment and assumed command of the regiment.

December 6th.—Captain Gould appointed Staff Captain, Mhow Cavalry Brigade.

December 16th.—The Division moved to a new area, the 2nd Lancers being billeted in Chépy, with half a squadron at Monchaux.

December 31st.—2nd Lancers won the divisional Marathon race.

January 3rd, 1916.—Lieut. Whitworth lent to 37th Division as Divisional M.G.O., returning on February 17th.

January 6th.—Lieut.-Col. L. L. Maxwell appointed to the command of the Sialkote Cavalry Brigade. He remained in command of that brigade until it was broken up in the spring of 1918, and did not serve with the regiment again.

January 30th.—Lieut. Peck and 55 I.O.R. were lent as a digging party to the 37th Division, and employed near Souastre.

February 1st.—The Machine Gun Section of the three regiments of the brigade were amalgamated into a Machine Gun Squadron, which was commanded by Capt. Humfrey, 6th Inniskilling Dragoons.

February 6th.—Lieuts. W. Lyng and J. A. Nash, of 3rd Reserve Regt. of Cavalry, joined the regiment.

February 17th.—2nd Lancers and 38th C.I.H. competed at mounted wrestling and tug-of-war. The 2nd Lancers won the former, and the C.I.H. the latter.

February 27th.—2nd Lieut. Murphy joined the regiment.

March 5th.—The Indian Cavalry Corps ceased to exist as a corps. The 1st Division was attached to the 3rd Army, and the 2nd to the 4th Army.

Our Indian Cavalry regiments perhaps only learnt the true value of the Indian Cavalry Corps when it existed no longer. To General Rimington and his staff the Indian cavalry was not an enigma and our regiments felt that at Indian Cavalry Corps H.Q. they would always be understood and dealt with

sympathetically.   General Rimington was immensely popular
with all ranks and his departure was much regretted.

March 11th.—2nd Lieut. V. W. Smith, I.A.R.O., joined the
    regiment.

March 19th.—The 2nd Lancers, having previously beaten the
    19th Lancers in the second round of the divisional mounted
    wrestling, beat the 29th Lancers in the final.

March 24th.—A march to a new billeting area ordered for
    to-day postponed owing to a heavy snow.

Chépy, 25th March 1916.

Brigade marched at 10 a.m. to new area halting for one night en route.
2nd Lancers at ONEUX and NEUVILLE.

Neuville, 26th March 1916.

Marched from Neuville at 9.45 a.m. and reached new billets at 12.15 p.m.
2nd Lancers distributed as follows :—H.Q., B and C Squadrons in BEAL-
COURT, A Squadron at FROHEN LE PETIT, and D Squadron at ST ACHEUL.

27th March.—2nd Lieut. F. T. Commeline joined the regiment. (He was
the fourth officer now in the regiment whose father had also been in the
2nd Lancers.)

1st April.—Major P. B. Sangster rejoined from staff employ.

15th April.—Major Knowles attached to 37th Division to train divisional
cavalry and cyclists.   A. L. D. Kehar Singh won the open mile at the
10th Battn. Royal Fusiliers' Sports.

Bealcourt, 22nd April 1916.

Marched to ST. RIQUIER training ground, 2nd Lancers billeted in
YVRENCHEUX and GAPENNES.

Here followed a period of training.   Within the training
area we were allowed to ride over the crops, and realistic
training was thus possible.   On May 4th a tactical exercise
was done before General Gough, who was then commanding
the Reserve Corps.   This was followed by the departure of
some of the more senior of the brigadiers of the two Indian
cavalry divisions.   On May 7th, the division returned to its
former billets.

Bealcourt, 10th May 1916.

Division moved to new area near R. CANCHE.   2nd Lancers billeted in
IVERGNY (H.Q. and B Squadron), BEAUDRICOURT (C Squadron, D Squadron,
and B Echelon), and OPPY (A Squadron).

May 24th.—Inspection of the regiment by Sir Douglas Haig.
June 1st.—First issue of steel helmets to the regiment.

June 18th.—Digging party of 300 all ranks sent up to assist 51st Division in work in front line.

June 28th.—Digging party returned. Steel helmets withdrawn.

Ivergny, 30th June 1916.

Brigade marched to AUTHUILLE, the whole brigade being concentrated in the one village.

Authuille, 2nd July 1916.

The brigade moved to a new area. 2nd Lancers billeted in MAIZICOURT, C and D Squadrons moving later to BERNATRE.

Maizicourt, 19th July 1916.

Marched to a new area. 2nd Lancers billeted in GRAND CAMP, ROCOURT, and BOIRIN.

July 20th.—Capt. F. Jackson joined the regiment.

July 27th.—Lieut. W. Lyng wounded when carrying out a reconnaissance of XVIIth Corps front near Neuville St. Vaast.

August 1st to 9th.—Working party of 306 all ranks away digging in 17th Corps area.

August 7th.—Major P. B. Sangster appointed to temporary command of 29th Lancers. This appointment afterwards became permanent and he did not serve again with the regiment.

Grand Camp, 10th August 1916.

Marched to MAGNICOURT SUR SOMME.

11th August.—Lt. H. G. Monks, who had been serving in the Royal Flying Corps, rejoined the regiment.

16th August.—Regiment moved to Mons en Ternois (1½ miles). A working party of 300 men was away continuously throughout the month. reliefs of half the party being carried out every five days.

Mons en Ternois, 3rd September 1916.

Marched to LIGNY SUR CANCHE.

Ligny sur Canche, 4th September 1916.

Marched to GUESHART, D Squadron being in COMONVILLE.

Gueshart, 5th to 10th September 1916.

In training on the ST. RIQUIER training area.

It was here that we first saw tanks, at that time a very jealously guarded secret. They were training for their first appearance, namely the attack on Flers.

CHAPTER V

ATTEMPTED BREAK THROUGH AT GUEDECOURT—WINTER BILLETS AT LANCHÈRES

Gueshart, 11th September 1916.

Marched *via* AUXI LE CHATEAU to MEZEROLLES.

Mezerolles, 12th September 1916.

Marched *via* DOULLENS to AMPLIER.

Amplier, 13th September 1916.

Marched to QUERRIEU. The 1st Indian Cavalry Division being concentrated on the banks of the river north of QUERRIEU.

Querrieu, 15th September 1916.

Marched to a preparatory position near MORLANCOURT with a view to partaking in active operations in the neighbourhood of BAPAUME and LE TRANSLOY.

Here we found the whole of the Cavalry Corps concentrated in the same place. After waiting there for the rest of the day the Corps was opened out a little, the Mhow Brigade moving into the re-entrant which runs up from the river towards Morlancourt, where we bivouacked among uncarried stooks of barley. Tents were issued the next day luckily, for heavy rain began which lasted for three days. Everybody was soaked but very cheerful, for it seemed as though cavalry's chance had come at last. The first ray of sun which struck the camp after the three days' downpour was hailed with a spontaneous cheer from every tent in the brigade. The cheer was taken up by neighbouring troops, and seemed to spread for miles.

Morlancourt, 25th September 1916.

Mhow Brigade marched from MORLANCOURT at 5 a.m. *via* specially prepared track to forward position (in square K. 3. c. & d.) between BERNAFAY and TRONES WOODS, 38th C.I.H. and Brigade H.Q. remaining in MONTAUBAN. Watered at MAMETZ en route. Considerable difficulty in watering arrangements at forward position, which was reached at 9.15 a.m.

Regimental H.Q.'s of 2nd Lancers and 6th Inniskilling Dragoons established in a trench 100 yards W. of WATERLOT FARM. Zero hour fixed at 12.35 p.m. At 3.25 p.m. information received that infantry had taken

" Brown line " (2nd objective). C Squadron, under Major Knowles, with two M.G.'s, under Lieut. Blomfield, and A Squadron Inniskillings moved to forward position in Square S.12.b.

The general plan of action for the cavalry was that when the infantry had captured Guedecourt (their third objective), and made a gap in the German line near it, the 2nd Lancers should pass through the gap, more or less make it good to enable the Inniskillings to pass through, and gallop to Le Transloy, following the valley which runs from one village to the other. C Squadron, 2nd Lancers, was to pass through first, and form a defensive flank to the right. It was to be followed by the leading squadron of the Inniskillings, which was in turn to be followed by B and D Squadrons, 2nd Lancers, which were to form a defensive flank on the left. The Inniskillings were then to gallop through the narrow bottle-neck formed by the 2nd Lancers, and, if successful in their attack, were to be followed by the whole division, if not the corps. The question as to the best way of initiating the move forward of the cavalry was always a burning one, and was never settled. In this instance the onus of starting a whole corps of cavalry on a great enterprise was laid on the most advanced squadron of the most advanced regiment, here, on Major Knowles, C Squadron, 2nd Lancers. Whether the ambitious scheme would have succeeded or not was never determined, for the infantry attack was not wholly successful, and the 2nd Lancers were not called on to perform what at least would have been a very difficult task. A Squadron, 2nd Lancers, was given the task of mopping up all the guns which the Inniskillings were to gallop through. The squadron commander (Capt. Robertson) was given a map of the valley, which showed the positions of all guns by green dots. Every day a new edition of the map was given him. As Zero day approached the number of green spots increased enormously, until finally he found that he had nearly as many guns to attack as lances with which to attack them.

In the move forward, the regiment passed through innumerable guns, beginning with heavies in the neighbourhood of Montauban, and traversing strata after strata of gradually diminishing calibre until the position of assembly was reached near Bernafay Wood between the 60 pounders and the 18 pounders. The bombardment was at its height, and the noise passed far beyond the capacity of the ear to hear it. The number of guns in this action amounted to one per six yards of front. Later, at Passchendaele this record was beaten, one gun being employed for every three and a half yards of front. Apart from a little wildly-fired shrapnel bursting far up in the air, no shells came near the brigade.

At 12.35 p.m.—Zero hour—there was a perceptible change in the sound of the bombardment as the barrages lifted and fresh batteries came into action, while the rate of fire generally seemed to slacken a little. Then came a long wait. Orders had been received that unless Guedecourt were taken by 4 p.m. the cavalry would not be used that day. At 3.25 p.m., C Squadron, 2nd Lancers, with two machine guns, followed by one squadron Inniskillings, moved to a forward position S.E. of Waterlot Farm, and came in for some shelling, which was presumably of a counter battery nature, for they were in dead ground, and no German plane at that time dared to come within even three miles of their own trenches. One or two, it is true, came over at an extreme height, but could have done no artillery spotting. Post-war German accounts of the Battle of the Somme testify to the disgust of their infantry at the lack of support given them by their flying service. At about 5 p.m., Lieut. Vaughan, who had been sent forward to reconnoitre, actually rode through the front line of our infantry, and only discovered the fact when, seeing nothing in front, he returned to them and asked them who they were.

Morlancourt, 25th September 1916.

6.15 p.m.—Information received that LESBOEUFS had been taken but attack held up at GUEDECOURT. Advanced squadrons ordered to rejoin.

7 p.m.—Orders received to water horses and return to MORLANCOURT. Arrived back in camp. Casualties 4 horses and 1 mule killed, 3 horses wounded.

Watering was carried out in Caterpillar valley, and was finished in the dark. Then followed a most confused night march, the whole division being mixed up with the usual night traffic of empty vehicles and disabled guns going back, and full vehicles and fresh guns going up. The brigade reached Morlancourt at varying times in " extended columns of lumps."

Morlancourt, 26th September 1916.
    In camp resting.

It was on this day that a squadron of the 19th Lancers, under the command of Capt. Fitzgerald, distinguished itself in the capture of Guedecourt, which was galloped and held till taken over by infantry.

On September 27th sudden orders were received for the division to march to a back area. The brigade marched at noon to Bussy les Daours. After a stop at Ponches Estruval, the regiment reached Raye sur Authie.

October 4th.—Lieut. P. Bannerjee, I.M.S., joined the regiment on appointment as Medical Officer.

October 6th.—Capt. W. P. G. Williams, I.M.S., on transfer to India, reported his departure.

At Raye sur Authie an unsuccessful drive for pig was attempted. The line of beaters met a party of French sportsmen in the middle of the wood. These turned out to be the owner and some friends. In the subsequent enquiry, however, the affair was ingeniously explained away. Ten boars were killed by the Indian Cavalry Division, some of great weight, but not fighters. They had very warm furry coats, not unlike bear.

Raye sur Authie, 1st November 1916.
    Marched 8 a.m. Arrived Quesnoy le Montant 2 p.m. and billeted for the night.

Quesnoy le Montant, 2nd November 1916.
    Marched 10 a.m. Arrived BRUTELLES 12 noon. Billets not sufficient for the whole regiment, 250 animals and 60 men being out in the open.

Brutelles, 7th November 1916.
    LANCHÈRES village added to the regimental billeting area and H.Q., B Squadron and B Echelon moved in there, the remainder of the regiment remaining in BRUTELLES.

During the foregoing period, most of the subaltern officers attended the Divisional School at Cayeux, where Major C. R. Terrot (6th Dragoons) conducted a series of courses, each lasting three weeks.

All Indian ranks of the regiment who were serving with the Mhow M.G. Squadron were returned to the regiment on November 21st, on the re-organization of the M.G. Squadron as a purely British unit. They had been in action at Beaumont Hamel during the first fortnight of the month.

A pioneer battalion, a new euphemism for a digging party, from the brigade, was sent to Fricourt and afterwards to Mondicourt, and those men who remained with the regiment were kept hard at work looking after the horses. The latter might naturally have been expected to be in a somewhat flabby condition by March 19th, when the monotonous routine of billet life was interrupted by a sudden order to move. That the casualties in horseflesh in the intense cold of the ensuing month were negligible reflects well on the regiment's horse management.

December 6th.—Lieut. B. C. Waller joined the regiment.   He
    remained with the regiment until December, 1917.

January 9th, 1917.—2nd Lieut. R. P. L. Ranking, 5th Cavalry,
    joined the regiment,

January 27th.—Capt. D. E. Whitworth rejoined from the
    Mhow M.G. Squadron and took over the duties of
    Adjutant.

February 27th.—Lieut. G. H. Monks rejoined from the Mhow
    M.G. Squadron.

March 12th.—Lieut. N. H. Broadway arrived from Rouen.

March 17th.—2nd Lancers Pioneer Coy. rejoined the regiment
    from Mondicourt.

CHAPTER VI

MARCH 19TH, 1917 TO NOVEMBER 30TH, 1917.

THE MARCH FROM THE SEA TO MIRAUMONT—ATTEMPTED
BREAK THROUGH AT BULLECOURT—ST. CHRIST—ATHIES—THE
TRENCHES AT VILLERET AND LE VERGUIER—FIRST BATTLE OF
CAMBRAI

Petit Laviers, 19th March 1917.
　Marched from Lanchères to PT. LAVIDIERS.

St. Ouen, 20th March 1917.
　Marched to ST. OUEN.

Aveluy, 21st March 1917.
　Marched to AVELUY. The regiment bivouacked at Square W 163 (Ref.
Sheet 57 D 1/40,000) at 8.30 p.m.　B Echelon halted at HÉRISSART.

Miraumont, 29th March 1917.
　Marched to bivouacs quarter of a mile N.E. of MIRAUMONT.

In these marches jhools were carried round the horses'
necks.　The weather at this time was abominable, snow or
sleet alternating with rain in endless succession.　The roads,
when not frozen, were inches deep in liquid mud, which hid
the shell holes and made marching hideous.　It was extraordinary the way in which the Indian troops withstood all
this cold, and did not seem to feel it even as much as the
Britisher.　At the Miraumont camp the horses were picketed
on a shell-pitted slope, which was so covered with pieces of
shell and other battle debris that it was necessary to clear the
horse standings very carefully before picketing them.
Officers and men were accommodated in bell tents, pitched
here and there wherever a reasonably level or sound piece of
ground could be found.

The reason for our sudden forward move was now made
known to us.　We were to take part in an attack on Bullecourt,
which was to be made by General Gough's 5th Army.　The
general plan was that Bullecourt was to be squeezed out,
the Anzac Division attacking on the right of the village, and

the 62nd Division on the left. Should the Anzacs' attack
succeed in making a gap, the 1st Indian Cavalry Division was
to move round the E. side of Longatte, Sialkote Brigade leading, and take up positions to the rear of Bullecourt.

Miraumont, 1st to 9th April 1917.

The regiment furnished working parties on the roads near IRLES. 5th
April, Capt. D. E. Whitworth appointed Adjutant vice Capt. D. S. Davison
resigned.

9th April.—10 p.m. Received Mhow Brigade's O.O. No. 4, giving time
of starting 1.30 a.m. (destination Sq. B 28, half a mile S.E. of MORY).

10th April.—1.30 a.m. Marched to B 28 (Sheet 57 C). A Echelon to
square H 9. B Echelon to BIHUCOURT.

7.50 a.m.—Returned to camp in accordance with Mhow Brigade's B.M. 2.

6.45 p.m.—Received Mhow Brigade's B.M. 3 ordering Brigade to return to
B 28 starting 2.45 a.m.

11th April.—2.45 a.m. Marched to B 28 arriving 5 a.m. Echelons
moving as before.

4.45 p.m.—Returned to camp at MIRAUMONT in accordance with verbal
order from Mhow Brigade.

12th April.—Ordered to stand to at two hours notice of moving.

Our first move to Mory was made on a pitch dark night
with a gale of wind blowing the rain in our faces. On arrival
there it became obvious from the lack of gunfire that no big
action was imminent, and soon after daybreak the order to
return confirmed this. We returned to camp in driving snow.
We were never told exactly why we were sent up on this first
occasion. The second move up was made in slightly more
favourable weather. At about 7.30 a.m., word came that
the Sialkote Brigade had moved forward, and the brigade
began to move over the Mory ridge. Hopes ran high for a
few minutes ; but we had barely reached the top of the ridge
when " troops right about wheel " was given. At the same
time a few riderless horses of the 17th Lancers came galloping
back. It afterwards appeared that they had been called
up prematurely. They were met by an artillery barrage and
forced to return. The remainder of the day was spent in the
position of assembly. Heavy snow began to fall in the afternoon, and shortly after the order came to return. The march
back was a depressing one. Many horses fell frozen and
exhausted at the side of the track and had to be shot and the
intensity of the wind and cold increased with the falling

darkness. On April 13th the brigade marched back to rest billets. The regiment was at Orville. There we remained until May 14th, resting and getting the horses fit again.

The regiment had lost only one horse since leaving Lanchères and a foal was born in D Squadron and was kept alive. Other units during the same period had lost up to 50 or 60 horses from exposure.

May 15th.—Marched to Heilly (where a very attractive teashop, first visited by 2nd Lancer officers from Beaucourt in 1916, was revisited).

May 16th.—Marched to Laneuville, near Bray sur Somme, and camped in an old prisoners-of-war camp.

May 17th.—Marched to billets in St. Christ, a half-ruined village on the Somme.

We were now in the devastated area, where all the villages had been blown up by the Hun, who had put himself to great pains to make things as uncomfortable for the oncoming British as possible. Every tree in the country had been cut down or partially sawn through to ensure its dying ; every important cross road had been mined, in some instances employing a newly invented slow action fuze, which was set to detonate the charge some weeks after the retreat. Traps of many kinds were set with the true spirit of German frightfulness. Here and there houses were left intact with cunningly laid mines beneath them in the hope of enticing the headquarters of high formations to occupy them. Hidden spikes were set in bathing places. A piano at one place is said to have been left filled with dynamite and the B flat electrically connected with a detonator—a rather doubtful story. Trip wires were attached to buried bombs, and the clearing of old horse lines and similar places had to be carried out with the greatest caution. In short, every resource of perverted ingenuity was employed in the attempt to lower the morale of our troops. Actually the only effect produced was to exasperate them and to inspire plans of retaliation.

The country is a fine, undulating and open one, with big woods here and there. The going was magnificent, except for occasional patches of shell holes or wire. Grazing was abundant and in every way it was ideal country for cavalry. For the rest of our stay in France we remained in this area, and trench parties were employed almost continually in various sectors between St. Quentin and Cambrai. From June onwards, polo was played regularly on the " Leighton Park Polo Ground " at Ennemain, where brigade headquarters was located. Ponies were fairly plentiful, and included old ponies from India, such as Rabies, Mejidie, Bullseye, Puck, Abdul, Bijli, Kiss, and " the Farrier Major's grey." When a large number of officers were in the trenches, those who remained behind had plenty of ponies, and polo sometimes ran to seven days a week. The ground was somewhat small, and there were big whirlpool shaped indentations, a common phenomenon in French pastures, in two of the corners ; nevertheless there were some quite fastish and good games. Later on in the summer there was a little partridge shooting to be had just behind the trenches, round Vermand and Ascension Farm, and in the autumn a few courageous duck faced a nightly barrage on the Somme. Riding partridges, and riding hares with polo sticks had now become almost a recognised British sport, and here the open nature of the country and the absence of crops was in favour of it. At St. Christ an attempt was made to spear carp in the Somme, with the aid of an Aldis signalling lamp covered with red cloth, and a lance, on the end of which Armourer Bishen Singh had fixed a trident. This venture was unsuccessful, and fishing generally was not much more so.

May 22nd.—A mixed trench party took over from the reserve battalion of the 176th Brigade at Templeux le Guerard, and bivouacked in a large quarry. Working parties were furnished daily on a rear line of trenches.

May 28th.—The quarry was shelled by two 8.5 in. naval guns. Only one man was wounded, although about a dozen shells landed in the quarry.

May 29th.—The trench party, which consisted of detachments of the 17th Lancers, 19th B.L., and 2nd B.L., under command of Lieut.-Col. Turner, took over a subsector in front of Le Verguier.

June 4th.—Trench party relieved by 36th J.H., and whole regiment concentrated at Hamelet.

June 15th.—A 2nd Lancers' trench party, under Major Knowles, relieved a party of the 6th Cavalry in the trenches at Villeret.

June 17th.—The regiment marched to Athies. This was a permanent billet until February 2nd, 1918.

June 28th and *29th.*—Trench party at Villeret relieved by another party from the regiment.

July 10th.—Trench party at Villeret relieved by two companies 22nd Northumberland Fusiliers.

July 23rd.—A working party, strength 60, under Lieut. Commeline, proceeded to Vendelles. This was relieved by parties on August 4th and 12th.

August 6th.—A second working party of 135 proceeded to Vendelles. This was reinforced on August 19th by a party of 82, and went into the trenches opposite St. Hélène.

September 14th.—The trench party was relieved by the Lucknow Brigade.

September 22nd.—A trench party, strength 271, under Major Salkeld, relieved a party of the Sialkote Brigade near Le Verguier.

September 30th.—Trench party at Le Verguier relieved by the 8th Battn. The Buffs.

During the foregoing period our portion of the front was comparatively quiet. A very successful raid made by the Inniskillings on Cologne farm was answered by an unsuccessful German one a little to the south. Night patrol fighting was taken up with great vigour, and to such effect that it was not long before the Germans kept to their own trenches, finding the Indian sowar too much for them in the dark. One patrol, led by Lieut. L. Hearsey, actually succeeded one night in passing right through the German trenches at St. Hélène. Casualties during the summer months were very light, and were caused mostly by gunfire.

Two horse shows took place in September, the 4th Cavalry Division show at Brie, and the Cavalry Corps show at St. Pol. At both of these the Regimental trickriders gave very successful performances.

October.—During the whole of this month the regiment remained at Athies, making permanent horse standings and billets for the coming winter out of the debris of the village, and such R.E. stores as could be obtained. There was great competition among the five messes of the regiment. For comfort that of A Squadron was perhaps the best, though H.Q., having the Quartermaster, was naturally more grandiose. Training was also carried out in preparation for the Cambrai offensive.

November.—The War Diary for this month is missing, but as the 4th Cavalry Division did not take any active part in the first battle of Cambrai, which opened on November 20th, it suffices to state that the Mhow Cavalry Brigade twice marched from the Athies area to a position of readiness at Fins and back, but saw nothing of the fighting. The attack, which is partially described in a letter which follows, written by Capt. Peck, was designed to break through the formidable trench system known as the Hindenburg Line, by a sudden attack of infantry and tanks, carried out with no preliminary bombardment. Its object was to break through and prepare a gap through which the cavalry might pass, and exploit the success of the other arms.   In order that the passage of the Hindenburg Line by the cavalry might be made with a minimum of delay it was necessary to clear a broad track through the wire and over the trenches and fortified sunken roads.   This task was carried out by a dismounted working party from the 4th Cavalry Division, which advanced with the attacking infantry and by its magnificent efforts had completed its task long before the cavalry were thrown into the fight.   No description of the first battle of Cambrai can be attempted here : suffice it to say that the attack, like every previous attack in trench warfare, and also like every subsequent one, succeeded only in driving a salient into the enemy's line.   By the end of the third week in November the British attack had been stopped, and the Mhow Brigade returned to its billets morosely resigned to an indefinite continuance of dismounted trench warfare.

The following officers joined the 2nd Lancers in this month from the advanced base at Rouen :—

2nd Lieut Pritchard.
2nd Lieut. C. E. L. Harris.
2nd Lieut. G. Wilkinson.
2nd Lieut. G. Lawler.
2nd Lieut. G. L. Silver.
2nd Lieut. E. St. J. King.

AN ACCOUNT OF THE MAKING OF THE CAVALRY TRACK AT CAMBRAI.

Extracts from a letter from Capt. L. J. Peck, M.C., to the compiler.

[Captain (then 2nd Lieut.) Peck, was the " Track Leader " of the Cavalry Track at Cambrai, and for his work there received the first M.C. to be awarded to the 2nd Lancers.]

" I am afraid I cannot give you a good narrative of the

Cavalry Track work in November 1917, but I will jot down some details from my diary, and try to rake out some more from my memory in case they may be of any use to you for the regimental history."

.   .   .   .

" As regards my diary, I do not know if you want exact dates. I was warned for the working party on November 8th, and very sick I was too, for I thought that I had done more than my share in that direction.

" On the 10th, the advance party went to Misery. When we arrived there we found only sleet, disused trenches, and wire, and a ruined château with some half-flooded cellars. Colonel Bell (38th C.I.H.) arrived in the evening, and assembled us and told us that it was not the usual sort of working party, but a special stunt to be brought off in connection with a tank-cum-infantry attack followed by a cavalry drive. He also told us to keep quiet about the whole thing, as it was a bigger show than usual ; and that we were to impress this upon the men."

.   .   .   .

" We started work next day with the full battalion. No one knew anything about making roads across trenches ; so Company Commanders were allowed to take their companies away and experiment. . . .

" In the afternoon we practised moving parties across country, and getting them quickly on to their work on arrival, Bell's idea, and this turned out to be one of the most difficult and important jobs."

————

Capt. Peck then goes on to describe how Col. Bell decided that an officer was required to go ahead to lay out the track and allot work. Capt. Peck volunteered for and was given this duty.

On the 13th, he went with Col. Bell and a sapper officer to Albert to meet the tank commanders, and, for the first time, learnt the actual locality of the proposed attack.

————

" Later on I got an excellent air photo map (patched up from scores of different photos) covering the whole of the area

H

up to the canal. I pored over this for hours every day and found something new every time I looked at it. Bennett (the sapper) gave me a lot of help too. I eventually got the line of the track marked out as exactly as I could, and then marked out the table of obstacles, distances, and the size of parties required ; and from that we allotted the three companies (Mhow, Lucknow, and Sialkote) to the three systems of trenches (front line, Hindenburg line, and Hindenburg reserve line) ; and the companies themselves divided up into the larger and smaller parties for large obstacles or groups of small obstacles. I was told I was to be given 12 tanks with wire-pulling attachment (I eventually got 10 only) and that I need not take wire clearing into account in allotting the parties. I asked leave to liaise with the commanders of these wire-pulling tanks ; they were a new idea to me, and, I think, to everyone ; but it could not be arranged.

" Incidentally, before this, I received your orders to rejoin the regiment to go on ten days' leave home, with the leave warrant enclosed. I sent it back with deep regret, and I heard that I was heartily strafed by everyone for messing up other peoples' chances of leave by refusing to go when I got the chance. I could not explain, for I was sworn to secrecy."

The letter describes how track-laying was practised on the trenches round Misery, and each individual thoroughly trained in his own particular duty. Capt. Peck and the sapper officer made a reconnaissance of the front line on November 16th. As a result of this Capt. Peck was relieved of all responsibility for the track as far as our own wire.

" We were due to leave by lorry for Fins on the evening of the 19th (" Y " day). I forget the number of lorries requisitioned ; but anyhow the M.T. people made a mistake and sent ten less. It was a most horrible shame. We could hardly cram all the men in, with their marching order, rifles, picks, shovels, T-heads, rammers, sandbags and all the rest of it. They were crammed so tight that several of them fainted on the way. The night was cold, but no snow. We passed through Peronne, where we saw the French Mobile Division in reserve. We reached Fins at 10.15 p.m., and marched up by slow stages to Gouzeaucourt. I left the battalion just outside Gouzeau-court, where they got some sleep, and went on to liaise with a fellow named Hopkins, who was commanding the wire-pulling tanks. We had never met before ; and I had had to fix the rendezvous (Partridge Road) by messages passing through about a dozen people, so I was very nervous that we might miss ; moreover it was a very dark night. It was then between 4 and 5 a.m., Zero hour being 6.20. I then took my track-laying party up to the rendezvous, and got there just before the 6.20 bombardment started. It *was* a show. You will remember that the scheme was the first in which there was no preliminary bombardment. The whole show was kept as quiet as possible, which was rendered easier by the fog and mist of that month which made aerial reconnaissance impossible. But on this particular night, as luck would have it, a tank caught fire about 3 a.m. and blazed to the skies, and the Boche began shelling heavily. We thought the show was given away ; but he stopped after about half-an-hour, and there was an uncanny silence up to 6.20 a.m., when the sudden roar was stunning. The first tank-cum-infantry attack went over at 6.25, and the second at 6.35. I had to wait for the third tank line, so I started off about 7 a.m. ; I confess I felt better when once I got on the move. I had not realised how slowly tanks move, so I decided to work inde-pendently of them. I therefore left Edwards (the young sapper) with them to follow me up and show them where to clear the wire on the line of the T-heads I put up. I saw the tanks again later on, but I cannot remember seeing Edwards.

Before leaving the Boche line, I overtook the third and second attacks ; and I struck the Boche wire just in the right place, much to my relief. It was invisible till we were close to it, and I was working on a compass bearing I had taken on the 16th. . . . I had three men from each regiment whom I left at the regiment's obstacles to guide the parties to position ; and I left a note with each, to hand to the commander, con-taining any particular information that might help him. I was not allowed to take the aeroplane photo with me : they said I might be captured with it. And they refused to give it back to me afterwards. I thought it was my " Haq," but some sapper bagged it as a souvenir.

" I ought to add that they told me afterwards that I had not put up enough T-heads, and they had difficulty in some places in tracing me ; but I could not carry an unlimited number of them.

" I cannot give you an account of the day in detail. I found all sorts of obstacles that the air photo had not shown ; and several times the ground looked quite different from my mental picture of it, and I thought I had gone wrong. The wire was ever so much thicker than I expected : I think there were four triple belts and two single belts in front of the Hindenburg line alone ; and, of course, I had to climb through it before it was cleared. Of course, the fighting tanks had crushed it enough for us to crawl through : but it was slow and tiring work. Also I had to do a lot of searching right and left to choose the right place for the track to cross the trenches, and in one place I had to alter my plan, and divert the track some distance to avoid obstacles I had not reckoned on.

" Several incidents stand out in my mind. (1) A couple of tanks knocked out in No Man's Land, and the infantry sitting down and looking at them, because the tank man was their guide and they did not know where to go without him. (2) In the Boche front trenches on the firing steps large carriers of hot coffee, untasted, as the Boche had bolted. (3) The Boche hung on in La Vacquerie and enfiladed us from the right ; but we had to go on and ignore them. They were cleared out afterwards. (4) As I was going across the open behind their front line, laying out T-heads, an infantry battalion, climbing along a Boche communication trench beside me was stopped by its C.O. who was seized by a sudden horror that he had gone round in a circle, and was leading his battalion back to Gouzeaucourt. I tried to reassure him. (5) Shells from nowhere as we were climbing through the Hindenburg wire : everyone swore they were our own. (6) About the Hindenburg line any number of snipers and machine guns lying up hidden ; they were brave enough, and they made things rather nasty. I saw one such nest rushed by a party of infantry just after they had shot the subaltern ; they hauled them out, held them up, and shot them on the spot. (7) In the front trench of the Hindenburg system a brigade waiting for nothing. The man I struck was the

Brigade-Major. I asked him what the situation was, and he said that the Boche were rallying in force in their reserve lines, that our supports had not come up, that our flanks were exposed, that our tanks had had such heavy casualties that they were retiring, and that it would be fatal to go any further. We certainly were being shelled rather nastily, but not more than we might have expected ; also a good number of our tanks had been knocked out just beyond ; for the Boche had got his anti-tank guns to work. Still, I did not see that I had any right to wait, so I climbed out again into the open, and Lahora Singh came with me. I went on and put up T-heads ; and when I had got about half a mile on, I saw the first battalion of that brigade coming out and following me. I found out later that there were as a matter of fact some of our infantry already further in front of us. (8) When I had laid out as far as the last trench in the Hindenburg reserve system I went down towards Masnières to verify my position. It was fairly clear beyond that ; but there was some odd wire about, so I put up more T-heads to guide the cavalry through. There was, however, no need to bring any working parties on so far ; so I went back . . . I should mention that I had sent back messages by runner to Col. Bell from each trench system. I had pressed for a field telephone to bring with me, but it was not allowed. I am told (I do not know if it is true) that Bell sent on my reports to the C.R.E., and the C.R.E. to the Cavalry Corps ; and that Cavalry Corps moved on the strength of them, not having heard from the Infantry Corps Commander. Whatever the explanation may be, it is at least a fact that the first cavalry brigade did not come over the track for two hours after it was fit to take them. This, coupled with the idiotic tank episode in which the Masnières bridge got broken, is enough to account for the failure to develop the situation as it then stood. While the working parties were at it, I wandered back along the track to see if everything was going all right. The men were working like heroes ; but there were readjustments to make every here and there, and I found plenty to keep me busy. After the cavalry started to come through, and when the rain began, it seemed that the track in some places would not last out, so we had to widen it and divert the cavalry on to the alternative track, while we strengthened the original one.   The ramps down into sunken roads and out again were the worst bits to keep shipshape.   We worked up to late at night, when the cavalry and artillery who had got through on to the clear ground beyond were ordered to dismount and slacken girths, where they were.   Lots of them had not the faintest idea where they were.   A gunner major (it was pitch dark then) asked me when they were going to reach the German trenches, and was incredulous when I told him he had already passed the Hindenburg line.

" We then withdrew our parties by degrees to Gouzeaucourt. . . . . "

" Lahora Singh's I.D.S.M. was turned down, and he did not get it till about two years later—and then it was not an immediate award—which makes all the difference."

L. J. Peck.

United Services Club,
 Calcutta.
  August 7th, 1921.

The letter from which these extracts were taken was a personal one to the compiler and was not intended for publication in its original form.   There are two strong reasons, however, for leaving the text untouched.   Firstly, it is a document of historical importance and furnishes valuable evidence on the vexed question of whether the cavalry advance at Cambrai was delayed unduly, a stout bone which enthusiastic pro-cavalry theorists and their bitter anti-cavalry opponents will worry and fight over for years.   Its value of first hand evidence would have been impaired by rewriting it.   Secondly, it gives a most interesting description for the benefit of post-war officers of what a battle is actually like ;   how little the execution resembles the plan, and not seldom the subsequent reports of the combatants ;   who, being only human, do not dwell upon any petty errors committed by themselves, and generally refrain from mentioning the errors of others, on the principle of " You scratch my back and I'll scratch yours." To have toned it down from the first person would have meant losing much of the colour.

D.E.W.

CHAPTER VII

NOVEMBER 30TH, 1917, TO MARCH 28TH, 1918
SECOND BATTLE OF CAMBRAI—DECEMBER 1ST—FRESNOY—
MARSEILLES

ON November 30th began the great German counter attack known as the second battle of Cambrai, which drove in our infantry. The cavalry, in this instance the two Indian cavalry divisions, were called up and on the last day of November and the first of December were able to put into practice what our arm has always preached, namely, that cavalry must sacrifice itself for infantry. These two Indian cavalry divisions were thrown into the gap which had been made in the infantry line and, afoot or on horseback, it was their action, combined with that of some staunch infantry formations, that stayed the German attack and saved the situation. It was a rough and tumble business, as such affairs must be. In one quarter of the field Guards were mixed with and fought shoulder to shoulder with Indian cavalry ; Guards officers commanded Indian troopers and Indian cavalry officers commanded Guards.

At daybreak on November 30th, a large trench party, under the command of Major Robertson, left Athies for the trenches. They went mounted, and the whole party, including the horseholders, amounted to nearly the whole of the regiment. There remained in the village only about forty of all ranks, and the transport. At about 11 a.m. the Brigade Major (Gould) rang up the Adjutant and gave orders to turn out at once every man available. The Colonel, who was just going out for a ride, was only just stopped in time. An hour later the " regiment " marched out. It consisted chiefly in pack horses (those of the Hotchkiss without their guns, which had gone up to the trenches in limbers), farriers, trumpeters, and salutris. In two G.S. waggons were taken all the swords and lances, for the trench party had naturally only taken rifles with them. The brigade rendezvous was near Estrées en Chaussée. Here there was a delay of more than an hour.

The march continued, with various halts, through Hancourt and Roisel to Villers Faucon. Thence, after darkness had set in, the brigade moved to the depression just N. of St. Emilie (Sheet 62 c Sq. E 18). Here at about 10 p.m. the trench party turned up and the regiment was complete. The trench party had spent a dreary day marching backwards and forwards between Templeux and Lempire. Everything seemed to be in confusion and they could find no one to give them any orders. Gas shells added to their discomfort. In the evening they received orders to rejoin the brigade at Villers Fauçon.

The reorganization of squadrons took place in the pitch dark. The sword and lance waggons were somewhere in rear and only turned up barely in time for the attack next morning.

At 4.15 a.m., operation orders were received from the brigade. The Mhow Brigade was to take part mounted in an attack on Villers Guislain. Our task was to gallop Targette, Quail, and Pigeon ravines, and form a defensive flank to the S.E.

At 5.30 a.m. the brigade concentrated just west of Peizière, and passed through the village to a position of readiness on the north edge of it (behind the railway cutting in Square X 25 a, Sheet 57 c). As the head of the regiment emerged from the village the Colonel rode off to join the Brigadier, telling the Adjutant to lead the regiment to an open piece of ground on the left of the Inniskilling Dragoons. As the regiment was beginning to form up a barrage of 77mm. H.E. came down, and by the orders of Major Knowles the regiment withdrew to a sunken road a hundred yards in rear. There were surprisingly few casualties, although the formation was mass and the shells were falling right amongst the horses.[1]

[1] Remarks by an eye witness :—" When daylight came I could see the Mhow Cavalry Brigade about a thousand yards from us standing quietly in mass close against the northern edge of Peizière. There were probably good reasons for so dense a formation. The German guns were soon on to so excellent a target. For a long time I watched shell after shell fall into those closely packed ranks. Save for occasional flying fragments of man or horse there appeared no movement or unsteadiness whatever. I was profoundly impressed by the total unconcern exhibited by those three regiments, the Inniskillings, the 2nd Lancers, and the 38th Central India Horse. At about 8 a.m. they filed away and were lost to sight beyond the

At 7 a.m., definite orders for the attack were given out, and the Colonel took all the British officers across the railway bridge (X 25 a) to see as much as possible of the ground we were to move over. A few battered gables of Villers Guislain stood up on the horizon. Otherwise the bare and undulating nature of the ground made identification of any useful points difficult.

At about 8.30 a.m., the waggons containing the swords and lances turned up, and a hurried issue began. This was not over when the order to move off was given. Weapons were being thrown to the men of the rear half squadron as they passed the waggons. The final orders were that we were not to leave Peizière by the railway bridge from which the officers had made their reconnaissance, but that we were to move through Peizière and Epéhy (a conjoined village), and go out by the level crossing E. of Epéhy Cemetery. It is not possible to state the exact strength of the 2nd Lancers as we rode out of Epéhy. Capt. Vaughan in a careful estimate puts it at 440 of all ranks, including 10 British batmen. We were followed by Capt. Moncrieff's squadron of the Inniskilling Dragoons, and a section of machine guns under Lieuts. Hollis and Oakes.

(For the doings of the remainder of the Inniskillings and of the C.I.H. see Mhow Brigade narrative, Appendix I : page 184 *et seq.*)

Just forward of the level crossing we passed through the trenches of our own very astonished infantry. In front of us the road forked at a Crucifix. The road to the left ran over the ridge, which runs from Peizière in an E.N. easterly direction, and down to our objective, Targette Ravine. The road to the right ran down the side of the valley which leads to Catelet Copse. C squadron was leading, and Major Knowles led them down the valley to the right. On the Adjutant remarking this, the Colonel said "Let him go. We will get more cover that way." The orders to squadrons were to

railway embankment. For what purpose they had gone we knew not then, but we knew a little later that two most gallant mounted attacks had been made ; one, by the three squadrons Inniskillings, which had failed, and one, by the 2nd Lancers and one squadron Inniskillings, which had got right home into the German trenches, through the wire and all, and had remained there."

advance in open column of line of troop columns extended. The order of squadrons was C, D, A, B.

Before us lay a shallow valley of a width averaging about four hundred yards, covered with rank, dead grass, and pitted here and there with fresh shell holes. On the high ground on the right was a plantation of smallish trees, and on the left was a bare slope up which slowly climbed the road from the Crucifix. On the roadside, about a mile away, were four prominent elm trees, near which lay " Limerick Post," which the enemy had taken the day before. C squadron seemed to have barely started down the valley when there was a tremendous outburst of machine gun fire from both sides, and the pace was increased to a gallop. The apparently deserted landscape became alive with running grey figures, but that all had not run was obvious from the intensity of the fire which was now brought to bear on the regiment. Although the air seemed to be full of bullets, and the flying turf showed that not all were going over our heads, very few casualties were noticeable ; in fact, there was no apparent diminution in the strength of the regiment when we dismounted for action two miles further on. Except for the shell holes, the going was splendid, and the pace must have been at least fifteen miles an hour. The number of German machine guns in action is uncertain, but there must at least have been half-a-dozen. Firing from both sides of a narrow valley, according to all the then known laws of musketry they should have annihilated a regiment of cavalry coming down it, at whatever pace. As it was, the effects of their fire were tactically negligible, a fact which must be ascribed to badly shaken nerves on the part of the enemy machine gunners. That, beyond the moral effect of the charge and its pace, there was nothing to prevent the German machine gunners from inflicting heavy casualties, was proved when the slower moving led horses of A and B squadrons returned by the same route a quarter of an hour later, and suffered heavily in doing so.

C squadron had now come across a line of wire which protected a fortified sunken road named " Kildare Lane." Two gaps were found, through which they passed, and then scrambled down on to the road. (Risaldar Mukand Singh was sent round to the right at the same time to outflank the enemy.

In doing this he found a single apron of wire between him and the retreating Germans. This he and his troop jumped, and went in with the lance.) The squadron in the meantime had got down the bank successfully. Lieut. Broadway and others climbed the opposite bank and went in pursuit of the Germans. Eyewitnesses say that Lieut. Broadway was approaching a German officer who was holding up one hand, and apparently wished to surrender, when the latter, drawing the other hand, in which was a pistol, from behind his back, fired, killing Lieut. Broadway instantaneously. A moment later, Acting Lance Dafadar Sahib Singh killed the German officer with a hogspear.

D squadron (Capt. Duke) which was following C, had now passed through the wire and entered the road on C squadron's right. Colonel Turner and regimental Headquarters were following D. The Colonel had just passed through one of the gaps in the wire when he was hit in the body by a burst from a machine gun, and killed instantly. His orderly Hidayat Ali, and Trumpet Major Ganga Ram remained with his body throughout the day, lying in a shallow shell hole, the former being wounded while doing so. Woordi Major Dhara Singh, who had been shot through the ankle, also remained there for some time.

A squadron (Major Robertson) and B squadron (Major Salkeld) dismounted at the foot of the slope leading up to Kildare Lane, and, as there was no room for the horses in the road, the led horses were forced to return by the way the regiment had come, passing between the two late British posts now held by the enemy. As already related, their casualties on the way back to Epéhy were very heavy, especially in horses. They were led by Ris. Azim Ali (22nd Cavalry).

Of the men of the led horses, Kote Dafadar Nihal Chand, of B squadron, was dismounted by having his horse shot and was himself shot through both thighs. Some Germans from a post to the right rear of Kildare Lane now came out and took some of these men prisoners. (By a coincidence, one of the Germans in this post was afterwards taken prisoner by the regiment at Beisan ten months later). They stripped Nihal Chand of his haversack, waterbottle, and accoutrements, and began to carry him towards their post. At this moment other

Germans, who were attacking Kildare Lane from the same post, were counter-attacked by B squadron under Major Salkeld. The men carrying Nihal Chand, then dropped him and ran back to their trenches, whereupon Nihal Chand dragged himself by his hands to the shelter of a shell hole. Here he remained all day, and that night he dragged himself in the same way towards Epéhy. Daybreak found him half way there, and again he had to lie up till dark, being without food or water. Early next morning he reached the wire of the British trenches, where he managed to attract attention, and was taken in. In dragging himself he had worn out the toes of his boots, and his lacerated toes had become frostbitten, necessitating afterwards the amputation of both feet, and the loss to the regiment of a very stout man.

Major Knowles was now in command of the regiment. He had been slightly wounded in the left shoulder, but was able to carry on. The regiment was joined almost immediately by Captain Moncrieff's squadron of the Inniskilling Dragoons and a section of the Mhow Machine Gun squadron.

The sunken road was now held from right to left by D, A, B, C squadrons 2nd Lancers, and A squadron Inniskilling Dragoons. Machine guns were posted at either end of the position. The road, which was narrow and fairly deep at the left, or northern end, gradually became shallower as it descended the hill, until it was only about three feet deep where it passed Catelet Copse. In the deeper part there were about half a dozen dugouts burrowed into the banks, and here too were two felled trees lying across from bank to bank. The road was littered with German knapsacks, rifles, machine-gun belts, and great coats. Lying on the top of the bank were two light pattern machine guns which had been abandoned at the last moment before the arrival of C squadron. Several men of A and B squadrons were lying outside the road. These were brought in, under heavy fire from Limerick Post. The most prominent of the rescuers was A.L.D. Liakat Hussain.

The horses of C and D squadrons stood between the two felled trees in the deeper part of the road. Here anybody passing up or down the road had to clamber up the bank to get round the horses. To the front of the position a convex rising slope allowed only a view of fifty or sixty yards. About one hundred yards from the right flank lay Catelet Copse. Beyond it was lower ground, where a continual barrage of heavy H.E. shells and machine gun fire went on all day. its purpose doubtless being to protect the German left flank, which in this place was somewhat in the air. Further away, on rising ground, stood Little Priel Farm. To the right rear, about twelve hundred yards away, on the south side of the valley, was the German post from which the dismounted men of the led horses had been captured. (X 27 c 8.0.) To the left flank, rising ground gave a short field of fire, and to the left rear, about a thousand yards off, was visible Limerick Post (X 27 b 5.9), from which machine gun bullets, coming through non-bullet-proof parapets, caused the Inniskillings several casualties. The limits of the position were about from X 28 a 9.9 to X 28 b 1.1. The enemy was obviously very uncertain of the strength of the force in Kildare Lane, or of the limits of its position, for two or three patrols attempted to approach from the left and left front. The Germans in the two posts behind us were probably completely cut off from their headquarters and could give them no information, for a fat bundle of German telephone wires which was found passing through the sunken road had been cut by our signalling officer.

At about 10 a.m. our right flank gained touch with our own infantry, which was found to be holding the ground round Little Priel Farm, but the barrage beyond Catelet Copse made any communication difficult. Soon after, an attack was delivered from the German post to the right rear. This was driven back by a counter-attack made by about thirty men of B squadron, led by Major Salkeld, although the Germans must have numbered three times as many.

About 11 a.m. an attack on our left flank died away under our fire. Two or three times afterwards parties of Germans advancing along the trenches from the direction of Limerick Post were driven off by bombing parties of the Inniskilling Dragoons.

At this time volunteers were called for to carry a message, giving our position, to Brigade Headquarters, which was situated on the outskirts of Peizière, at about X 25 b 2.8. Of those who came up, Lance Dafadar Gobind Singh (28th Cavalry, attached) and Sowar Jot Ram were selected. They were given duplicate messages, and started off at a gallop. Jot Ram took a right handed course and passed close by Limerick Post, from which he was seen to be shot down. Gobind Singh, taking the lower ground to the south, got about half-a-mile before his horse was killed by machine gun fire. For some time he lay still close to his horse. Then, when he judged that he was no longer watched, he got up and began to run. When fired at again he tumbled over as if shot, and by repeating this process, varied by wriggling along the ground, he reached Brigade Headquarters unhurt at 10.50 a.m. A return message had now to be sent, and he volunteered to take this too. He was given another horse and started back, taking the high ground on the south of the valley until he neared the German post, then dipping down and across to the sunken road. This time he had covered two-thirds of his journey when again his horse was shot, and he made his way, running, and falling, into the sunken road. An hour later ánother message had to be sent from the regiment, and Gobind Singh came forward again. He was told that he had already done his share, but he insisted that he now knew the ground better than anybody else, and said that he intended to take a new line. On the strength of this the Adjutant allowed him to go. He started from the lower end of the road, turned right-handed past Catelet Copse, and went straight through the barrage in Epéhy. Half-way through Epéhy, his horse was cut in half by a direct hit from a shell just behind the saddle. Gobind Singh then ran on and eventually got into dead ground in the re-entrant which debouches into the valley at X 27 d 6.0. Thence he made his way out of the sight of the enemy to Peizière. Arrived there, 11.55 a.m., he volunteered to make the journey for a fourth time, but was not allowed to do so. For his splendid gallantry he was awarded the Victoria Cross.

From noon onward no important move was made by the Germans. A few shells fell on the right flank of the position, but the heavy bombardment, which might have been expected, never eventuated. A low flying German plane had flown down the length of the position, and was fired at by everyone who had a rifle, but went off apparently untouched. Whether it took any information back or not, nothing came of it.

In the course of the afternoon, Lieut. V. W. Smith, the

signalling officer, managed to send a few messages to Peizière by lamp from a very exposed position ; but any reply from the brigade immediately evoked heavy shelling from the German guns, by whom their light could be seen.

At 3 p.m., the Adjutant (Capt. Whitworth) was sent to try and get orders from the brigade through the infantry on our right. Getting through the barrage in safety he succeeded in finding Battalion H.Q. where he was able to get into touch with the brigade by telephone. He got orders for a retirement from Kildare Lane and returned to the regiment, being slightly wounded on the way. He then reconnoitred a route for retirement.

Darkness set in at 5 p.m. and the moon was due to rise at 6 p.m., so that the evacuation had to be done quickly.

In anticipation of the retirement, the ground beneath the lower fallen tree had been dug away to allow of a horse passing beneath it, and as soon as dark fell, a bridge over a trench at Catelet Copse, which had to be crossed, was covered with earth to deaden the sound of the horses' hoofs. All horses unfit to move were shot. The line of retirement was past the east side of Catelet Copse and up the Lempire road. The retirement was begun from the left flank, a rearguard sending up red lights from a captured German Very pistol, this being the German signal for " This is a German position : raise your barrage." The German barrage on the low ground beyond Catelet Copse died away just before the retirement began and it was carried out without casualties.

It began at about 5 p.m. and by 5.40 p.m. the whole garrison of Kildare Lane, taking the body of Colonel Turner, their wounded, and all unwounded horses, were behind the British infantry line and marching up the Lempire road.

From Lempire the regiment marched back to Epéhy and joined the remains of the led horse party half a mile west of the village. Major Knowles reported at 9 p.m. to B.H.Q., and then went to a dressing station in Epéhy, whence he was sent to C.C.S. Tincourt. Colonel Turner's body, which had been tended with devoted care by Jemadar Abdul Latif and A.L.D. Hasan Raza, was taken to a mortuary in the village, and was brought back later for burial. Thanks to the energy of the Quartermaster, Lieut. Banister, the regiment found hot tea and food awaiting them.   It was a clear and intensely cold night, and the discomfort did much to destroy the rest which the men so needed.

December 2nd.—At 6 a.m. the next morning the regiment moved back to the northern outskirts of St. Emilie, where some " elephant shelters " afforded welcome protection. Orders were now received to organise a dismounted company in order to go back into action on foot, but nothing came of it.

At 11 p.m., the 1st Cavalry Division, which had been rushed up from its billets on the coast, took over from the 4th Cavalry Division.

December 3rd.—At 10 a.m. the brigade marched back to billets to rest and reorganise.

The casualties of the regiment were as follows :—

	Killed.	Wounded.	Missing.	Died in Hospital.
British officers ..	2	2	0	0
Indian ,, ..	1	1	1	0
Indian O.R. ..	6	50	47	3

N.B.—Of the 48 missing, 36 were killed, the remainder being prisoners of war.

The death of Colonel Turner was much deplored by all ranks.   His strength of character, absolute impartiality, and kindness had gained for him a very deep respect and affection among the Indian ranks, not only of the regiment, but also of the men attached from other regiments, and their devotion to the 2nd Lancers was not a little due to his influence. Lieut. Broadway's death was also a great loss, for he was much liked by all who knew him.

It is undoubted that the sacrifices of the regiment in this action were entirely justified by results.   On the morning of December 1st, a German attack on Epéhy was imminent, and there was only a weak and disorganised force of British infantry to meet it.   The regiment's swift attack broke right into the German attacking troops, and caused such confusion that no attack on Epéhy could be made that day, and it is probably not an overstatement to say that a break through of the British line was avoided.

The following honours were awarded to the regiment :—
In the Cambrai Dispatch, the 2nd Lancers was the only

Indian Cavalry regiment mentioned by name by Sir Douglas Haig.

Victoria Cross.—Lance Dafadar Gobind Singh.

Bar to D.S.O.—Major G. Knowles.

D.S.O.—Major H. Y. Salkeld.

M.C.—Capt. D. E. Whitworth, Lieut. V. W. Smith, Risaldar Mukand Singh Br.

I.O.M. 2nd Class.—(1417) A.L.D. Sahib Singh, (2136) A.L.D. Liakat Hussain.

Bar to I.D.S.M.—(2026) A.L.D. Sobha Singh.

I.D.S.M.—Ressaidar Het Ram, Ressaidar Krishna Chandra Singh, (1515) K.D. Dharam Singh, (1861) Daf. Ram Singh, (1705) Sr. Mohar Singh, (2049) Sr. Amar Singh, (2152) Sr. Kehar Singh.

Croix de Guerre (Belge).—(2090) A.L.D. Bansgopal Singh.

Major J. F. Bennett was now in command of the regiment. After the return from Epéhy the regiment spent the next three weeks reorganizing and re-equipping. Another German attack was expected, and for the first week we stood to in the streets of Athies every morning from 6 a.m. to 7 a.m. About 80 remounts, the best batch the regiment had yet received, were sent up from Rouen.

December 23rd to 31st.—Digging and wiring parties were sent up daily for work in the Cavalry Corps sector.

January 1st to 26th, 1918.—Digging and wiring parties were sent up to the trenches.

January 27th.—A trench party under the command of Capt. D. S. Davison, strength 242, went into the trenches at Cote Wood two miles E. of Templeux la Fosse. This was the last trench party to be furnished by the regiment. The Indian officers in this tour were particularly unfortunate. Ress. Het Ram, I.D.S.M., and Jem. Jang Bahadar Singh were both wounded by the same bullet. Ris. Mukand Singh, Br., M.C., was wounded by a shell. Ress. Bhapur Singh was injured by shock from a trench mortar.

Rumours of a move to Egypt were now going about. These were confirmed when orders were received to march back to a back area.

February 3rd.—The regiment, less the trench party, marched to Guillacourt.

I

February 4th.—The march continued to Clairy.

February 5th.—The regiment marched into billets at Fresnoy au Val, a village to the S.W. of Amiens. H.Q., D and half C were in Fresnoy ; half C at Montenoy, A at Bussy, and B at Moyencourt. Here, for the first time during the war, a regimental mess was formed, and squadron messes were not again resorted to in Palestine. There were many big woods round about these billets, and an unsuccessful attempt to stick pig was again made.

February 15th.—The trench party from Cote Wood rejoined. The following parties now proceeded without horses to Egypt.

February 22nd.—Party of 106 (Major Salkeld) *via* Taranto.

February 24th.—Party of 29 (Lieut. Peck) *via* Taranto.

February 28th.—Party of 7 (2nd Lieut. Lawler) *via* Taranto.

March 1st.—Party of 39 (2nd Lieut. Mallam) *via* Taranto.

By those B.O.'s who now remained with the regiment the next few weeks will be well remembered. All went for a last leave to England, and those not on leave found distractions in the fine green rides which abounded round Fresnoy, and in frequent visits to Amiens, which town was now at the summit of its glory, as far as the entertainment of the British army went. Such names as the Cathédrale, Godbert, Les Huitres, and the Hotel du Rhin, la rue des Trois Cailloux, and la rue du Corps Nu Sans Tête, call up many pleasant memories.

March 20th.—The regiment entrained in three trains at Saleux, on the outskirts of Amiens, en route for Marseilles. On the next day the German offensive broke out over the very ground where we had spent the last year, and where we knew every little fold and wrinkle. There was no chance, however, of the regiment being recalled from Marseilles, as there only remained sufficient men to groom the horses.

CHAPTER VIII

THE VOYAGE TO EGYPT—TEL EL KEBIR—BELAH—THE FIRST
MARCH DOWN TO THE VALLEY—OUTPOSTS AT GHORANIYEH—
ACTION ON JUNE 17TH—OUTPOSTS AT HENU

AT Marseilles, the regiment was in camp at Mont Furon.

March 30th.—Major Robertson, with 8 men and 52 horses embarked in H.M.T. *Minominee* for Alexandria.

2nd Lieut. Silver, with 32 mules, embarked on H.M.T. *St. Pancras.*

April 12th.—The remainder of the regiment embarked in H.M.T. *Maryland.* The whole regiment crossed over to Alexandria without any casualties.

The voyage was made with every precaution against submarine attack. The convoy was escorted by Japanese destroyers and followed a zig-zag course : lifebelts were worn by all, day and night, there were masthead lookouts in addition to the ordinary ones, and troops were constantly practised at boat stations, especially in the dark. " Mucking out " was carried out as usual, but stable accumulations were dumped overboard at a given hour at dark so as to leave as little track as possible. By night extreme precautions were taken against showing the smallest ray of light, even sailing lights being dispensed with. The formation adopted by convoys depended on their size, but always aimed at covering as small an area as possible to be protected by the escort. The war appeared to have no effect on the food on board ship. It was as abundant, particularly in fancy breads, butter, sugar, etc., as before the war and provided a great contrast to the fare obtainable at that time in England.

April 21st.—The *Maryland* arrived at Alexandria, and the regiment disembarked into two trains which took them to Tel el Kebir, this being its second visit by the 2nd Lancers. Here the advance parties were absorbed, and the regiment reformed. Capt. Seton-Carr, late 92nd Highlanders, who was present with that regiment at the storming of the Tel el Kebir earthworks in '82, took a party of 2nd Lancers and 6th Cavalry officers over the ground and told the story of the long night march and attack at dawn.

April 25th.—The regiment marched to Quassasin and bivouacked.   It was at this place that the regiment had fought on September 9th, 1882.

April 26th.—Marched to Ismailia.

April 27th.—Marched to El Ferdan, on the Suez Canal.

April 28th.—Marched to Kantara.   Here all the transport vehicles were exchanged for others whose wood was said to have been seasoned to the dry climate.

A few other stores were also issued by ordnance, but we found that the rearward services in Palestine could in no way be compared with those of France.   It was not of course to be expected that the same amount or even quality of stores would be found here as were in France, but the bases of the E.E.F. seemed to generate a passive atmosphere which almost amounted at times to obstructive laziness, and was very annoying when first encountered.

April 29th.—The regiment entrained in three trains for Belah.   The men were accommodated in flat trucks with open sides and pent roofs, and the horses in cattle trucks. The latter were packed tight, head and tail across the trucks, ten in a truck.   From Kantara to Gaza a double railway line, which was constructed by the E.E.F., runs across the desert. Parallel to it runs a water pipe which supplied to the force as it advanced to Gaza water from the Sweet Water Canal in Egypt.   Here and there traces of the road, made by laying down wire netting on the sand, could be seen from the train. For motor transport this type of road is admirable, but it is liable to be cut up very quickly by horse traffic.   The railway is now a permanent one, and links Cairo with Haifa, Jerusalem, and Damascus.   A branch running direct from the Jordan at Beisan to Baghdad is also projected.   In the spring of 1918, the line ran as far as Ludd, which was General Allenby's G.H.Q.   A narrow gauge line from Jaffa ran through Ludd to Jerusalem, which was railhead for the Jordan valley.   A few months later the line from Ludd to Jerusalem was converted to broad gauge, so that a truck could run direct from the quays of Kantara to either Ludd or Jerusalem.   Immediately after

the advance of September 1918, the line was pushed on from
Ludd to Haifa, where it met the narrow gauge line which runs
through Beisan, Deraa, Damascus, and Rayak to Beirut.
At Rayak it meets a broad gauge line, the " Damas, Homs et
prolongements " railway, which joins the Berlin–Baghdad
railway at Aleppo.

At Belah, the regiment camped in deep sand. A five days
halt gave the first opportunity of getting off the dirt which
the horses had accumulated in the journey from France.
Here water for the horses was obtained from a well dug in the
sand quite close to the edge of the sea. We were told that this
way of getting water is feasible all the way along the coast
from Egypt to Palestine. It was probably employed by every
invading army from time immemorial on the way from Egypt
to Syria.

By great good fortune we now came again under the command of our late Brigadier and Divisional Commander,
General G. de S. Barrow, while our new Brigadier was Gen.
Godwin, who was our first Brigade Major in France. The
regiment, with the Dorset Yeomanry, and the C.I.H. now
formed the 6th Mounted Brigade, a designation altered a few
months later to the 10th Cavalry Brigade, the division changing at the same time from the 1st Mounted Division to the
4th Cavalry Division. This division, with the 5th Cavalry
Division and the Australian Mounted Division, formed the
Desert Mounted Corps.

On the arrival of the 2nd Lancers in Palestine, the campaign
in that country had temporarily subsided into one of trench
warfare, following on General Allenby's victorious offensive
of the winter of 1917–18, which included the capture of first
Beersheba and Gaza, and then Jerusalem. News of the latter's
fall had reached us at Athies shortly after the second battle
of Cambrai.

Although a little disgruntled at leaving the main theatre of
war at a moment when the Indian Cavalry might have rendered valuable service on the well-known country opposite
St. Quentin, the prospect of being used purely as cavalry in a
country where there was plenty of elbow room and no great
systems of wired trenches reconciled us to our lot. Palestine
is in many ways unique ; although the climate is on the whole

a good deal better than that of India, and the soil extremely
fertile, there are practically no trees except those of fruit
plantations. This naturally gives the country a somewhat
barren aspect. Stone-built monasteries and red-roofed
Zionist colonies surrounded by vineyards, fig, olive, and almond
plantations stand out in surprising contrast among dreary-
looking Arab villages and their primitive cultivation.

Rising from the coastal plain the mountains of Judaea and
Samaria dominate the whole country. In the spring they are
covered with an immense variety of wild flowers, but for the
remainder of the year they are sterile, barren and uninviting.
Viewed from the plain they remind one forcibly of the diagrams
on the first page of a school atlas which show the relative
heights of the mountains of the world. The range is a com-
plicated mass of spurs and re-entrants running roughly from
Hebron to Nablus, the Samaria of the Bible, and is for the
most part waterless, except during the months October to
February, when the heavy winter rains fall. From Nablus a
long spur stretches out to the north-west, terminating in the
rocky promontory of Mount Carmel, which forms the solitary
salient in the Palestine coastline. On the east side of this range
runs the deep depression of the Jordan valley : the holy river
actually rises seven feet below sea level and finally falls into
the Dead Sea, thirteen hundred feet below, one of the lowest
points on the earth's surface. Here the regiment was destined
to spend the four months in which it was supposed to be unfit
for human habitation, a supposition which all ranks heartily
endorsed. On the east side of the valley the ground rises in
terraced ridges to the plateau of Moab, about a thousand feet
lower than the highest points of the Judaean range, and two
thousand feet above the sea. The trench line at the time of
our arrival ran east and west from a point some ten miles
north of Jaffa to the Jordan, where it curled round to the south
to end on the northern shore of the Dead Sea. Two partially
successful raids to the east side of the Jordan on Amman and
Es Salt respectively had been made with the object of cutting
the Hedjaz railway and relieving the Turkish pressure on the
Shereefian forces, the latter being completed only a few days
before the regiment's arrival in " the valley."

One welcome change from the conditions of warfare in

France was afforded by the fact that gas could not be used in Palestine ; gas helmets were consequently withdrawn. We heard that the British had experimented with gas shells fired at a herd of goats tethered on a hill side. There was only one casualty, the unfortunate victim being killed by a direct hit.

Steel helmets were carried for the first few months, but were most uncomfortable in a hot sun : they were withdrawn in June, and not issued again.

May 4th.—The regiment marched to Gaza, in company with the C.I.H. and the Jodhpur Lancers.

May 5th.—The march continued to Mejdel. On this and the succeeding night heavy and unseasonable rain fell, making the tracks very heavy, and giving the regiment a chance of testing the new bivouac sheets which had been issued at Belah. Each man carried one sheet of coarse cotton drill, and a stick about three feet long. Two sticks and two sheets buttoned together formed a bivouac for a couple of men. The sticks were very difficult to carry in marching order, and as a rule soon became lost, and were replaced by swords with the scabbards stuck in the ground.

May 6th.—Marched to Junction Station.

May 8th.—Marched to Enab, via Latrun.

We were now following the ancient road from Jaffa to Jerusalem. At Latrun it enters a narrow defile and climbs in a gradual slope to Enab, past numerous olive groves. At Enab, which was one of the regular halts for mounted troops marching to and from the valley, the regiment camped on rocky ground among olive trees.

May 9th.—The march continued to Talaat ed Dumm. This march was invariably a night march, as the road beyond Jerusalem was under the observation of the enemy. From Enab the road descends a thousand feet into a narrow valley, then climbs slowly to Jerusalem. From there it drops down, over two thousand feet, past the inn of the Good Samaritan, to Talaat ed Dumm.

On this occasion the regiment started soon after dark and reached Talaat ed Dumm at dawn, after a march which seemed interminable. As always happened in this particular march, nearly every man slept in his saddle, only waking up at the halts. At Talaat ed Dumm, an almost indescribably desolate spot, the regiment bivouacked on a foul and fly-infested camping ground under a broiling sun.

May 10th.—Starting again soon after dark, the regiment took the old Roman road, which here branches from the modern road from Jerusalem to Jericho. It follows the line of the Wadi Kelt, and, after passing the Mount of Temptation, descends in a steep slope to Jericho. As the regiment descended, the air became closer and closer until we finally entered the stifling heat of " the valley." Our first camp was situated about two miles N. of Jericho. We were on dusty ground sparsely covered with low bushes. Just as we were settling down, a German plane came over and dropped a few bombs in the vicinity, but caused us no casualties. The discomfort of this camp can be imagined from the fact that our only cover from the sun consisted in our bivouac sheets, which were so thin, that British officers, at any rate, had to wear a helmet under them, and so low that it was not possible to sit up under them unless a hole was dug in the ground beneath. There were many other discomforts : the myriads of flies made all meals taken during the day a torture ; dead camels seemed to be scattered all over the valley ; scorpions were very numerous ; and, as a final touch, a dust storm began every afternoon at two o'clock and raged until half past five. Under these conditions, it was hardly surprising that both officers and men began to go sick in increasing numbers. The rations of both men and horses were as a rule of very inferior quality, and were blamed equally with the dust and flies for the many cases of diarrhoea and dysentery which occurred. Henceforth, until the regiment was made nearly up to strength for the September offensive, the low strength of squadrons made the heavy demands for guards and fatigues on the part of the Woordi Major very hard to meet.

For the first fortnight, the regiment was principally employed in finding fatigues for work in connection with ration dumps, and anti-malarial work on streams and marshy ground. The beds of all small streams were cut as straight as possible to avoid pools or eddies, and all vegetation was cut down within five yards of their banks. During the same period, officers' patrols visited the whole of the front line in the Jordan valley.

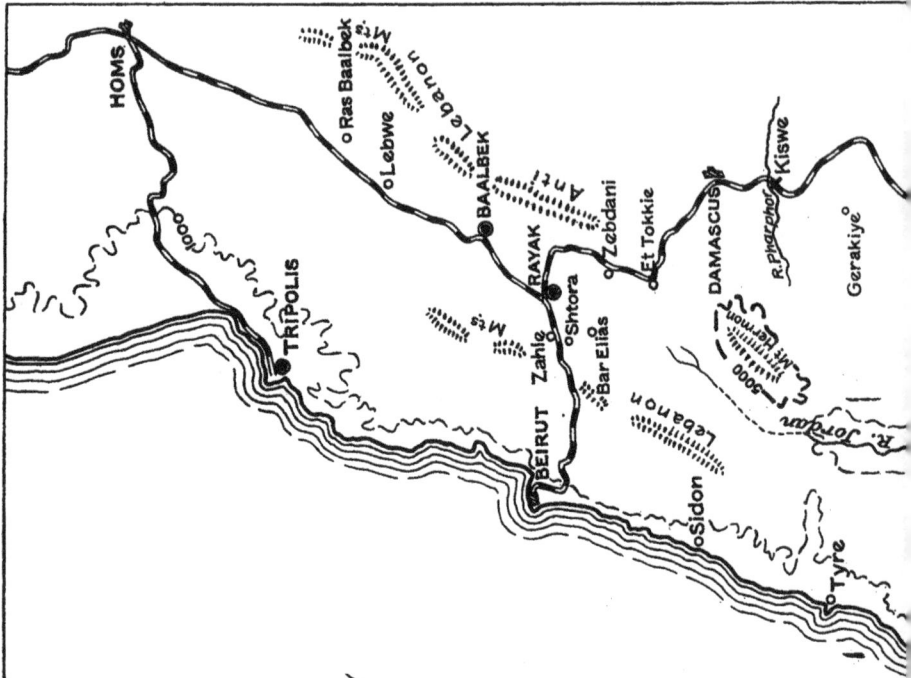

SKETCH MAP

TO ILLUSTRATE THE MOVEMENTS
OF THE 2ND LANCERS
IN
PALESTINE AND SYRIA
1918 – 20.

HOMS

o Ras Baalbek
o Lebwe
● BAALBEK

TRIPOLIS

RAYAK
Zahle
o Shtora
Bar Elias

BEIRUT

Zebdani
o Et Tokkie
DAMASCUS
R. Phacphor × Kiswe
Gerakiye o

Mt. Hermon
9000

R. Jordan

Lebanon Mts

Anti Lebanon

Mts

Lebanon

o Sidon

o Tyre

MEDITERRANEAN SEA

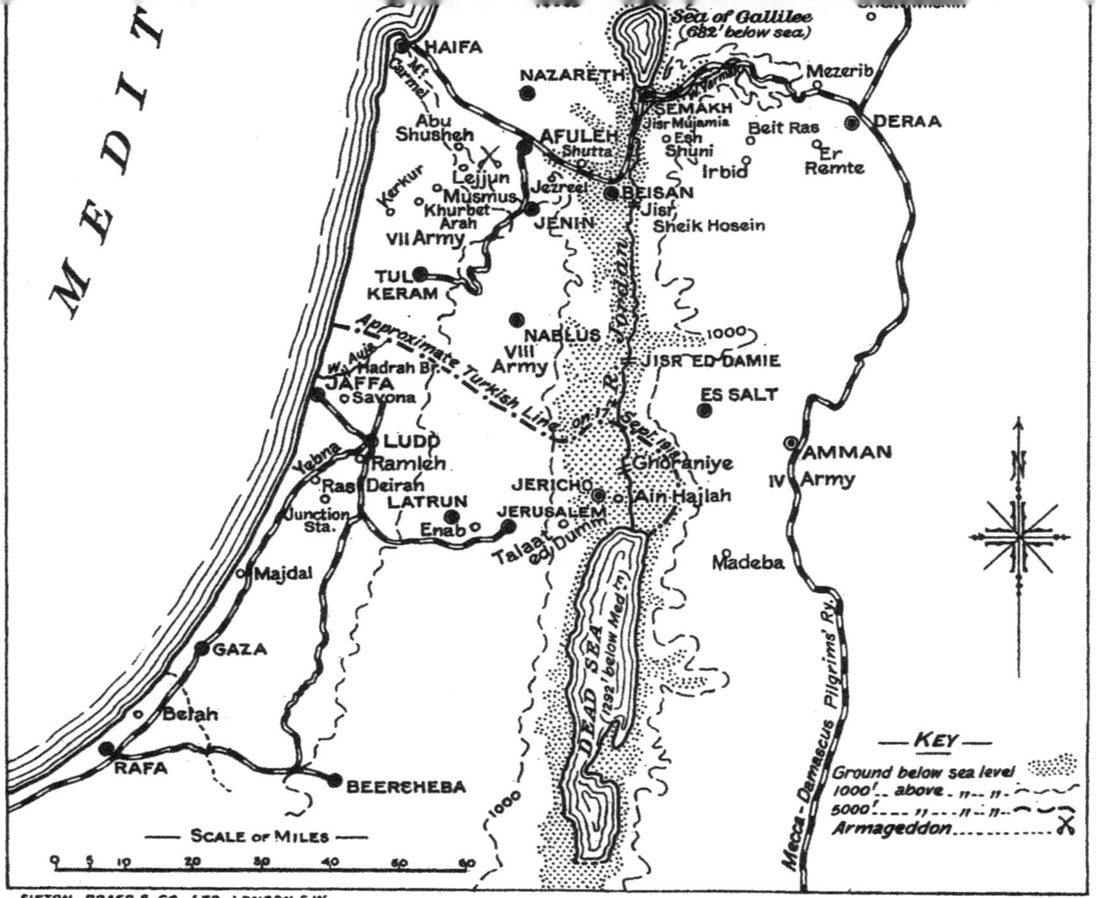

SIFTON PRAED & CO., LTD., LONDON S.W.

May 31st.—The regiment marched to the Ghoraniyeh Bridgehead, and took over from the 29th Lancers the duty of finding forward outposts in No Man's Land. The bridgehead was covered by a semicircle of trenches about a mile and a half

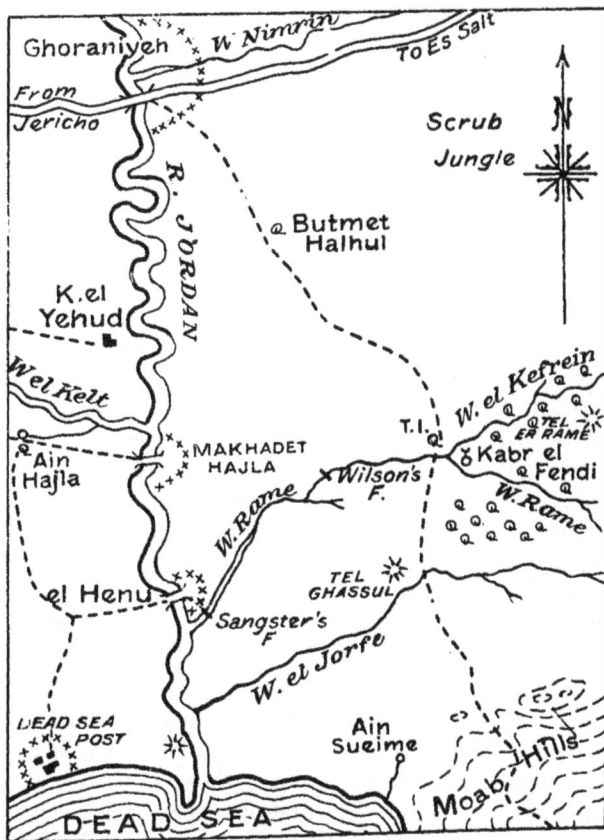

The JORDAN from GHORANIYEH to the
——— DEAD SEA ———

Scale of Miles

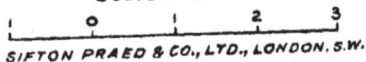

SIFTON PRAED & CO., LTD., LONDON. S.W.

in diameter. These were held by a brigade of Imperial Service Indian Infantry. In front of the bridgehead the ground, which was covered with bush jungle of varying density, mounted gradually up to the foothills of the plateau of Moab, along the foot of which lay the Turkish trenches. A prominent hill named El Haud gave the enemy an excellent observation post from which the whole of the valley was over-looked.   In this vicinity No Man's Land was about four miles across.

The Jordan, in its lower reaches, has cut for itself a straight bed running north and south, about half a mile across, and nearly a hundred feet below the level of the plain, and within this bed the river winds about in a most intricate manner. The remainder of the bed is filled with dense jhow jungle. Neither the river nor the jungle on its banks, is visible from the level of the plain.   The ground immediately on either side is cut up by deep and tortuous nullahs, and is in most places quite impassable, and then mounts in gentle slopes to the foothills of Judea on the west and of Moab on the east, whence it again mounts in a succession of hills to a height of two thousand feet above sea level.   The Jordan at Ghora-niyeh is 1,250 feet below the sea, and the Dead Sea, which is entered eight miles further south, is 1,292 feet.

The regiment was bivouacked in the mouths of two nullahs debouching on the river bed.   Here rough overhead cover of branches was made for the horses, both for concealment from aeroplanes, and for protection from the sun.   As a precaution against aerial bombing, each man dug himself a narrow trench about two feet deep, to which he could run when necessary.

Each squadron took it in turn to find the outposts for the day, the remainder staying in the bridgehead.   For the first week or so, when the patrols went out at dawn, there was always a sporting chance of mopping up some belated Turkish patrol on its way home.   The first instance of this occurred on June 2nd, when a patrol of C squadron, commanded by Daf. Sanjam Singh (the son of Ris. Kala Singh Br.), met such a patrol of Turks, and attacked them with the lance, killing three and capturing the rest.   This action of the patrol was com-mended in Brigade Orders.   During the day frequent patrols were sent out from the outposts towards the Turkish trenches.

At sundown, another squadron of the regiment put out night picquets in front of the infantry's trenches, and the day outpost squadron then retired through them to camp.   This

outpost work gave squadron leaders a splendid chance of
training their N.C.O.'s and men in patrol work, and to pick out
by experiment the boldest and most cunning of their patrol
leaders.   The Turks made two or three, usually unsuccessful,
attemps to ambush our early morning patrols.   On June 12th,
a case of this sort occurred when one man of A was killed and
two became missing.   On another occasion a patrol of C was
ambushed, and one man's horse was shot.   Lieut. L. Hearsey,
the patrol leader, then rode up to him under close rifle fire,
and taking the man up behind his saddle, rescued him.   For
his gallantry on this occasion Lieut. Hearsey was awarded the
Military Cross.   A few half-hearted attacks were also made on
our night outposts, but the readiness of the 2nd Lancers to
use the lance, and a practice which was started of outpost
squadrons taking a rapid sweep round No Man's Land, as soon
as it was light enough to see, soon convinced the Turks of the
advisability of keeping within their own wire.   (See map
page 121).

June 17th.—On this date the regiment was relieved of outpost duty by a regiment of Australian Light Horse, in order
to take part in a " demonstration " on the N.E. shore of the
Dead Sea.   This was to be of the nature of a reconnaissance
in force, and was intended to strengthen the enemy in the
opinion, which it was hoped that the two raids on Es Salt
in March and April had caused him to form, that Allenby's
next move would be on the Eastern flank.   On the night of
the 16th, the brigade concentrated at Wilson's Ford, a crossing over the Wadi Rame, a stream which flows from the east
into the Jordan two miles from the Dead Sea.   The orders
were that a squadron of the 2nd Lancers was to start from the
ford as soon as light permitted, and gallop a knoll called Tel
Ghassul, a point usually held by the enemy.   The remainder
of the regiment was then to follow, and the leading squadron
was to push on to a point S. of Tel er Rame.   The Dorset
Yeomanry was to come up on the left of the 2nd Lancers
and the 36th Jacob's Horse was to take up a position on the
right.

The C.I.H. was to be in reserve.   Tel Ghassul was accordingly galloped by B squadron (Capt. Whitworth).   It was
found to be unoccupied.   B and C squadrons then pushed on

to a point on the Wade Jorfe, about a mile in front. The
Dorset Yeomanry, who were advancing towards Tel er Rame,
were now held up in some bush jungle to the right rear of
B and C squadrons, by what must have been a strong night
patrol of the enemy returning towards their own lines.   At
the same time, one troop of A squadron 2nd Lancers
charged into the bush jungle from the direction of Tel Ghassul.
Capt. Whitworth then sent Lieut. Ranking with half C squadron
to co-operate on the right of A, Ris. Mukand Singh following
with the other half of C in support.   Here what might have
been a dangerous mistake was made, for Regt. H.Q. was not
informed at once of C squadron's move.   Lieut. Ranking,
finding a crossing over the Wadi Rame, led a very spirited
charge from the south, killing over 40 Turks with the lance.
Ris. Mukand Singh's half squadron was not so successful, as
they were unable to find a crossing over the wadi.   The troop
of A squadron's advance had also been held up.   The Dorset
Yeomanry in the meantime were in action, dismounted.
Lieut. Ranking's charge finished the fight, for the enemy made
off at once.   B squadron now came in for some heavy shelling
from the hills in front.

At this point orders were given for the withdrawal of the
two brigades, and the troops returned to camp.   The casualties of the regiment in this action were :

	Killed.	Wounded.	Taken prisoner.
I.O.'s	—	—	1 (Jem. Attar Mohd, wounded).
I.O.R.	2	9	9 (3 wounded).
Horses ..	32	9	—

On returning to camp the regiment was visited by Gen.
Allenby, who congratulated Col. Bennett on the 2nd Lancers'
" brilliant little scrap."

June 18th.—Outpost work at Ghoraniyeh continued.

June 20th.—The regiment was relieved by the 29th Lancers,
and marched back to a camp near Jericho (Tel es Sultan).
As before, when in reserve, large fatigues had to be found
daily, and no one was sorry when the regiment again went
into the line.

June 28th.—Marched to El Henu, and took over outpost
duties and a small bridgehead.   The bridgehead, which

covered a swinging pontoon bridge, was held by half a squadron with a British officer, and each squadron took it in turn to find the garrison for 24 hours. The duty was not a coveted one, for the mosquitoes were very bad there. Another squadron found mounted patrols for outpost work. The bridge, which was hidden under trees by day, was swung into position, to allow these patrols to cross, just before dawn, and again just after dark.

A third squadron held three posts W. of the Henu crossing.

The enemy was at this time meditating an attempt to recapture Jerusalem, and an attack was expected at Henu. The 2nd Lancers were intended to remain at Henu until this attack took place. On the night of June 29th–30th, a party of Turks attacked the Henu bridgehead. Firing continued for some time and died away by about 3 a.m. At dawn Jem. Brij Lal's troops went out on patrol, and found, just outside the wire, 15 armed Bedouins with about 500 sheep, which he captured and brought back. The Bedouins claimed to be servants of the King of the Hedjaz, and that they were bringing the sheep as a present to the British army. Both Bedouins and sheep were sent back to Corps Headquarters. Then followed a weary succession of days, but the expected attack did not come.

July 13th.—The regiment was relieved after dark by the Jodhpur Lancers, and marched to Talaat ed Dumm. As we climbed the hill behind Jericho the valley was lit up by gun-fire. At Talaat ed Dumm we were ordered to stand fast for 24 hours, but were not called on to reinforce. The enemy's attack was a fiasco. On the Wadi Auja nearly a battalion of Germans was captured, and opposite Henu a Turkish force was routed by a brilliant charge by two squadrons of the Jodhpur Lancers commanded by Major Gell.

CHAPTER IX

JULY 14TH TO SEPTEMBER, 10TH, 1918

A SPELL ON SEA-LEVEL AT RAS DEIRAN—SECOND MARCH TO
THE VALLEY—AIN HAJLAH

July 15th.—Marched to Enab.

July 16th.—Marched to Ras Deiran. Here we remained
until August 12th, resting from the hardships of the valley
and training. Brig.-Gen. Howard-Vyse, B.G.G.S., Desert
Mounted Corps, now took over from Brig.-Gen. Godwin, the
two exchanging appointments. From Ras Deiran all British
officers went on leave to Cairo. The regiment played polo
again, and won two matches against the Desert Corps School
at Richon le Zion.

August 12th.—The brigade began to march back by short
stages to the valley, camping the first night at Latrun.

August 13th.—Marched to Enab.

August 14th.—Marched to Bethel (just beyond Jerusalem).

August 15th.—Marched to Talaat ed Dumm.

August 16th.—Marched to Jericho.

August 17th.—Marched to Ain Hajlah (two miles N.W. of
Henu). Here the British officers had a very pleasant camp
under the shade of a big banyan tree, where also a cement
reservoir made a very good swimming bath. From here one
squadron a day found the outposts in front of Makhadet
Hajlah bridgehead, held by the C.I.H. A post at Kasr el
Yehud was also held by a troop of the regiment.

August 20th.—Relieved the C.I.H. in Makhadet Hajlah
bridgehead, three squadrons in the line, one squadron in
reserve.

August 25th.—Relieved by the Worcester Yeomanry and
returned to the Ain Hajlah camp. Outpost work resumed,
taking alternate days with the C.I.H. The outpost squadron
going out in the morning first crossed the bridge over the
river at Makhadet Hajlah, then passed through the bridgehead
trenches, and made for an old tomb known as Kabr el Fendi el
Faiz, which was situated at the junction of the wadis El

Keffrein and Rame, and just below which was a ford, known from its map reference square as " Tock one ack." In this place the enemy made several attempts to ambush British patrols, for the ground was admirably suited to that purpose. Thick bushes lined the banks of either wadi, and riflemen hidden among them were invisible at distances of even ten or fifteen yards ; the roof of the tomb itself too was a good position for a machine gun, which, hidden by the surrounding trees, could fire through them in any direction. The deep and winding nature of the wadis, and the dense bushy growth which lined the tops of their banks, made retreat towards the Turkish lines a matter of no difficulty. The approach of this position by the outpost squadron was therefore made with the greatest caution, and demanded much ingenuity on the part of squadron leaders to avoid a stereotyped manner of making it good. The wadi Rame could be crossed a mile lower down, at Wilson's Ford, so that the squadron leader had the choice of approaching from the north or south. The wadi Rame could also be crossed at one or two places above the junction, as for instance at the spot found by Lieut. Ranking on June 17th ; there was no good crossing however over the wadi El Keffrein, nor could it be approached and so any attempt to encircle and cut off an ambushing party was out of the question. The Turks attempted no fewer than six ambushes at this place, but never when the regiment was on outpost duty there. They were in a position between the Kabr and Tel Ghassul when charged by the Jodhpur Lancers on July 14th.

At this time several special reconnaissances were made by the outpost squadron. In one of these, B squadron was required to report on the condition of the track which runs from Ghoraniyeh, past Tel Ghassul, to Madeba, as far as the crossing over the wadi Barrakat, a point about three miles S.E. of Ain Sueime. This was carried out by two troops under Capt. Whitworth. As the party approached the foothills, fire was opened from a small Turkish post which covered the road. A British aeroplane which happened to be flying over assisted in locating this by first dropping a message on B squadron, and then firing a red light directly over the post. Our party now made good a small hill opposite the Turkish post ; from this one troop came into action with rifle and

Hotchkiss fire, while Capt. Whitworth with the other slipped up the road. After a steep climb of nearly 1,200 feet, the wadi Barrakat was reached, its identification being made by compass bearing on the Dead Sea Post. An hour had elapsed since entering the hills, and there was a possibility of the party being cut off if it returned by the way it had come ; the descent was therefore made by a series of goat tracks to Ain Sueime. The other troop (Ress. Devi Chand) which had retained its original position, and was still carrying on an intermittent fire-fight, now retired. They had no casualties, though several Turks were seen to be hit. The party then returned to the outpost squadron H.Q.

September 3rd.—Lieut.-Col. J. F. Bennett relinquished the command to take up an appointment in Remounts in India. Lieut.-Col. G. Knowles, D.S.O., now assumed the command, but was evacuated sick a few days later. The command then devolved on Capt. D. S. Davison, who commanded the Regiment until the arrival of Major G. Gould, D.S.O., on September 23rd, from England.

September 5th.—A mixed brigade of Turks appeared opposite Henu. The outpost squadron of the C.I.H., who were on duty that day, found Kabr el Fendi el Faiz strongly held, and a battery, covered by Turkish cavalry, came into action from Tel Ghassul. There was an indecisive fight at the Kabr, in which a good charge was made by a troop of the C.I.H. On two more squadrons of the C.I.H. coming out to reinforce their outpost squadron the Turks retired. They were probably intended to reconnoitre the bridgeheads below Ghoraniyeh, for by now, in addition to those at Henu and Makhadet Hajlah, two more dummy bridges, with roads cut to approach them, had been constructed. There was a certain amount of speculation now as to where operations would begin in the autumn, but none of the troops had any inkling of the plan which had actually been made. That something was in the air was obvious, for A echelon of the transport was being re-organized to carry two days' emergency rations for man and horse, and classes of instruction in demolition work were being conducted by R.E. officers.

A series of night marches began, which indicated on which flank Allenby's stroke was to be made.

CHAPTER X

SEPTEMBER 11TH, 1918, TO SEPTEMBER 24TH, 1918

NIGHT MARCHES TO SELMEH—THE BREAK THROUGH—PASSAGE
OF THE MUSMUS PASS—THE CHARGE ON ARMAGEDDON—
CAPTURE OF AFULEH—BEISAN—JISR MUJAMIA

September 11th.—Marched to Kilo 17 (just beyond Talaat ed Dumm).

September 12th.—Marched to Enab.

September 13th.—Marched to Junction Station.

September 15th.—Marched to Ramleh, where we drew some new equipment and a few remounts.

The following narrative is taken from the *History of the 19th Cavalry Brigade Operations, September and October,* 1918, compiled by Brig.-Gen. W. G. K. Green, C.M.G., D.S.O., with omissions where paragraphs do not concern the 2nd Lancers, and with a few interpolated notes (in brackets) on matters affecting the regiment only.

2. On the night of the 16th–17th September, Divisional H.Q., Divisional Troops, 12th Cavalry Brigade, and the Dorset and Middlesex Yeomanry regiments, arrived at Ramleh from El Mejdel, and the 4th Cavalry Division was thus completed.

3. During the one day's halt at Junction Station and two days at Ramleh the Brigade was fully occupied in re-adjusting equipment and stores, and in the many necessary details of preparation for the offensive, The night marches from the Jordan Valley had been tedious, and the daytime with its customary routine, added to the annoyance by flies, dust and other worries of the hot weather, had afforded little real rest to the troops. Considering the many weary weeks they had spent through the summer in the valley, subjected to the perpetual torment by flies and mosquitoes, their spirits and morale on the eve of the operations were wonderful. A great deal of abnormal labour was expended

in the return of surplus kit to the ordnance depot at Ludd, and the drawing of complementary equipment that had been awaiting the troops' arrival from the Jordan Valley. All brigades had to carry out this work simultaneously, with the result that the congestion of traffic on the road entailed waiting about for many hours on the transport and loading parties.

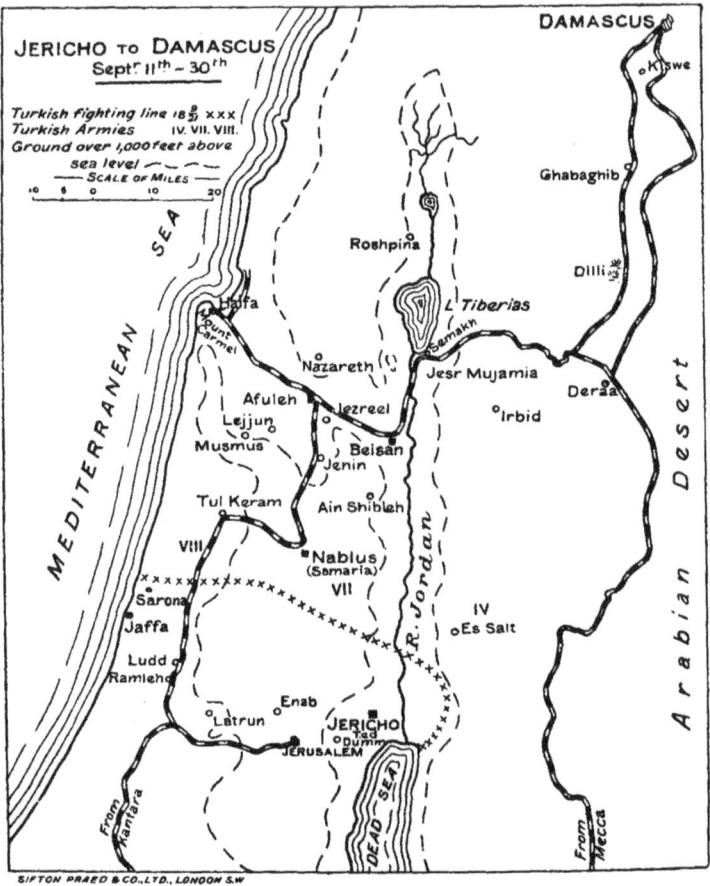

4. At 10.00 on the 17th September, a conference of all commanding officers was held at Divisional Headquarters camp, and the details of the scheme for the coming operations were explained. At 10.30 the Commander-in-Chief, General

Sir Edmund Allenby, arrived and made a short address to the assembled commanding officers. The afternoon was employed in the issue of final orders, and distribution of maps to units. Preparations for the campaign had hitherto been rightly kept so secret that it was not until this day that squadron and troop leaders became aware of the plan of action.

(The plan of attack was to employ every means possible to induce the enemy to believe that the main blow would be delivered east of the Jordan. To this end dummy roads, bridges, and camps were constructed in the Jordan valley, realistic lines of horses made of reeds being made as has already been described. Ostentatious preparations were also made for the establishment of G.H.Q. at Jerusalem. In the meantime three cavalry divisions and four infantry divisions were secretly moved to the coastal sector, marching by night, and hiding in plantations by day. The air force at the same time made a very successful effort to prevent enemy aircraft from discovering these movements. The task of the infantry was to roll back the Turkish right flank on the coast and make a way for the cavalry to pass. The latter were then to cross the ridge which ends in Mount Carmel, and, by establishing themselves on the Turkish lines of communication at Haifa, Afuleh, and Beisan, to cut off the VIIth and VIIIth Turkish armies which were west of the Jordan. This was carried out so swiftly and successfully that the plan was enlarged to include the capture of Damascus and then of Aleppo.)

5. After dark on the 17th September, the brigade moved to the 4th Cavalry Division's next place of assembly in the Selmeh-Sarona area and was here disposed in orange groves, which gave complete concealment from aeroplane observation during the 18th, the eve of the advance.

6. All troops were fitted out with bare necessities only, all dispensable equipment and clothing being left behind at Ludd, such as greatcoats, extra blankets and heavy tethering gear. Every man carried one iron ration, and two days' emergency ration in addition to the unexpended portion of the day's issue. Twenty-one and a half pounds of grain[1] were carried on the horse in addition to one day's grain ration per horse, loaded on the A echelon limbered waggons. Each

[1] Chiefly barley, carried in nosebags.

regiment was allowed to take with the fighting column one water cart and one limbered waggon, loaded as desired ; also one mess cart. These were well horsed and were able to keep up with the guns over any country.

SELMEH TO BEISAN

7.   Before dawn on the 19th September, the brigade moved out of its bivouacs in the Selmeh-Sarona orange groves, and marching the four to five miles over the sand dunes to Hadrah Bridge watered on the north bank of the river Auja. Thence it moved on to its appointed position of readiness nearly two miles S. of El Jelil. Arrived here at 08.25, horses were off-saddled and fed.

8.   The bombardment of the enemy's lines, in which the horse batteries of the division took part, commenced at 04.30 and very shortly afterwards the infantry attack was launched. It went with such dash and success that the 4th Cavalry Division was able to start on its mission earlier than had been anticipated. Regimental pioneers had been concentrated the previous night behind our front line under a divisional staff officer ; and in the morning, following on the heels of the infantry, they cut the wire and prepared the track over our own and the enemy's trench systems for the cavalry advance.

9.   The 11th Cavalry Brigade was the leading brigade of the division and passed through the gap at 08.58.

10.   The 10th Cavalry Brigade, leaving its position of readiness at 09.30 and following the 12th Cavalry Brigade, passed the Turkish wire at 10.30, in the following order of march :—

Dorset Yeomanry ..	..	(Lt.-Col. Mason, D.S.O.).
2nd Lancers ..	..	(Capt. Davison).
17th M.G. Squadron	..	(Major Patron, M.C.).
Berks Battery R.H.A.	..	(Major Landsberg, D.S.O.).
38th C.I.H.—less 2 sqdns.		(Major Hutchison).
10th Cav. Field Amb.	..	(Capt. Humphreys, M.C.).
1 Squadron C.I.H.		

The Berks Battery, R.H.A., which had been in the line for some days, and had taken part in the bombardment at 04.30, joined the brigade before crossing No Man's Land. One squadron of the C.I.H. was absent on escort duty to the first

line transport which had all been divisionalized, and was to
follow the division at its own pace.

11. The march continued throughout the morning and
afternoon, except for a halt from 13.00 to 14.00, without
incident. At 11.30 the brigade had come up on the left of
the 12th Cavalry Brigade, and had advanced parallel with it
in open formation as far as Shel Alif. The country here
consisted chiefly of rolling downs—ideal going for cavalry.
The infantry (XXIst Corps), after breaking through the
enemy's lines, had wheeled eastwards towards the hills, and
the fighting in that direction could be heard as the brigade
moved on towards the north.

12. At 14.55 the brigade received orders to march from
Shel Alif to Mejdel, where it was to water and feed. The
Dorset Yeomanry were detailed as advanced guard, but
mistaking situation of Mejdel, since it existed only on the
map, they arrived at Jedd, a village some 1,500 yards beyond.
From here they reported only two small wells, so it was decided
to push on to Kerkur-Beidus, where a plentiful water supply
was known to exist.

13. At 17.50 the 2nd Lancers were sent forward, with
one Subsection M.G., as advanced guard and with orders to
cover the brigade while watering at Kerkur-Beidus. The
Dorset Yeomanry was ordered to rejoin the brigade.

14. The 2nd Lancers reached Kerkur-Beidus at 19.00
and put out one squadron to hold an outpost line to the east
to cover the brigade while watering near the railway crossing
just north of the village. A squadron of the 36th Jacob's
Horse (11th Cavalry Brigade) was already holding the village,
with protection out towards the north.

15. Meanwhile, at 18.10 the 11th Light Armoured Motor
Battery, having reported its arrival for duty with the advanced
guard through the Musmus Pass, was directed to join the 2nd
Lancers and push forward patrols as far as Kh. Arah cross
roads, supported by one squadron of the 2nd Lancers.

16. The brigade commenced watering (probably about
19.30—records are slightly contradictory on this point) in a
stream about one mile N.E. of Kerkur-Beidus.

NIGHT MARCH THROUGH MUSMUS PASS

17.   The division had issued at 18.30, the following orders (time of their receipt at Bde. H.Q. is uncertain, but it was evidently not earlier than 19.30) :—

" The advance will be continued to-night through the Musmus Pass on El Lejjun, moving from Kerkur through Kh. Es Sumrah.   Units will leave Kerkur in the following order :

" 10th Cavalry Brigade, 11th Cavalry Brigade, 12th Cavalry Brigade.

" Divisional H.Q. will move at head of 11th Cavalry Brigade. 10th Cavalry Brigade will leave Kerkur at 22.00.   Other units will time their march from present bivouacs so as to follow in above order at Kerkur.   No. 7 (? 11) L.A.M. Battery will leave Kerkur at 21.45 and will reconnoitre the pass in advance of the 10th Cavalry Brigade.   Enemy are reported to have retired last night on Nazareth and El Lejjun but no guns with column.   Acknowledge.   18.30."

18.   At 19.30, the Brigade Major was sent on to the 2nd Lancers to direct them to advance forthwith with the L.A.M. Battery to Kh. Arah and hold the cross roads.   The 2nd Lancers record orders to the following effect, received at 20.15 :—

" The brigade will act as advanced guard to the division in its march to El Afuleh.   The 2nd Lancers will be leading regiment of the brigade and will move off at once and make good the cross roads at Kh. Arah.   Only two squadrons may be employed in order to make good your objective.   But the whole regiment may be made use of to retain it when gained. The attainment of your objective will be reported to Brigade H.Q. and you will then await the arrival of the remainder of the brigade."

The O.C. 2nd Lancers (Capt. Davison) was given to understand that the remainder of the brigade would not move from Kerkur till his report had been received, so that he might expect to be at Arah for about 4 hours.

19.   At about 20.30 (19.30 ?) the brigade was disposed thus :—

2nd Lancers	..	At Tel Asawir ready to move on
1 Subsect. M.G.S. ..		Kh. Arah.
11th L.A.M. Batty.		

C.I.H. (less 1 sqdn.)   At Tel Asawir.

C.I.H. (less 1 sqdn.)
17th M.G. Sqdn (less
 1 Subsect.)   ..   ⎬ Watering N.E. of Kerkur-Beidus.
Berks Batty. R.H.A.

Dorset Yeomanry ..   En route from Jedd to rejoin Bde.

C.F.A.   ..   .. ⎫ Moving on Kerkur Beidus.
Field Troop.   ⎭

20. At 20.45 the Brigadier verbally explained to liaison
officers of units that it was his intention to push on to El
Lejjun at 01.00 (20th September) and that the 2nd Lancers
were to advance as soon as the head of the brigade was in
touch with them. But at 21.30 the Divisional Commander
(Maj.-Gen. Sir George Barrow) arrived at Brigade H.Q. and,
having heard the dispositions of the brigade, directed a modifi-
cation of the Brigadier's arrangements, and himself motored on
to the 2nd Lancers to push them on at once to El Lejjun.
He ordered the remainder of the brigade to follow as soon as
possible.

21. Meanwhile the 2nd Lancers had moved off from Tel
el Asawir at 20.45.

Advanced guard : 1 sqdn. (Capt. Vaughan), L.A.M. Batty.
Main body :   1 sqdn. Subsect. M.G.S., 2 sqdns.
The advanced guard was spread out in small packets, strength
one troop each, at about 100 yards distance. The L.A.M.
Battery followed the leading troop. The main body followed
the advanced guard at 400 distance. The whole regiment
was in column of half sections, as movement off the road was
impossible. The orders to the advanced guard were :—
" In the event of your being fired upon, the leading troop will
charge at once and try to rush the position. If this fails you
will take no further action pending orders from Regimental
H.Q."

22. Soon after crossing the railway line by Tel el Asawir,
the advanced guard came upon the rear of a column of Turkish
transport and stragglers retreating towards El Lejjun.
These surrendered without fighting. Nearly 500 prisoners
were taken before reaching Kh. Arah, and were sent back to
Brigade H.Q. in batches under small escorts of about 2 men
to 30 prisoners. Arah was reached without further incident

and by 23.30 the advanced guard had taken up a line of outposts covering the cross roads.   Information from prisoners and inhabitants showed that a considerable column of Turks with three guns, moving towards El Lejjun, had passed shortly before the 2nd Lancers' arrival.

23.   At this moment, 23.30, the Divisional Commander drove up and, after ascertaining from the O.C. 2nd Lancers the situation, ordered him to push on to El Lejjun, and make good the exit from the pass.   At the same time he ordered the armoured cars to go ahead and find out whether or not the enemy were holding the strong position by Umm el Fahm towards the eastern end of the pass.

10TH CAVALRY BRIGADE MAIN BODY GOES ASTRAY

24.   At 23.00 the remainder of the brigade commenced its march from Kerkur-Beidus   to   follow   the   2nd Lancers. Near the railway crossing, the track to the Musmus Pass was missed and the brigade proceeded on another track leading in a more northerly direction.   The 11th Cavalry Brigade in turn followed on its heels, but after one regiment of the latter had filed off, the Divisional Commander arrived on the spot and, discovering the mistake that had been made, halted the remainder of the column.   He thereupon put the 12th Cavalry Brigade on the right road and directed them to push on up the pass behind the 2nd Lancers, and the 11th Cavalry Brigade to follow the 12th.   The 10th Cavalry Brigade wheeling its head eventually struck the road leading to the pass further east of the railway and, after a rough passage over stony and broken country, in the growing moonlight came into column of route behind the battery of the 12th Cavalry Brigade.   In this position it passed through to El Lejjun, the 2nd Lancers being now temporarily attached to the 12th Cavalry Brigade.

25.   It was imperative that the   heights at   El Lejjun, commanding the entrance to the pass, should be secured before dawn.   The accomplishment of this object was entirely due to the energetic personal action of the Divisional Commander, who never spared himself for one moment, through these anxious hours of unexpected toil.

26.   The track through the historic Musmus Pass had been made practicable for troops and vehicles only in this war.

Previously the narrowest parts admitted of passage only in single file. The western end is a valley about 500 yards in breadth. This gradually becomes narrower, until at Umm el Fahm the hills rise abruptly on either side from near the road itself. The track surface was rough and stony, as was also the space on either side.

27.   At 23.45 the 2nd Lancers proceeded on its advance from Kh. Arah in formation similar to that in which it had entered the pass, with the exception that the L.A.M. Battery had gone on ahead and a fresh squadron was put out as advanced guard. Capt. Vaughan's squadron on outpost duty, fell in rear after the regiment had passed.   The Umm el Fahm position was reported clear by the armoured cars and was reached by the regiment at 00.30 on the 20th September.

28.   El Lejjun was reached by the 2nd Lancers without opposition at 03.00.   About 100 Turks were taken sitting round a fire, with their arms piled, at the exit from the pass. This party was probably the advanced guard of a force sent from El Afuleh to hold the pass, the main body of which was encountered later in the morning.

29.   The leading squadrons (2nd Lancers) took up a line of outposts covering the exit from the pass and the rear squadron a supporting position in rear, to cover retirement if necessary. While watering was in progress, at 04.30 the head of the 12th Cavalry Brigade arrived at El Lejjun and Capt. Davison's troops came under the orders of its Brigadier.

30.   He received orders from the Brigade Major to occupy points on the plain of Esdraelon, as pivots of manœuvre. A Squadron was directed to make good Tel el Mutasselim and Kh. el Khuzneb on the left ; C Squadron to occupy Point 193 in the centre, on the Lejjun-Afuleh road ; and B squadron to send one troop to seize Tel ed Dhaheb on the right.   While these movements were being carried out, the G.O.C., 12th Cavalry Brigade, gave orders for the 2nd Lancers, accompanied by the L.A.M. Battery and subsection M.G.'s, to advance and capture El Afuleh and to destroy the railway lines there, leading to Haifa, Beisan, and Jenin.

31.   At 05.05 the O.C. 2nd Lancers issued the following orders :—" The regiment will advance and take El Afuleh. C Squadron will move along the direct Lejjun-Afuleh road.

and attack from the front.   A Squadron will cover the left
flank and moving N. of Birket-el-Fuleh (marsh), will
attack from the north, making the station their objective,
in co-operation with C Squadron.   B Squadron will cover the
right flank and attack from the south, also in co-operation with
C Squadron, making the aerodrome their objective.   D
Squadron and Subsection M.G. will be in reserve.   11th
L.A.M. Battery will accompany C Squadron.   Demolition
Troop will follow D Squadron."

32.   Daylight was now coming on.   Mt. Tabor stood up
clear and bold against the dawn.   To the left of it could be
seen the hills about Nazareth.   The Plain of Esdraelon,
or Armageddon, was half hidden, as was also Afuleh, by
the low lying morning mists.   The direction of Afuleh was
determined by compass bearing, but away to the right could
be discerned the village of Tel ed Dhaheb perched on a low
knoll.

(Squadron commanders of the 2nd Lancers were as follows :
A : Lieut. King ; B : Capt. Whitworth, M.C., also 2nd in
command ; C : Lieut. Turner ; D : Capt. Vaughan.)

ACTION AT MEGIDDO (ARMAGEDDON)

Report by Capt. Davison, 2nd Lancers (Capt. Davison was
awarded the D.S.O. for this action).

33.   As squadrons moved off a steady fire broke out from
the direction of Point 193 at 05.30 hours.   Leaving Capt.
Vaughan to bring along the reserve, I rode forward to find out
what was happening, and on approaching Point 193 I received
a verbal message from the O.C. C Squadron to the effect that
he was held up by a force estimated at 80 rifles.   I found the
situation to be as follows :—

(a) The Turks were holding a position in the open about half
a mile east of Point 193.

(b) C Squadron had dismounted 1 troop under R.M.
Mukand Singh, and their Hotchkiss troop, and were engaging
the enemy with fire at about 800 yards range, while the remainder of the squadron was concentrating in rear with a view
to moving round the enemy's flank.

(c) The 11th L.A.M. Battery were in action about 300 yards
in front of C Squadron and were engaging the enemy with

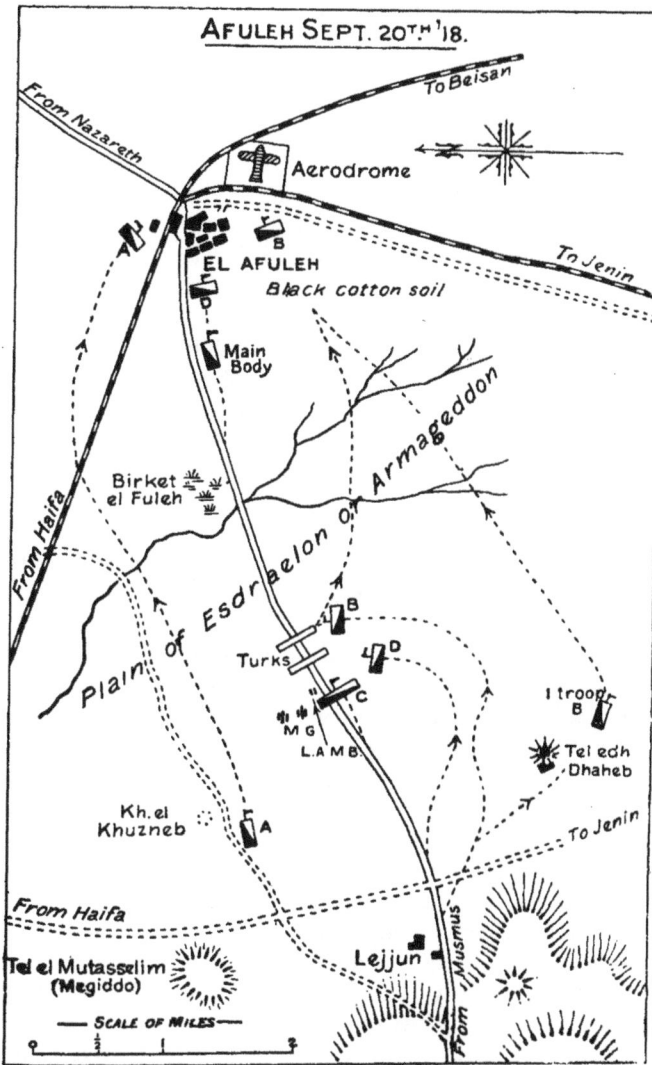

AFULEH SEPT. 20TH '18.

From Nazareth

To Beisan

Aerodrome

To Jenin

EL AFULEH

Black cotton soil

Main Body

Birket el Fuleh

From Haifa

Plain of Esdraelon or Armageddon

Turks

M G

L.A M B

Kh. el Khuzneb

I troop B

Tel edh Dhaheb

To Jenin

From Haifa

From Musmus

Tel el Mutasselim (Megiddo)

Lejjun

SCALE OF MILES

SIFTON PRAED & CO., LTD., LONDON, S.W.

machine gun fire. From the high ground about Point 193
the enemy's position could be seen, and was fairly well demarcated by the dust raised by his rifle and machine gun fire, and
I realized that the estimate of 80 rifles was much below the

mark. The soil was black cotton in this particular place and was not so bad as to stop horses galloping. The enemy's flank could be distinguished, and, as there seemed to be no obstacle to hold us up, I decided to turn his left flank and gallop the position.

34. I accordingly directed the O.C. D Squadron (Capt. Vaughan) to left shoulder, pointed out the enemy's position and ordered him to go slow for five minutes to enable me to get the machine guns into action, and then to turn the enemy's flank, and charge. I then ordered the O.C. M.G.'s to come into action in the neighbourhood of Point 193. In the meantime, I had despatched the Adjutant (Capt. Ranking) to get into touch with the O.C. A Squadron, who at this time was on the road about half way between Lejjun and Kh. Khuzneb, and order him to work round the enemy's right flank. Owing to the distance that this message had to go and to the fact that A Squadron was rather scattered when the order was received, the fight was over before the order could be acted upon.

35. By the time I had got the machine guns into action I could see that D Squadron was well round the enemy's flank in column of troops, and almost immediately they wheeled head left, formed squadron and charged in open order, rolling up the Turkish front line, capturing or killing every man. R.M. Mukand Singh, on seeing D Squadron charge, mounted his troop of C Squadron and charged from the front with good results. In the meantime, O.C. B Squadron (Capt. Whitworth), seeing what was happening, decided to co-operate with D Squadron on his own initiative. My original intention had been to leave B Squadron out to watch the right flank, but the necessary orders did not arrive in time ; so, seeing what was happening, I sent a message to Jem. Sargit Singh, who was commanding the troop of B Squadron sent to seize Tel ed Dhaheb, to remain out as flank guard. As things turned out it was just as well that O.C. B Squadron acted as he did, for the Turks were found to be holding the position in two lines, one immediately behind the other, and some 300 yards apart, and had D Squadron been alone they might well have suffered heavy casualties from the fire of the second line. The O.C. B Squadron realizing this, swung round outside D Squadron and charged the Turkish support line, rolling it up.

(Narrative by Captain Whitworth, O.C. B Squadron :—

" As we debouched from the pass dawn was breaking, and we saw a broad plain covered with low mists. Captain Davison had explained our formation for the forward march. My squadron was to move on the right flank, and I was to detach one troop to Tel ed Dhaheb as a flank guard. I sent Jemadar Sarjit Singh with his troop on this duty, and the squadron moved to its position with only thirty lances. The formation was squadron column.

" Hardly had the regiment begun to move forward when heavy rifle and machine gun fire broke out from the direction of the road. Bullets were coming unpleasantly close and I increased the pace to a hand gallop and edged towards the right with the intention of locating the enemy's left flank. Almost immediately I saw the reserve squadron (D) moving out in my direction, and I guessed that the C.O. intended making an enveloping movement from the right. There was no time to receive orders, so I decided to co-operate with D. Just then B Squadron ran into a wire fence hidden in the jowar which covered that part of the plain. I was on ahead and left it to my second in command (Ressaidar Jang Bahadur Singh) to reform the squadron, which he did with great celerity.

" Bullets were coming thick and fast now, and I imagined that the squadron had had pretty heavy casualties ; added to this I was in a blue funk of striking an uncrossable nullah, for the map showed a tributary of the Kishon between me and the enemy. From our experience of the inaccuracy of the Palestine maps, I might have equally expected a hill as a nullah, but in the flurry of the moment I became obsessed with the fear of sharing the fate of Sisera's host on the same field, and the words ' that mighty river Kishon ' kept ringing through my head.

" Up to now I had not caught a glimpse of the enemy. Looking back I saw that B was crossing D's line, and I galloped back to lead the squadron off more to the right. There seemed to be plenty of the men left, and the formation was still tolerably good. We were moving at a good fifteen miles an hour by now. It was just then that I caught sight of the Turks. They were formed in two lines in column with a distance of two hundred yards. The men saw the enemy at

the same moment, and I was just able to direct the leading
troop on the rear line of the enemy before they all saw red and
broke into a hell for leather gallop.   It now became a question
of who could get in first, but I was still in mortal terror that
the Turks' determined stand might be fortified by the knowledge that a deep nullah lay between themselves and us.
We had overtaken our ground scouts long ago.   However,
I need not have worried, for we were in for it now.   I could
hear yells from D on my left rear.

" Before I realized it we were right on top of the enemy,
and it was only when I saw a young Turk deliberately aiming
at me that I realized that I was still holding my map in my
right hand, and had forgotten to draw my sword.   The little
brute missed me and ran under my horse's neck, and tried to
jab his rifle in my stomach.   I had just time to draw and
thrust over my left knee.   The point got him somewhere in
the neck and he went down like a house of cards.   My next
opponent was a moustachioed warrior, probably an N.C.O.,
who was hopping about with a fixed bayonet, and a blood-
thirsty expression.   I suppose he had never met an opponent
going at fifteen miles an hour ; at any rate he had not begun
to point when I poked him in the ribs.

" All the Turks on the left flank had now had enough of it,
but a few ran out of the ranks on the right and fired down the
line at us.   It did not take long to polish them off.   I made for
one who had murderous intentions, but changed his mind at
the last moment.   My point caught him plumb between the
shoulders, and the shock nearly dislocated my arm ; perhaps
he was wearing a pair of steel braces.   During this time I was
naturally preoccupied with saving my own skin and saw little
of what was going on round me.   I only remember my orderly
Lal Chand, on my second horse, Advocate, who had the
regimental flag furled round his lance, dragging along the
ground a Turk who had stuck on the point, and I distinctly
saw Jemadar Gobind Singh, V.C., deliver a magnificent cut
at an opponent, but as his sword was not made for this sort
of thing, the Turk was not damaged.

" The men stopped killing directly all resistance ceased,
but rallying them was an awful business.   I was just beginning
to do so when I saw that D had just reached the front line,

which must have been considerably shaken by B's success on their supports.

" While we were rounding up the prisoners I became aware of a fat officer doubling about in circles. He finally fetched up in front of me and fell on his knees, shouting ' Spare my life. I am a Syrian,' to which I answered 'All right, old cock. Go and join your pals over there.' This evidently conveyed nothing, so I tried less colloquial English, and then found that he understood none, but had prudently acquired his one sentence against a rainy day.

" All was over now bar the shouting, which, rather to my surprise, was provided by the prisoners, who burst into song as they were marched to our rear.

" After rallying the squadron I sent a patrol back along the route of the charge to give first aid to our wounded, and we then found to our immense astonishment that although about half-a-dozen horses had been hit, not a single man was wounded. One horse which had been hit by a bullet which passed between the back tendons of the off hind did not even go lame. All the hits were in the legs or belly, and I have noticed the same report in the case of other cavalry actions. It therefore seems that a machine gunner who has the misfortune to be charged by cavalry should, if he is cool enough to remember it, aim high.

" My batman, Nagington, by profession a stable boy from Auteuil, was not with the squadron, but saw the charge from the mouth of the Pass. I asked him that evening what he thought of the show, and he answered ' I thought that Advocate went fine.' To him it was obviously a species of race.")

36. During the advance B Squadron ran into a wire fence and became considerably disorganized while under heavy fire from rifles and machine guns. Ressaidar Jang Bahadur Singh however rallied his men with great coolness and reformed the squadron in time to co-operate with D Squadron. For his coolness and ability on this occasion, Ress. Jang Bahadur Singh was awarded the Indian Distinguished Service Medal.

The Turkish force was found to consist of a battalion with three machine guns. Of these between 40 and 50 were killed and the remainder taken prisoners. None got away. The

prisoners numbered 470. Our casualties in this action were
one man wounded and about a dozen horses, which had to be
destroyed. For his skilful leading on this occasion, Capt.
E. W. D. Vaughan was subsequently awarded the Military
Cross. Capt. D. E. Whitworth, M.C., was mentioned in
despatches.

37. Comments (Capt. Davison). The reason why an
immediate attack was made on the Turkish position, without
waiting for any more extensive reconnaissance than was
possible from a general survey from Point 193, was that :—
This battalion was evidently moving up to hold the Musmus
Pass. Their advanced guard had been captured in its entirety
two hours previously. As far as I (Capt. Davison) knew, no
one had got away to give information of our approach, and the
chances were that the first intimation that the Turkish commander had of our arrival was when our leading patrols were
seen approaching. The Turks had therefore to take up their
position where they stood and could not select their own
ground. Hence an immediate attack was indicated before
they had time to better their position and before the surprise
occasioned by our appearance had time to wear off. The great
value of surprise and mobility, and the moral effect of the
lance were clearly exemplified in this action. The battalion
was a fresh one and had not been shaken by previous defeat.
They fought well and kept up their fire till we got right into
them ; but the moral effect of the lance, combined with the
surprise and unnerving effect of an attack from both front and
flank, caused them to throw down their arms as soon as we got
in. Their shooting may not have possibly been up to the
standard of continental armies, but this alone can hardly be
held to account for the successful carrying out, with practically
no casualties, of an operation which has hitherto been set down
as impossible, namely, the charging by cavalry of unbroken
infantry armed with modern rifles and machine guns. Its
complete success must be largely attributed to the moral effect
of a quick-moving force attacking from the flank with the *arme
blanche.*

The O.C. B Squadron acted rightly in co-operating on his
own initiative in the attack. This squadron had been detailed

as right flank guard and had received orders framed to achieve a certain object, viz., the capture of Afuleh.   While engaged in carrying out these orders it was confronted with a new contingency to meet which no orders had been issued.   Events moved so quickly that new orders had not time to reach the squadron commander, but he could see what was taking place and co-operated on his own initiative.

The L.A.M. Battery afforded very great assistance both during the advance through the Musmus Pass, when they went on in advance of the regiment and reconnoitred the road, and during the action itself.   In the former their presence was found to add considerably to the confidence of the advanced guard, and the steady flow of negative information they maintained was most comforting.   In the latter the cars moved down to within 500 yards of the Turkish position and maintained a steady machine-gun fire on the Turkish left flank. They ceased fire just at the right moment, as D Squadron charged home, and it was undoubtedly largely due to their effective support that our casualties were so negligible. Action of Hotchkiss rifles :—The only Hotchkiss rifles which came into action were those of C Squadron.   The led horses of these rifles and of R.M. Mukand Singh's troop were about 100 yards in the rear of the fighting line in the open.   Slight cover from view was given by a patch of tall thistles and grass.   No bullet proof cover was available.   Orders to the H.R.'s of B Squadron (Capt. Whitworth) were to join in the mounted charge in order to increase the moral effect.   This squadron only consisted of three troops, one of which was the H.R. troop, one troop under Jem. Sargit Singh was at Tel ed Dhaheb, so that only one troop of lances was available for the charge.   The Hotchkiss troop formed on the left of this troop and charged with them in order to make the numbers appear greater than they were.   D Squadron consisted of three troops of lances and one troop of Hotchkiss ; so the H.R. troop and packs were dropped, and followed 200 yards in rear of the squadron, ready to cover the retirement should one be necessary. Both squadrons charged in line.   The going was fairly good, though over cotton soil.   The route followed by B and D Squadrons afforded slight cover for part of the distance passed over in the approach manœuvring.

L

CAPTURE OF EL AFULEH (2ND LANCERS). REPORT BY
CAPT. DAVISON

39. A halt of half-an-hour was made to allow for reorganization, during which patrols were sent from B and D Squadrons
to reconnoitre El Afuleh. These patrols reported that on
approaching the village they had been fired on by rifles and
machine guns ; but that the place did not appear to be strongly
held, and that the Turks appeared to be evacuating it as fast
as they could.

40. At 06.30 the advance was resumed, the armoured cars
pushing on in advance. The order of march was now as
follows :—A Squadron on the left on the line of the Kh. El
Khuzneb—Afuleh track ; D Squadron in the centre on the
Lejjun—Afuleh road ; B Squadron on the right on the line
Tel Ed Dhaheb—Afuleh ; C Squadron and machine guns
in reserve on the Lejjun—Afuleh road. The cotton soil,
which up to this time had been passable at all places, now
became so bad that it was impossible for the squadrons in the
centre and on the right to move out of a walk. The going on
the left was better and as a result A Squadron got somewhat
ahead of the general alignment.

41. As we approached El Afuleh streams of lorries could
be seen moving out along the Beisan road. When we were
about a mile from the village a German aeroplane rose from the
aerodrome and flew over D Squadron. It fired a couple of
bursts from its machine gun without effect and then flew away
towards Beisan.

42. While B and D Squadrons were still about half-a-mile
away from the village, A Squadron had got into position north
of the village and, as he was coming under rifle and machine
gun fire, Lieut. King decided to gallop the village at once.
This was carried out in good style, the squadron clearing the
village and reaching the aerodrome at its southern end. For
his handling of his squadron on this occasion, Lieut. King
was awarded the Military Cross.

43. On reaching the aerodrome, A Squadron was almost
immediately joined by B Squadron ; while D Squadron went
through the village from the front. At the aerodrome over
100 German air mechanics were found, who tried to get away

on motor lorries but were prevented by Hotchkiss fire. A considerable quantity of munitions of various kinds, including 3 aeroplanes, 10 locomotives, and 50 rolling stock, was taken at the aerodrome and in the station. No. 11 L.A.M. Battery captured 12 motor lorries driven by Germans endeavouring to escape by Beisan. El Afuleh was in our hands by 08.00 on the 20th September. B and D Squadrons were left out to hold an outpost line while the demolition troop carried out the destruction of the railway as ordered.

44.   Shortly after the outpost line was posted a closed car approached the aerodrome, and being taken for one of our own cars was allowed to approach the picquet. When some 80 yards away it stopped and nine Turks jumped out and opened fire on the picquet. Considerable confusion resulted owing to the unexpected nature of the attack, but Daf. Chuni Lal kept his head and got a Hotchkiss into action, killing two of the Turks and wounding one. He then seized a rifle and bayonet and attacked the remainder single handed, upon which they surrendered. For this gallant action, Daf. Chuni Lal was awarded the Indian Order of Merit, and Acting Lance Dafadar Nun Singh, who actually fired the gun, the Indian Distinguished Service Medal. Somewhat later six lorries full of Turks were seen approaching from the direction of Jenin. The armoured cars were turned on to deal with these. The Turks deserted their lorries and took to their heels.

45.   On arrival of the 12th Cavalry Brigade, the relief of the squadrons on outpost was begun. While the relief was in progress a German aeroplane, not knowing that we held the place, attempted to land, discovered its mistake as it touched the ground and opened fire with its machine gun. . . . (Fire was opened by a Hotchkiss rifle and by the machine guns of the armoured cars. The propeller of the aeroplane was broken by the first burst, and the pilot promptly put his hands up. The observer was wounded.) On relief B and D squadrons joined the remainder of the regiment.

AFULEH TO BEISAN

46.   Leaving one regiment temporarily at El Afuleh to close the exits north until relieved by a detachment of the 5th Cavalry Division, the whole division marched down the

plain of Jezreel in the afternoon, to occupy Beisan in the
Jordan Valley, and so bar the only remaining route, west of
Jordan, for escape northwards of the broken VIIth and VIIIth
Turkish Armies.

47.   The brigade was now reassembled, under command of
the new Brigadier (Brig.-Gen. W. G. K. Green, D.S.O., 36th
Jacob's Horse), and received orders to march at 13.00 as
advanced brigade of the division.   Owing to the necessary
delays in collecting the scattered units it was impossible to
actually start before 13.30.   Order of march :—Advanced
Guard :   Dorset Yeomanry, 1 Subsection M.G.—Main Body :
C.I.H. (less 1 squadron) with 2 squadrons as right and left flank
guards, Berks Battery R.H.A., 2nd Lancers, Field Troop, Field
Ambulance.

48.   The O.C. Dorset Yeomanry disposed his advanced
guard across the plain with parties central and lateral, with
requisite support, and a central reserve.   After the advance
had been commenced in this order the Brigadier decided that
the nature of the country made progress so slow that there was
danger, not only of holding up the Division, but of failing to
reach Beisan before nightfall.   The ground was of a cotton
soil nature—dry, hard, and intersected freely by large cracks
—which rendered movement out of a walk almost impossible.
Orders were therefore sent to the O.C. Dorset Yeomanry to
concentrate and move principally by the road.   The flank
guards, moving parallel under the hills on either side at a
distance of one to two miles, were clearly visible from the road.
Also a certain amount of risk was warranted by the evident
helplessness of any small groups of enemy that were in the
neighbourhood, and by the distance (17 miles) to be traversed
before the enemy's next line of retreat northwards could be
reached.

49.   The distance was covered at a rapid pace, which was
well maintained by the tired troops and horses, with one
principal halt at Shutta.   Several prisoners were captured
en route.   Some of these were accompanying small waggons
laden with clothing and other rubbish concealing rifles.
All that could be done was to remove the bolts of the rifles
and break their stocks, then pass the prisoners to the rear of
the column.   A few machine guns were also captured.

50. The leading troops entered Beisan village, a mile south of the railway station, soon after 16.30, and by 16.55 the remainder of the brigade had assembled near the station. The village fell into the Dorset Yeomanry's hands after slight opposition and about 100 prisoners were taken. Among other booty captured were three 5.9 in. Howitzers at the station with

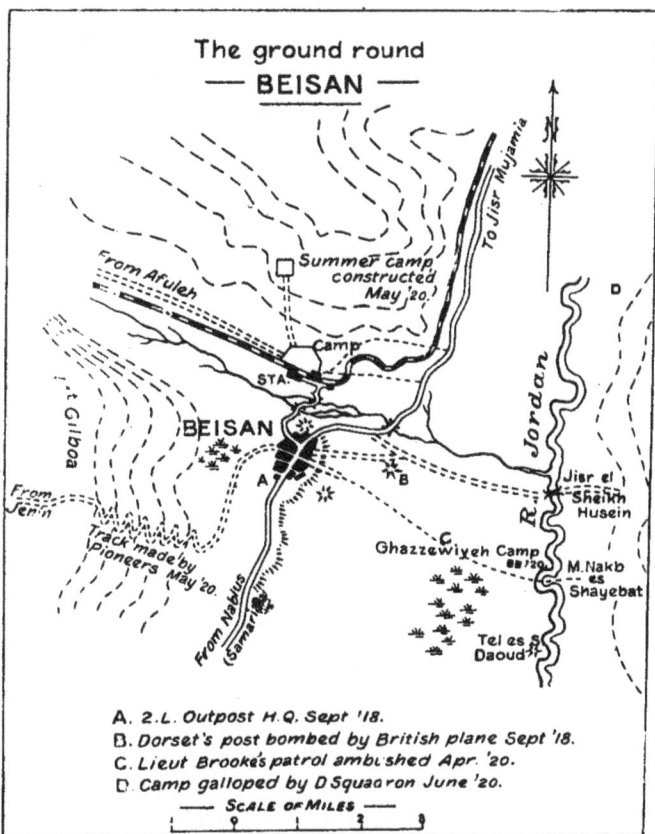

The ground round
— BEISAN —

A. 2.L. Outpost H.Q. Sept '18.
B. Dorset's post bombed by British plane Sept '18.
C. Lieut Brooke's patrol ambushed Apr. '20.
D. Camp galloped by D Squadron June '20.
SCALE OF MILES

SIFTON PRAED & CO., LTD., LONDON. S W

a quantity of ammunition. The division soon had these manned by the artillery and put into action to command all roads leading into Beisan from the south. On arrival at Beisan it was learnt that, shortly before, a party of 30 Germans, who had been sent to place the locality in a state of defence, had departed rapidly for the north in motor lorries. One of our aeroplanes bombed them on the Jisr Mujamia road and wrecked most of their lorries.

51. At 17.35 the 2nd Lancers and C.I.H. put out an outpost line encircling the whole division's bivouac area which lay between the neighbourhood of the railway station and the village of Beisan.

52. In this march from the Selmeh orange groves to Beisan the brigade had covered a map distance of 68 miles in 35 hours, including halts and delays. The actual distance covered by smaller parties, such as patrols and despatch riders, and many officers, in the same time was nearer 80 miles. The total casualties in horses evacuated to the Mobile Veterinary Section at the end of it were 15. This, after a month in the Jordan Valley, followed by night marches aggregating 65 miles to the point of concentration, with only one day at Ramleh to refit.

BEISAN

53. During the night September 20–21st, which passed quietly, several small parties of enemy stragglers were made prisoners by the troops on outposts. From the information they gave it was gathered that the Turkish command was as yet unaware that the cavalry had occupied Beisan.

54. At 09.00 on the 21st, the Dorset Yeomanry relieved the 2nd Lancers in the southern half of the outpost system and the latter were withdrawn to a well-earned rest in bivouac just north of the railway station, in one of the small buildings in which the brigade headquarters were accommodated. Divisional headquarters occupied the main station buildings.

55. Troops and animals were now running short of provisions, but, thanks to the energy of the Staff Captain (Capt. Whiston), by the evening considerable quantities of grain. fodder and flour had been collected by requisition and from enemy military stores. Water was plentiful and good in the aqueducts a few hundred yards below the station.

56. During this day a considerable number of prisoners came in through the outposts from the direction of Nablus, several of them straggling down from the hills on the west.

Aeroplane reports had been received that very large enemy forces were retiring northward on the Nablus-Beisan road.

(On the night of the 21st–22nd the Dorsets' outposts were attacked by a mixed force of Germans and Turks. The enemy were driven off with heavy losses. A troop of the C.I.H. co-operated in this fight and made a successful charge.)

59.   In the meantime, thinking it possible the enemy might break away eastward and endeavour to escape over the River Jordan by the Sheikh Hussein bridge, guarded at that time by only one troop of the C.I.H., the Brigadier ordered out two squadrons of the 2nd Lancers to move east and lie up for the enemy near the bridge. They remained out till early next morning.

60.   Extract from narrative of Capt. Whitworth, M.C., commanding these two squadrons :—
It was a bright moonlight night. The going was splendid, and we might have had a pretty scrap, but the Turks never came. They surrendered to the Dorsets next morning. Soon after dawn one of our planes came over. First it dropped a bomb on one of the Dorsets' picquets not far from us. Not wishing the same thing to happen to us, we began waving all our aeroplane flags and showing the white aircraft strips of American cloth. After a short chukker round, the aeroplane flew over the same picquet of the Dorsets and dropped a message to say that a large force of Turks was close to them, and that it would fly over the position and fire a red light there. It flew over *us* and fired its red light ; then made off, to the unbounded joy of the Dorsets and ourselves.

(On the 22nd, Major Gould, Major Robertson and Capt. Hearsey rejoined and Major Gould took over the command.)

63.   By nightfall on September 22nd, the division had accounted for over 4,000 prisoners and still more and more streamed in through the night.

65.   In the early morning of the 23rd the 11th Cavalry Brigade (Brig.-Gen. Gregory, C.B.) had moved down the valley, on both sides of the River Jordan, with the object of cutting off the retreat of the VIIth Turkish Army across the river. Their mission was most successful, after some hard fighting and many difficulties. They took many thousand

prisoners, dozens of machine guns, one battery of 77mm. guns, and 2 mountain guns.   They returned to Beisan on the 27th September.

67.   During the 22nd, 23rd, and 24th September, the 2nd Lancers had been fully employed in guarding and providing escorts for the ever growing crowd of prisoners.   These were temporarily accommodated on the open ground east of Beisan railway station, where they were fed on rations specially brought down for them in motor lorries.   Before leaving Beisan, the 4th Cavalry Division had taken 16,000 out of the total 40,000 prisoners reported up to that time as captured by the whole force.

(The C.I.H. who had been sent to Jisr Mujamia, were engaged on September 23rd in reconnoitring Semakh, which was strongly held by the enemy.   On September 24th, the C.I.H. made two attempts to cut the railway line to the east of the town.   The first was frustrated by artillery and machine gun fire ; the second was on the point of being successful when the demolition mule bolted, taking with him all the guncotton.   Semakh was taken on September 25th by a very dashing attack of a brigade of Australian Light Horse. On the 25th September, the 10th Cavalry Brigade moved to Jisr Mujamia, joining up with the C.I.H.)

CHAPTER XI

THE ATTACK ON IRBID—ER REMTE—DERAA—THE CAPTURE OF
DAMASCUS—BAALBEK—THE ARMISTICE WITH TURKEY

77.   At 22.35 on 25th September the following telegram was
received from Divisional Headquarters at Beisan :—
" 10th Cavalry Brigade will move not later than 08.00 from
Jisr Mujamia on 26th inst. to a position covering the bridge
just south of Es Shuni on the Jisr el Mujamia-Irbid-
Deraa road (distance 2½ miles). · Communication with division will be by wireless and D.R. service to Jisr el Mujamia.
Remainder of division will be prepared at one hour's notice
after 12.00 on 26th inst. . . . " The Brigadier had previously
been informed verbally by the Divisional Commander that he
might have to push on to Irbid on the 26th, a day's march
ahead of the division.   The above quoted order was therefore
taken to signify only a preliminary move, and all necessary
preparations were made for the immediate march to Irbid.
78.   At 07.57 the division despatched the following priority
message by wire :—" 4th Turkish Army H.Q. is reported
moving *via* Remte to Deraa.   4th Cavalry Division will move
on Deraa.   Lawrence's Arab force is in area and will co-
operate with us.   Following moves will take place to-day.
10th Cavalry Brigade will move from Jisr el Mujamia to
Irbid and endeavour get touch with Lawrence.   12th Cavalry
Brigade will leave Beisan at 10.00 and move to a position
covering bridge just South of Es Shuni.   Divisional H.Q.
and 11th Cavalry Brigade will leave Beisan at 13.00 and move
to Jisr el Mujamia. . . . "
(The Arab force had moved north to co-operate with the
general operations, making a wide detour into the desert to
do so.   Making every use of their great mobility they made a
series of destructive raids on the railways east of the Jordan,
and then proceeded to harry the flanks of the retreating
Turkish IVth Army.   At this point the 4th Cavalry Brigade

joined forces with them, and with them advanced on
Damascus.)

79. The advanced guard, 2 squadrons of the C.I.H., and
a subsection of machine guns, was in position, covering the
starting point east of the Jordan, by 08.00.   At 08.00 two
officers' patrols were despatched, one under Lieut. Silver,
2nd Lancers, with 1 I.O. and 15 other ranks, to Umm Keis,
to rejoin the brigade near Kharaj ; and the other under Lieut.
Reece, Dorset Yeomanry, by the road leading south to Wadi
el Hasa, thence *via* Et Taiyabe to rejoin the brigade north of
Kefr Yuba.   Their missions were principally :—(1) To get
touch with, or gain information of, an Arab force under Colonel
Lawrence believed to be operating N. and E. of the 4th Cavalry
Division ; (2) To ascertain the situation, strength and dis-
position of enemy forces, if any, met en route.

80. *Lieut. Silver's patrol* : the first part of the route was
very rough and negotiable only in single file.   From Tahunet
el Firsan a well built road led to Umm Keis, very narrow and
passing through cliffs on either side to gain access to the east
end of the village, which was reached at 10.20.   One of the
Christian colony there informed Lieut. Silver that on the
previous evening 200 Germans had quitted Umm Keis for
Semakh, leaving 20 Turks with 2 machine guns to hold the
village.   The latter had left the village at 09.45 when they
saw our patrol emerge from the wadi at Tahunet el Firsan.
They further said that there were now no formed bodies of
enemy in the neighbourhood,   Proceeding eastward the patrol
had a few shots fired at it from the high ground north of the
road, which was too steep to be ridden over.   On the strength
of the above information the patrol commander paid no attention to the firers.   From El Kabu to Kharaj parts of the
tracks were so bad that horses, even when led, moved with
difficulty.   Some Arabs fired at the patrol from the village of
Kefr Esud.   The patrol merely broke up their rifles and
passed on.   On gaining the main road they fell in with some
friendly Arabs from Kamm and a patrol of the C.I.H.   No
information of Colonel Lawrence and his Hedjaz forces was
gained by any of the patrols.

(The brigade watered at Esh Shuni.   The 2nd Lancers

then relieved the C.I.H. of advanced guard duty. C Squadron became vanguard. Owing to the inaccuracy of the map the road was lost in the Wadi Zakar, and it was found impossible to go on. B Squadron was then pushed out on the right road, and the march continued. This, and the partial breaking of the bridge over the wadi, caused great delay, and it was past noon when the whole brigade got moving again.)

83. Between Kharaj and Kamm was met a friendly Arab sheikh with three or four attendants, mounted and armed, who greeted the brigade warmly, and reported that Irbid was held by about 2,000 Turks who, he thought, would willingly surrender. This party accompanied the Brigadier and was found useful as a guide, for the road over the plateau ran further south than as shown on the map in use, and in many places was deceptive and poorly demarcated. The country here was thickly covered with stones and generally it was only where the surface had been scraped to form the track that troops could move at anything more than a walk. Time was limited and the column was hurried on at every opportunity. The 2nd Lancers had got well ahead at Kharaj with the object if possible of seizing Irbid before dark, in order to secure a water supply for the night.

84. About 3 miles short of Irbid a serious defile was encountered in the deep gorge of the Wadi el Ghafr. The new Turkish road runs down to the bottom and crawls tortuously up the other side to the plateau facing Irbid. The surface was of sharp stones and the tired horses could make no better pace than a walk. It was therefore impossible for leading units to push forward at an increased pace for more rapid deployment on the far side.

ACTION AT IRBID

85. In the meantime the 2nd Lancers had crossed the defile and their advanced patrols had been fired on from the village of El Bariha and also from the ridge between Beit Ras and Irbid. Capt. Whitworth, M.C., commanding the leading squadron (B) despatched a troop (Jemadar Gobind Singh, V.C.) to take El Bariha. The village was galloped with success and a few Turks retired at a run from its eastern end

to Irbid.   The regiment being in view of some of the houses
of Irbid moved into hollow ground near the road which gave
them a covered way tò within 1,500 to 2,000 yards of Irbid.

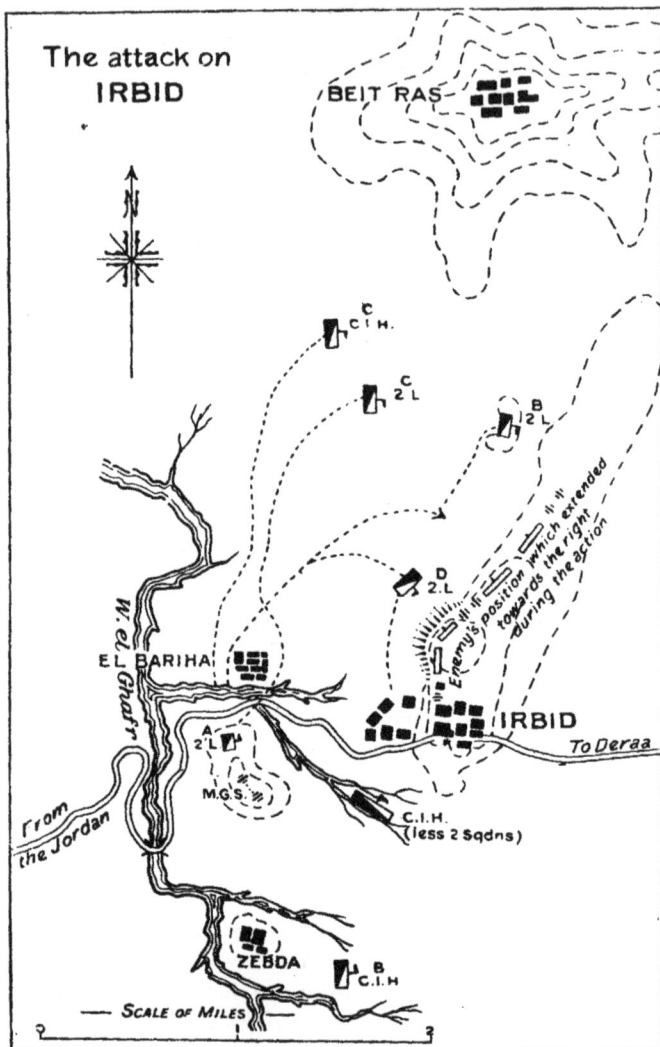

The attack on
IRBID

86.   It was now 16.00 and nightfall was approaching.   The
O.C., 2nd Lancers, (Major Gould, D.S.O.), fearing that darkness

would supervene, leaving Irbid in the enemy's hands and the
brigade without water for the night, decided on immediate
energetic action.   Seeing that El Bariha was clear, and as
yet the fire of only one machine gun, from the northern half
of Irbid village, had been heard, he opined that no very
protracted resistance was intended.   The following verbal
orders were issued :—

B Squadron (Capt. Whitworth, M.C.) now in advance, will
move *via* Bariha and try to work by the north round behind
Irbid.   As soon as B Squadron has passed Bariha, D.
Squadron (Capt. Vaughan, M.C.) will follow B Squadron and
attack mounted from north to south.   C Squadron (Capt.
Davison, D.S.O.) will advance at the same time as D Squadron
and attack from the south of the village northwards, as nearly
simultaneously as circumstances will permit.   Subsection
M.G. Squadron will support the attack and encircling movement by fire on hostile machine guns.   A Squadron (Captain
Hearsey, M.C.)—less 2 Troops on flank guard—in reserve, and
also to cover the deployment from the defile of the brigade's
main body.

(These orders were not so understood either by B or by D
squadrons.   O.C. B had only a H.R. troop in hand when the
attack was ordered : D Squadron led the attack and B followed
D until they were clear of El Bariha and then swung out to
their left to support their attack with Hotchkiss fire, as the
narrative proceeds to describe.)

87.   The position of Irbid was a formidable one consisting
of the village at the southern end of a high ridge (1882 ft.)
extending about 500 yards from its northern edge towards
Beit Ras, and terminating in a steep slope.   On its western
and southern sides it was surrounded by an open glacis slope.
(Note : Published maps give a false representation.   The
Wadi el Ghafr proper does not run immediately below the
western front of Irbid, but as shown in the accompanying
sketch.)

88.   The squadrons and machine guns moved off . . . and
El Bariha was cleared without opposition.   Enemy machine
gun fire now became more pronounced along the whole position.
. . . B Squadron took up a position 1,200 yards north of the

village and brought Hotchkiss fire to bear, at 1,100 yards range, on the hostile machine guns in support of D Squadron's attack. D Squadron having brought their Hotchkiss rifles into action at Bariha prior to moving N.E., came under heavy fire as they moved southward to the attack, and Capt. Vaughan led them in a most gallant charge on the machine guns. The ground was almost impassably stony. When within 200 yards of the enemy, Capt. Vaughan realised that he was not as far round the flank of the position as he ought to have been. There was very rough ground between him and the northern end of the ridge the enemy were holding, which itself appeared too steep to gallop in the face of the intense fire which was now going on. He accordingly swung the squadron half-right into the village, which protruded further to the west than the line of the ridge. His advanced troop was too far to recall and he thought he might obtain a footing in the village until rein-forced. The advanced troop had made a most gallant effort, Ressaidar Raj Singh himself reaching the position, where he and the majority of the troop were killed.

89. When giving the signal to head for the village, Capt. Vaughan was wounded in the knee, and his horse was mortally wounded but carried his rider as far as the village square. Here the squadron commander found he had with him Jem. Basti Singh, Ress. Kheri Singh (both wounded), some half dozen men and four wounded horses. There were roads running S., E., and N., by the latter of which they had entered. On reconnoitring those on S. and E. they came under heavy machine gun fire. Having too few rifles to hold on and seeing no signs of the other squadrons, Capt. Vaughan ordered a retirement, adding that anyone who reached the regiment should report what had happened. Clambering over or through the houses they escaped from the village westward being under continuous fire. Capt. Vaughan had his left arm shattered by machine gun bullets when 150 yards from the village, and 50 yards further on his left thigh broken. He was carried, with magnificent devotion, by his Indian orderly to a place of safety within the advanced line of the C.I.H., just before the battery opened fire. (For this act of gallantry the orderly, A.L.D. Nand Singh, was awarded the I.D.S.M.)

This squadron's losses were 1 I.O. killed ; 1 B.O. and 2 I.O. wounded ; 9 I.O.R. killed and 20 wounded, of whom 4 subsequently succumbed to their wounds.

Though the attack failed in its immediate object, there is little doubt that the determined effort much increased the enemy's desire to quit the position. It was, in fact, afterwards learnt that 500 enemy left the village immediately the advance started, and streamed away N.E. and E. (For his leading in this action Capt. Vaughan was awarded da Solidaridad of the Panamanian Republic.)

90. C Squadron, meanwhile, had unfortunately mistaken El Bariha for Irbid as the village to be attacked. The squadron commander discovered his mistake when he saw D Squadron attacking Irbid, and when it was too late to co-operate. He decided therefore to move up and attack in support of D Squadron. Seeing D Squadron's failure, and realizing that an attack from this flank unsupported by one from the south, was hopeless, he established his squadron under cover 1,200 yards W. of where B Squadron was in position. The latter squadron's Hotchkiss rifles now came in for serious attention from the enemy. They were lying in a stony ploughed field without cover and one man and two horses were killed. Capt. Whitworth moved them out of action and eventually collected his squadron under cover of a ridge between Beit Ras and Irbid. His patrols from here were met by heavy machine gun fire. As darkness came the firing died down.

91. *Machine guns with 2nd Lancers.* The two subsections of the 17th M.G. Squadron (Lieut. Bence) accompanying the 2nd Lancers had, after clearing the Wadi Ghafr defile, come into action on the knoll about 1,700 yards W. of the southern end of Irbid. Their object was to support the 2nd Lancers' attack on the position. This was found difficult. In the first place, on reaching the knoll the right subsection came under heavy M.G. fire from the high ground between Zebda and Irbid. These enemy machine guns were engaged by the subsection and retired out of range to a position S.E. of Irbid. In the second place, the nature of the ground, sloping steadily towards the hollow below the village made further advance impossible in face of the brisk fire from the

enemy position. The four guns were accordingly directed against the position, but the distance, 2,700 yards, militated against effective fire on the actual point of attack. These machine guns remained in this position through the night of 26th–27th September.

92.   We must now hark back to the doings of the remainder of the brigade. As the 2nd Lancers were nearing Irbid the Brigadier hurried on to get in touch with them and to make a personal reconnaissance. He came up with them at 16.15, just after their D and C squadrons had moved off. The situation was explained to him by the O.C. 2nd Lancers and the sight of large numbers of the enemy hurrying across to take up positions on the Irbid ridge clearly indicated the urgency for getting the battery into action. But the defile behind, as already explained, was all against rapid debouch-ment ; and it was 17.10 before the battery, which was in rear of the M.G. Squadron and C.I.H., could open fire, too late to be of assistance to the 2nd Lancers' attack. Shooting was difficult owing to the failing light and the uncertainty of the location of our troops. It is most probable however, that the battery's fire assisted in dissuading the enemy from any inten-tion he may have had of holding on to the position.

93.   Prior to the battery coming into action the Brigadier had given verbal orders for :—

(1) Two subsections (Lieut. Thom, M.C.) of the M.G.S. to move into action E. of the village of Bariha.   Escort 1 troop C.I.H.

(2)   The C.I.H. to move southward and eastward joining up if possible with the flankguard squadron and circumvent the enemy from the S.E.

It was here that a dangerous complication was initiated by some confusion either in the delivery or in the interpretation of the verbal orders.

(The O.C. C.I.H., understood his orders to be to follow a squadron of the 2nd Lancers down the wadi leading past the S. end of Irbid.   The C.I.H. accordingly moved down this wadi till held up by fire, when they dismounted and came into action against the enemy in Irbid.   The right flank guard of the brigade (Capt. Williams' squadron of the C.I.H.) attempted to co-operate in the attack on Irbid from the S.E., but was held up by fire.)

The night passed quietly, the 2nd Lancers remaining in position, and the remainder of the brigade concentrating S.W. of the village. Owing to the uncertainty of the situation, saddles could only be removed for a short time by portions of the force, and the weary animals got no rest and no water for the night, after the fatigue of the action added to the most exhausting march that the brigade had yet performed.

The casualties of the 2nd Lancers were :—

			Killed.	Wounded.	Missing.
B.O.'s	..	..	—	1	—
				(Capt. Vaughan)	
I.O.'s	..	..	1	2	—
			(Ress. Raj Singh)		
I.O.R.	..	..	11	23	4

(The regiment lost in Ress. Raj Singh a very promising young Indian officer. He was the son of Ris. Ram Singh, a retired I.O. of D Squadron.)

111. At dawn on 27th September, patrols from the 2nd Lancers and C.I.H. approached the village of Irbid and found it clear of the enemy. The inhabitants stated that when the brigade came in sight the previous evening there were in and about Irbid not less than 3,000 Turkish troops of all arms, some said as many as 10,000, with a great number of machine guns. As soon as the 2nd Lancers' attack began in earnest, the Turks had begun to stream away north-eastward by cross country tracks towards Mezerib, leaving a strong rearguard to cover the retirement. It was now all too evident that lack of sufficient daylight had deprived the brigade of a big success.

112. Comments. The question arises as to the wisdom of having committed the troops to the offensive on insufficient information of the numbers and morale of enemy at Irbid. Certainly experiences since the 19th September justified the opinion that our troops could attack and defeat very largely superior numbers of the enemy, and that rapid movements round their flanks invariably threw them into confusion. At the same time no accurate knowledge of their strength was available. Unless an effort to seize the village was made

M

immediately, it was probable that nothing beyond reconnaissance could have been effected, because of the short space
of daylight remaining.   It was for this reason that Major
Gould decided to seize the village before the arrival of the
remainder of the brigade.   He would have been better advised
to make a more thorough reconnaissance before committing
the majority of his regiment to the assault.   This might have
put the Brigadier in possession of more complete information
by the time the main body had debouched from the defile and
it is possible a better plan of action would have been devised.
As, however, the 2nd Lancers were on their way to attack, the
only sound course appeared to be to send another regiment
immediately to threaten the enemy's left rear and cut in on
his line of retreat.   Taking into consideration the general
state of the enemy's morale, there is little doubt that the
desired effect would have been achieved had there been no
miscarriage of orders.   A short reconnaissance from M.G.
knoll by the O.C., C.I.H., before actually launching his
regiment towards Irbid would have saved valuable time.
The brigade's lack of success here made no difference to the
final result, for the whole of this enemy force was eventually
smashed and captured near Damascus by the Australian and
5th Cavalry Divisions.

(After making good Irbid and watering, the brigade immediately moved on Er Remte (the ancient Ramoth Gilead),
the Dorset Yeomanry in advance.   The village was found to
be occupied by the enemy.   They were driven out by a dismounted attack made by the Dorsets, and a mounted pursuit
was carried out by the C.I.H., who followed the enemy to the
first of the two ridges which lie between Er Remte and
Deraa.   Good and plentiful water was found at Er Remte
in ancient subterranean reservoirs.   The C.I.H. took up an
outpost position N.E. of Er Remte and the remainder of the
brigade watered and went into bivouacs on the W. side of the
village.   Towards evening they were joined by Divisional
H.Q. and the 12th Cavalry Brigade from Jisr Mujamia and
Es Shuni.)

125.   At 15.00 the 2nd Lancers relieved the C.I.H. on
outpost duty and before dark pushed forward to the eastern

edge of the hills overlooking Deraa.   From here a clear view
was obtained of the old town and standing apart, to the north
of it, the station and other buildings.   On the roof of the
largest of these was marked a Turkish crescent, denoting a
hospital.   The building and rolling stock and railway were
then all intact, but a great deal of movement was observed
northwards from the place and from the east towards it.
These were reported to our division as enemy columns on the
move, though eventually they proved to be chiefly members
of the Sherifian army added to hordes of local Arabs engaged
in looting and carrying off all the Turkish government property
they could lift from the station buildings and their environ-
ments.

127.   A quiet night was passed in the brigade bivouac,
and divisional orders were issued for an early morning start
for the occupying of Deraa, believed to be still in the enemy's
hands. . . . During the night a representative of the Sherifian
army reported the arrival of some Sherifian troops in the
vicinity, but it was still unknown that Deraa was actually
in their hands.

128.   Consequently at 04.30 on the 28th, the 10th Cavalry
Brigade moved out from Er Remte and marched to the hills.
Two regiments were disposed in position to cover the assembly
of the division.   Deraa station settlement was now seen to
be in flames ; the roof of the large hospital which was seen
to be intact the previous evening had fallen in and much of the
rolling stock on the railway was black and smouldering.   The
outposts reported having seen the red glow of fires during the
night, and early morning patrols brought in information that,
though the place did not appear to be held, there was a great
deal of firing going on in the streets.   At 07.00 the brigade
was ordered forward to Deraa.   On the eastern edge of the
hills the brigadier met Colonel Lawrence with some of his
Arab irregulars.   He stated that the Sherifian troops had
entered Deraa soon after noon on the previous day.   He
accompanied the brigade to the railway station where he was
shortly joined by the Divisional Commander, about 09.30.

129.   Words fail to describe the appalling scenes that the
station settlement presented.   Many Turkish dead and

wounded were lying unheeded and in agony about the roads
and buildings ; hordes of local Arabs were hurrying hither and
thither carrying off furniture and other loot ; the whole area
was littered with books, papers, machinery and quantities of
property wantonly destroyed and scattered abroad by the
marauders. Locomotives and railway carriages had been
burnt, broken up and stripped of important accessories for no
other reason, than sheer lust for destruction. The cruelty
exhibited by irresponsible Arabs to the miserable vanquished
Turks was abominable in the extreme.

130. After the brigade had picqueted the station and
principal routes some measure of order was established and
looting ceased. The enemy wounded were collected and
attended to by the medical establishments and steps were
taken to bury the dead. The brigade bivouacked for the night
on an open space S.W. of the station. . . . The night passed
quietly with the exception of some firing by the inhabitants of
the old town, who had amassed a goodly collection of rifles
and ammunition that had been cast away by the fleeing Turks.
This was the first real night's rest that the brigade as a whole
had had since leaving Beisan. Some of the squadrons had
only had their saddles off for two hours since starting from
Jisr Mujamia until they settled down at Deraa.

131. . . . (In accordance with orders from the division)
at 07.30 on the 29th, leaving a composite squadron from the
2nd Lancers and the C.I.H. under Lieut. Turner, 2nd Lancers,
to guard the railway station and rolling stock, the brigade
commenced its march northwards, and joined on behind the
division at Sheikh Miskin. Its bivouac site for the night
29th–30th was two miles S. of Dilli beside an old Roman
aqueduct with good and plentiful water. The march had
passed without incident ; the country was flat, stony and
uninteresting. Several stray Turks were collected on the
way, the severely wounded being brought along by our ambu-
lances as long as they had capacity to do so. There was
evidence all along that any stray Turk fared badly at the hands
of the villagers and Bedouins, and if left unguarded stood every
chance of being killed and stripped of the little they still
possessed.

(The next morning the division continued its advance towards
Damascus, the 10th Cavalry Brigade being in rear.   The
brigade bivouacked at Zerakiye after a slow and tedious
march along a particularly stony road.   The country on either
side was equally stony and covered with blocks of basalt rock
and so offered no relief.   On this evening the 11th Cavalry
Brigade came into contact with and routed a Turkish column
near Kiswe.   This was the last occasion in which the division
was in action.   At the same time the Australian Mounted
Division crossed the hills commanding the Damascus-Beirut
road, and the 5th Cavalry Division being to the S.W. of
Damascus, all its exits were closed.)

135.   The advance was continued on the 1st October and
the 10th Cavalry Brigade bivouacked on the night of the 1st–
2nd October near the vineyards about 4 miles S.W. of Damascus and the following morning moved S.W. to a new bivouac
near Daraya, on El Kuneitra—Damascus road, that being
the only route by which the division could be fed.

(The regiment bivouacked amongst vineyards, the grapes
of which are of the very large kind of which muscatel raisins
are made.   They were just ripe, and very welcome after
twelve days on the simple diet of iron rations.   Since leaving
Ramle the rations of the Indian ranks had consisted of tea,
jam, milk, and biscuits only.   They had consequently under-
gone far greater hardships than the British ranks, who could
eat preserved meat.   The question of whether preserved meat
cannot be made in such a manner that caste scruples will be
overcome is a very important one.   In the advance of the 4th
Cavalry Division, a satisfactory solution of the problem would
probably have reduced the numbers evacuated sick by 30
per cent.   Two officers were sent into Damascus to forage for
the mess.   They came back with two bottles of alleged pre-
war whisky and a big drum of cocoa ; in their elation at finding
the whisky, however, they had failed to notice that the capsule
of one of the bottles was adorned with a bunch of grapes, a
style of decoration not usually affected by Scotch distilleries.
It contained aniseed in fact, but the second bottle held the
genuine article.   In addition to these supplies a few eggs and
some sourish black bread were all the extras that the mess
could find.   This was a somewhat serious matter, for many of

the British officers were by now suffering from digestive troubles.)

136.   Since starting from Selmeh on the 19th September, the 10th Cavalry Brigade had covered 180 miles in 9 days' marching, and captured many thousand prisoners, three 15 cm. guns, 15 machine guns, 4 aeroplanes, 7 motor-cars, and a vast quantity of stores and material which passed through the division too quickly to be counted. . . . The horses bore the strain well, the total losses in the brigade being 230, of which 91 were casualties caused by the enemy.

137.   *Supplies.* The brigade left Selmeh on the 19th September with one iron ration and two days' special emergency rations per man, and 21½ lbs. grain per horse, all carried on the horse. In addition one day's grain for horses was carried on the 1st line transport limbered waggons.   On leaving Beisan the above scale was again made good, but it was not until the morning of the 3rd October that any further rations were issued by the supply column.

139.   On the 2nd October, a representative detachment of the Desert Mounted Corps, consisting of one composite squadron from every regiment in the three divisions present, and one battery from each division marched through Damascus. The populace must have been greatly impressed by this immense procession of mounted troops and guns, but the men in the ranks could see little of either the spectators or the city by reason of the dense clouds of dust that were raised by the column.

DAMASCUS TO BAALBEK AND THE FEVER EPIDEMIC

140.   On the 6th October, the 4th Cavalry Division commenced its move to the Zaahle area in support of the 5th Cavalry Division which had already marched there, the Australian Mounted Division being left in charge of Damascus.

141.   Great difficulties had now begun through the appearance of a virulent epidemic, partly malignant malaria and partly a form of influenza. The late strenuous operations had rendered the personnel susceptible to such forms of disease, after their previous long sojourn in the Jordan Valley. Added to this came the five days' stay at Beisan, where malaria was

rampant and there was no protection from the swarms of
mosquitoes.   This epidemic raged for a fortnight before any
appreciable diminution could be detected.   Men fell sick
suddenly on the march as well as in bivouacs.   The death rate
was high, being in the 10th Cavalry Brigade over 10 per cent.
of admissions to the Field Ambulance. . . .

142.   The large numbers of sick evacuated daily naturally
threw more work, in the way of surplus horses to tend, on the
shoulders of others, and the patience and fortitude shown by
all ranks, in many cases sick themselves but sticking to their
work till they were too sick to stand, were beyond all praise.
. . . The final result of this infliction was that after reaching
Baalbek the division, through having evacuated about
3,600 to hospital of whom nearly 400 succumbed, was too weak
to further follow in support of the 5th Cavalry Division which
had advanced to the occupation of Aleppo.   It was some time
before the ranks could be replenished by reinforcements
from the base and men released from hospital, and the de-
pleted units had to carry on as best they could.

143.   The brigade marched out from its bivouacs near
Damascus at 07.00 on the 6th October at the head of the
division and halted for the night two miles W. of El Hame
on the Beirut road.   In the gorge just W. of Damascus, it
passed through the horrible debris resulting from the surprise
of the Turks by the Australian Mounted Division on the 30th
September.   Australian troops were now hard at work
clearing the defile of dead animals, baggage, and broken
transport of all sorts.   Much of this was being destroyed in
huge fires to obliterate causes of the nauseating effluvia that
pervaded the whole area.   Soon after the bivouac area was
reached a violent storm with torrents of rain came on and
lasted through many hours of the night.

144.   Next morning, starting at 09.45, the brigade moved
7 miles only and halted at Dimez (3,500 ft. above sea level) . . .

145.   . . . The brigade moved north to Zebdani at the head
of the Barada (Abana) valley.   This was a pleasing spot with
a plentiful supply of water, but there was a shortage of fodder.
It was therefore impossible to remain here for any length of
time.

146.   On the 12th October, all troops at Zebdani moved back to Et Tekkie, 7 miles, and on over the hills the next day to Shtora (3,000 ft.) in the Zaahle area, where a halt was made over the 14th.   This is a magnificent fertile valley irrigated from the Nahr el Litani (River Leontes).   Fruit trees are numerous in the valley itself, which is also a rich grain growing district ; while along the foot of the Lebanons stretched miles of vineyards supplying fruit for the Shtora wine factories.

147.   The brigade, with the remainder of the division, moved to Baalbek (3,675 ft.), on the 15th October, a day's march behind the 12th Cavalry Brigade, which went on next day to Lebwe, 17 miles N. of Baalbek.

148.   Baalbek stands on the stony foot slopes of the Anti-Lebanon range, about 4 miles east of the fertile plain, and on the watershed between the two valleys, the Litani running south, and the Orontes running north.   It has a copious water supply from perennial springs, and a considerable quantity of fodder (tibbin) was procurable in the neighbourhood.   At this time of the year the sun's rays were strong, and the nights cold, and troops were in danger of being seriously affected by the bitter winds that swept the shelterless watershed.   A large supply of warm clothing, brought up by sea to Beirut, and thence by lorries, arrived none too soon. An armistice with Turkey was concluded on the 31st October.

(On October 31st, we were informed that an armistice with Turkey had been signed, and that the war, as far as we were concerned, was over.   This momentous news was received by the troops without any great demonstration of joy or excitement, perhaps because the idea, after over four years of war, was too stupendous to be taken in in a moment.   The compiler's only recollection of any mental reaction at the time is of the formation of a resolve to profit by the promised cessation of movement by enlarging the species of dog kennel in which he was then residing.   To this end he employed some old planks torn from a Turkish barrack.   During the night he discovered that these concealed about two battalions of man-eating bugs, and the pressing preoccupation of the moment effectually prevented a deliberate appreciation of the blessings of peace on the first day of its era.)

149.   After it was finally decided that a further move north-wards was out of the question, the division (less the 11th Cavalry Brigade, detached on the 27th October to relieve the Australian Mounted Division at Damascus) left Baalbek on the 25th November and moved in three marches to Beirut, arriving on the 28th, where it went into camp on the sand dunes near Bir Hasan for the winter.

(End of Gen. Green's narrative.)

2ND LANCERS' CASUALTIES, 19TH SEPTEMBER TO 28TH NOVEMBER

	Killed.	Wounded.	Died of wounds.	To hospital.	Died in hospital.
B.O.'s	—	1	—	5	—
B.O.R.	—	—	—	7	—
I.O.'s	1	2	—	7	—
I.O.R.	9	21	4	131	13
Foll'rs	—	—	—	7	1
Total	10	24	4	157	14

Lieut.-Col. G. Knowles, D.S.O., had rejoined the regiment at Baalbek from hospital, and taken over the command from Major G. Gould, D.S.O.

CHAPTER XII

October 24th, 1918, to December 28th, 1920

THE WINTER AT BEIRUT—SUMMER AT HOMS—THE MARCH BACK
TO PALESTINE—SARONA—JENIN—THE DEFENCE OF BEISAN—
FRONTIER WORK ON THE JORDAN—RELIEF BY THE 8TH CAVALRY
—KANTARA—SUEZ—THE VOYAGE TO INDIA—ALLAHABAD

At Beirut the regiment was camped on the seashore to the
south of the town. During the winter the weather alternated
between days of heavy rain and intervals of warm sunshine.
Bathing was general from February onwards, but was a
rather dangerous pastime, for currents were numerous and
many swimmers were washed out to sea. Many rescues of
drowning men were made by members of the regiment. On
one day three were rescued with the greatest gallantry by
Trumpeter Mangal Sain (B Squadron), for which he was
subsequently awarded the Albert Medal. The Beirut Turf
Club was instituted by Major Robertson, and most successful
race meetings were held weekly. Football and wrestling were
begun for the Indian ranks, and weekly regimental sports
became a regular institution until the regiment returned to
India.

In May, 1919, the brigade marched over the Lebanons to
Homs, a city of 70,000 inhabitants on the Rayak–Aleppo
railway : here also Divisional H.Q. was located, and a battery
of R.H.A. The Dorset Yeomanry were left at Beirut to be
demobilized, and the Stafford Yeomanry took their place in
the brigade. The latter were demobilized in July and were
replaced by the 16th Lancers, who had just arrived from
England, and were composed very largely of recruits. At
Homs two good turf polo grounds were made and polo was
played regularly ; the game was often spoilt by the high wind,
which blew every day from the direction of the sea. In
September there was a " Homs Week," the programme comprising an American polo tournament of mixed teams, brigade
sports, and a brigade horse show.

170

In the mounted sports the regiment won the following :—

Tentpegging, I.O.'s	..	1st, Ress. Kheri Singh.
		3rd, Ress. Het Ram.
Mounted Wrestling	..	2nd Lancers.
V.C. Race	.. ..	2nd Lancers.
Relay Race	.. ..	2nd Lancers.
Bending Race	..	1st, Lieut-.Col. Knowles' M.M. and Capt. Whitworth's Rupan (dead heat).

In the dismounted sports the regiment won the 100 yards, the long jump, and the high jump.

In the horse show, the regiment won :—

B.O.'s Chargers	..	1st, 2nd and 3rd (Lieut.-Col Knowles' Jimmy, and Lieut. Silver's Banbury and Peter Pan).
B.O.'s Jumping	..	1st, (Lieut. Lawler's Spider).
I.O.'s Chargers	..	2nd and 3rd.
I.O.'s Jumping	..	2nd and 3rd.
I.O.R.'s Jumping	..	1st and 2nd.

On September 20th, being " Afuleh Day," the regiment entertained Brig.-Gen. Green and officers of Divisional H.Q. to dinner. In October a serious outbreak of malaria began, which affected all units, more particularly the 16th Lancers, whose effective strength was reduced by nearly 80 per cent. Orders were now received to make winter camps on the high ground in the vicinity of the city, and work on these was begun, but never finished, for in November the British began their evacuation of Syria.   Directly the Syrians became suspicious of this they began to show strong opposition to the evacuation, one form of which was a strike on the Damas, Homs et Prolongements railway.   Trains were run by volunteers from the British army, and the brigade was employed in guarding railway bridges and embankments from possible sabotage. In the last week of November, the brigade began to march towards Palestine, *via* Baalbek, Beirut, Sidon, Tyre, and Haifa. At Haifa a halt of four days was made while accommodation on the railway was waited for.   Here torrential rains turned the regiment's camp into a marsh.   The move continued by rail to Ludd, whence the regiment marched to Sarona, arriving

just before Christmas. On January 3rd, 1921, Lieut.-Col.
G. Knowles, D.S.O., relinquished the command in order to
take up his appointment as Commandant of the 34th Poona
Horse, and the command devolved on Capt. D. E. Whitworth,
M.C. At Sarona, the Regiment's camp was surrounded by
rolling green downs, which made it about as good a cavalry
station as can be imagined. Troop, squadron and regimental
training were carried out in January and February, followed
by an inspection of the regiment by Major-Gen. Sir Henry
Hodgson, who in 1919 had succeeded Lieut.-Gen. G. de S.
Barrow in the command of the division. Polo was played
three days a week, and a pack of hounds, started by the
division, hunted on Wednesdays and Sundays. The weekly
regimental sports were continued, and much football and
hockey was played.

In April, the brigade (less 16th Lancers) was ordered to
relieve the 11th Cavalry Brigade on the Jordan. On April
12th, the regiment moved by rail to Jenin, where it remained
less the following detachments : B Squadron (Capt. Peck) at
Roshpina, N. of the Sea of Galilee, half a squadron at Beisan,
and half a squadron at Ain Shible, in the hills of Samaria
overlooking the Jordan valley. The Arab tribes on the
frontier at this time were in a very disturbed condition, and
raids into Palestine were becoming very frequent. On April
20th, the Military Governor of Beisan heard suspicious rumours
of intended lawlessness on the part of a large tribe called the
Ghazzewiyehs, who had camps normally on both sides of the
Jordan due E. of Beisan. He accordingly asked Lieut. Brooke,
who commanded the half squadron at Beisan, to bring a patrol
and accompany him on a visit to the sheikh of this tribe.
Lieut. Brooke did so with one troop of A Squadron. The
party did not reach the Arab camp until after dark. As they
were approaching it along a narrow path running through a
swamp, they were challenged, and immediately after they
came under the fire of about 100 rifles. A sharp fire fight
immediately began, but the Arabs soon made off, and in the
dark the patrol was unable to follow them. Three of our
horses were killed and two wounded, but no men were hit.
On news of this reaching the brigade, Capt. Whitworth was
ordered to take a squadron to Beisan at once, and, if possible;

punish the offending tribe. He took C Squadron (Lieut. Lawler) and arrived at Beisan at 9 a.m. the next morning. At the request of the Military Governor no action was taken that day, but on April 22nd a visit to the Ghazzewiyeh's camping grounds on this side of the Jordan was decided upon.

CAPT. WHITWORTH'S REPORT ON EVENTS AT BEISAN, 22ND APRIL AND NIGHT 22ND–23RD APRIL 1920

(See map, page 149.)

At 08.15 hours, 1½ squadrons 2nd Lancers (about 50 lances and 6 H.R.'s) under Capt. Whitworth, Lieut. Lawler commanding C Squadron, Lieut. Brooke commanding half A Squadron, and the Deputy Military Governor of Beisan (Lieut. Thornycroft) with 20 mounted police, left Beisan with the intention of discovering the new camps of Mohamed Zenati's Ghazzewiyeh Arabs, and to find whether any of their belongings remained on this side of Jordan. It was also intended to induce the Ghazzewiyehs to join battle.

The party passed through the tribe's old camping ground and struck the Jordan at Makhaded Nakb es Shayebat. The tribe's new camping grounds were now clearly seen. The northernmost, ascribed to Mohamed Zenati, appeared to be about Umm es Shukaf. The other, said to be Amir Bashir's, appeared to be about one mile S.W. of Kh. Fahil. Several men were seen on various spurs across the river, watching our party.

09.30. It now appeared that some cattle were grazing on this side of Jordan and an attempt was made by Lieut. Lawler with C Squadron to push through the high grass and dense weedy undergrowth of the river bed and drive these cattle back towards us. Circumstances combined to make this a very slow undertaking. Armed men were reported to be guarding the herd, and caution was necessary. The dense vegetation not only hindered progress, but sight also.

11.30. Finally at about 11.30 it became evident that the herd, which from the bluff overlooking the river bed seemed to be obviously on this side of Jordan, was in reality on the other side. Three houses said to belong to Mohamed Zenati were found near the tribe's old camp, about one mile N.E. of the ford. On being searched they were found to contain amongst other things much ammunition. They were fired, as also some miscellaneous belongings found in the old camp.

12.00. During the operation a mounted attack was made on our party from the direction of Tel es Sheikh Daoud by Ghazzewiyehs. They were promptly countered and driven back into the Jordan bed. A desultory fire action now commenced at long range from the bluffs on either side of the Jordan.

13.00. After about an hour of this, the O.C. 2nd Lancers decided to return to camp, as fire was dying away, and it seemed profitless to stay longer. (N.B.—It was forbidden for British troops to cross the river, then the frontier of Palestine.) The retirement was carried out the whole way to Beisan in bounds by alternate squadrons.

13.15. It was now that the enemy appeared and began to press strongly in considerable numbers. (Their strength was afterwards estimated at from 1,200 to 1,500.) Hotchkiss fire proved most effective for this rearguard work. The ground here was very marshy with occasional patches of thistles about five feet high, and our movements were very hampered.

14.00. As we approached Beisan, enveloping movements on both of our flanks developed, and it soon became evident that it was a race for the village.

14.15. A stand was made on the slopes E. of Beisan, and from here Lieut. Lawler with C Squadron was ordered to hold the southern exits of the village, while Lieut. Brooke with A Squadron held those to the west. About this time a party of Arab riflemen got above our right flank on the high ground S. of the village, and opened an effective flank fire, killing one H.R. gunner and wounding another. Lieut. Lawler, who had been showing marked gallantry in command of his squadron, appears to have gone to the assistance of the wounded man, and was himself severely wounded. He was dragged back under heavy rifle fire about half way to the village (about 70 yards) by Dafadar Buland Singh. Lieut. Lawler was then hit again, this time in the neck, and killed instantly. His squadron was taken over by Risaldar Jiwan Singh.

14.30. Our party now fell back to the outskirts of the village, and held the main exits of the village as follows ;—

S. entrance (Samaria road).

S.E. ,, (A small gully) C Squadron (Ris. Jiwan Singh).

E. ,, (Road towards Ghazzewiyeh camp) A Squadron.

N.E. ,, (Jisr Mujamia road) (Lieut. Brooke).

W. ,, (Road to Beisan station) D.M.G. and rifle picquet from C Squadron.

For the next two hours, the attack was pushed forward with great energy by the Bedouins. The exits were attacked independently by various gangs throughout the afternoon, the Bedouins often getting within 50 yards of the defences. The value of the Hotchkiss rifle was again strikingly exemplified ; attack after attack died away under its fire. The isolation of the various exits of the village rendered any co-operation between them impossible, while the small number of our men available to hold the exits made the provision of any central reserve impossible. The situation therefore at various times at certain exits was most critical. Penetration at any one point of the defences would have meant the loss of the village. That the defence was not broken was due in a very great degree to the leading of the squadron commanders, viz., Lieut. Brooke and Ris. Jiwan Singh. The latter's task was the more difficult in that his squadron was split into five posts, all of which he successfully kept controlled and supplied with ammunition. Ressaidar Abdul Wahid's defence on the Jisr Mujamia road was also noteworthy, especially in the repulse by six rifles of a very noisy and determined attack at about 23.30 hours. Communication with Brigade H.Q. at Jenin was difficult at first, as no B.O. could be spared from the defence to go to the signal office 1½ miles away at the station. The D.M.G. volunteered to go and telephone, but it was thought that his leaving the village would create a panic amongst the inhabitants, already sufficiently perturbed. The road to the station was free from any close fire from the enemy, and along it was sent the D.M.G.'s Local Advisor, whose verbal report to Brigade H.Q. was, it is understood, a little imaginative. He was followed by a trumpeter of the 2nd Lancers, with a short written message asking for reinforcements, ammunition, and ambulance arrangements. (No copy kept.) At about 16.00 hours (exact time uncertain), 2nd Lieut. Lloyd, Signal Service, appeared in the village with a cable waggon, and successfully linked the D.M.G.'s office, H.Q. of the defence, with the 10th Cavalry Brigade. This officer's resource and energy came as an unexpected help to the defence. He organized the 2nd Lancers details left behind at the station, and thus beat off a tentative attack on the railway from the south. He also sent up ammunition, and food for men and horses, all of which were much required.

18.30. At sundown the continuity of the attack began to lessen. This was probably due to the Bedouins running short of ammunition. Sporadic and isolated attacks were now delivered at odd points and at increasing intervals.

23.30. The last of any note was delivered with much shouting on Ress. Abdul Wahid's rifle post at 23.30 hours. This was made by the Bedouins living in the outskirts of Beisan itself, and was repulsed with heavy loss, some of the attackers being shot down at from 15 to 25 yards range. The rest of the night passed off quietly. The Bedouins profited by the darkness to drag off their dead and wounded. These, it is thought, could not have numbered less than 100, probably considerably more. Six corpses were found in the outskirts of the village in the morning. All were identified as Ghazzcwiyehs, and it is presumed that in the main the attackers were composed of this tribe.

03.30. Shortly before dawn, Capt. Hearsey with 1 Squadron 2nd Lancers appeared in the village, accompanied by one officer and 35 O.R.'s with three Lewis guns of the Somerset Light Infantry. The former had marched from Jenin, and the latter trained from Haifa. Three armoured cars despatched from Jenin overnight failed to reach Beisan before daylight, though one armoured car with six boxes of S.A.A. arrived at Beisan station at about 03.00.

05.00. Patrols from Capt. Hearsey's squadron at dawn found the plain to the Jordan E. of Beisan clear of armed Bedouins. It may be presumed that the attack on Beisan was pre-arranged for the 22nd April, as expert opinion holds that the Ghazzewiyehs could not ordinarily have made such a rapid concentration of their forces.

(End of Capt. Whitworth's report.)

On November 8th, 1920, the War Office published a report on the defence of Beisan, the gist of which is almost identical with the foregoing. It concludes with the following paragraph :—" The success of the defence was in a large measure due to the effective use made of the Hotchkiss rifles, whose fire continually broke down the Arab attacks. The handling of the Indian Troops by their British and Indian officers and the behaviour of the Indian other ranks left nothing to be desired." For the defence of Beisan the following decorations were awarded to the 2nd Lancers.

Bar to M.C.—Capt. D. E. Whitworth.

I.D.S.M.—Ris. Jiwan Singh, Sr. Dalip Singh.

Sowar Dalip Singh distinguished himself by the cool and gallant way in which he handled his Hotchkiss rifle, through which, in the course of the operations, he fired over 2,000 rounds without a stoppage, continuing to fire after both hands had been badly burned by the heat of the barrel.

April 23rd.—At 9 a.m., A and C Squadrons returned to the camp at the station, leaving D Squadron 2nd Lancers, one platoon Somerset Light Infantry, and three armoured cars to hold the village.

It was found that the telegraph wires to Jisr Mujamia had been cut, and 2nd Lieut. Lloyd of the Cable Section took out a patrol to investigate. He met a party of some 300 Arabs and was pursued back towards Beisan. Other patrols in this direction reported large forces of Arabs in this vicinity. The day was spent in making a defensive perimeter round the station camp.

During the night 23rd–24th, two companies of the 53rd Sikhs arrived as reinforcements.

April 24th.—At 7 a.m., the British manager of the railway arrived at the station with a breakdown train, and it was decided to send a small mixed column to open communications with Semakh, which was held by the C.I.H. Accordingly, three flat trucks were attached to the train, and on them were constructed rough stone parapets over which the men could fire from a lying position. Two platoons of the 53rd Sikhs, with two Lewis guns, and two Hotchkiss rifles of the 2nd Lancers manned the train, which was escorted by two troops C Squadron (Lieut. E. C. Johnson), and two armoured cars of the 11th L.A.M. Battery. This mixed column made its way to Semakh, repairing the telegraph and telephone lines, also, in one place, the permanent way, as it went. On approaching Jisr Mujamia the column was fired upon from the direction of the Jordan by a body of about 400 Arabs. The armoured cars were sent to deal with these, and the column continued on its way, Semakh being reached at 7 p.m. It was found that the C.I.H. at Semakh had been attacked from the east and south by a strong force of Arabs, and with the aid of four bombing aeroplanes had driven them off, inflicting losses estimated at 200 killed. The casualties of the Semakh garrison were 7 wounded.

On the afternoon of the same day, the garrison of Beisan was further reinforced by a section of an Indian Mountain Battery, commanded by Capt. Pugh, R.G.A.

April 26th.—Major R. MacLeod, D.S.O., arrived at Beisan from Sarona with two squadrons 19th Lancers, and took over command of the Beisan troops from Capt. Whitworth.

Various schemes were made for the punishment of the Ghazzewiyeh tribe, whose camps on the far side of Jordan could be seen from Beisan, but political considerations prevented their being carried out. Cavalry patrols towards the Jordan were fired on almost daily as they approached the fords.

April 29th.—Lieut.-Col. W. K. Bourne, O.B.E., who had relinquished the command of the 2/35th Sikhs, arrived and assumed command at Beisan, and of the 2nd Lancers.

In the first week of May, all the troops at Beisan were withdrawn with the exception of C Squadron 2nd Lancers, one platoon 30th Punjabis, and two companies 53rd Sikhs. A permanent fortified camp was made to protect Beisan station, and when it was finished, the 53rd Sikhs also withdrew. A squadron of the regiment was kept at Beisan throughout the summer to patrol the frontier and prevent raids.

June 7th.—The regiment made a raid on a camp of the Ghazzewiyehs beyond Jordan, with the intention of looking for some stolen cattle, supposed to be in the tribe's possession. The camp was galloped successfully by D Squadron (Capt. Hearsey) under rifle fire. One man of D was wounded. No stolen cattle were identified, and D Squadron, moving north, recrossed the Jordan at Jisr Mujamia, the remainder of the regiment moving parallel to them along the river, leaving detachments at the fords. The regiment then returned to Beisan.

Headquarters of the regiment remained at Jenin until November. Polo was played regularly on a small, and rather inferior ground, and football and hockey grounds were constructed. In September, C Squadron (Hon. Lieut. Mukand Singh) relieved B (Capt. Peck) at Roshpina.

In November, the 8th Cavalry, from India, arrived on the frontier, and took over the regiment's horses, and the regiment moved by rail to Kantara.

December 3rd.—The regiment moved by rail for Suez.

December 12th.—Embarked on the Union Castle's S.S. *Edouard Woermann,* an ex-German ship, in which the accommodation for the Indian ranks was very cramped, and sailed for India.

December 25th.—Arrived at Bombay harbour on the morning of Christmas Day, but not allowed to land.

December 26th.—Disembarked at the Alexandria Dock, and entrained for Allahabad.

December 28th.—Detrained at Allahabad 7 p.m. and marched to the Cavalry Lines.

The regiment had been on active service out of India for a continuous period of over six years. It signalised its return to India by getting both its polo teams into the final of the next Connel Cup Tournament, and by Capt. Davison winning the Kadir Cup, two happy auguries for the future.

CHAPTER XIII

February 15th, 1921.—All private buying and selling of
horses was stopped—Government having taken over the
mounting of all Sillidar regiments.

March 21st, 1921.—From this date Government took over
the regimental horse run at Sarghoda, together with all credits
in that fund.

Two polo teams of the regiment, A and B, competed in the
Connell Cup Tournament at Allahabad, A team defeating B
in the final.

Captain D. S. Davison, D.S.O., won the Kadir Cup 1921,
this being the first occasion on which it has been won by an
officer in the regiment.

Major and Brevet Lieut.-Col. H. C. S. Ward, C.I.E., O.B.E.,
took over officiating command vice Colonel W. K. Bourne,
O.B.E., proceeding on furlough.

A Squadron under Captain J. H. Wilkinson, proceeded to
Poona on April 26th to relieve a squadron of the 34th Poona
Horse; C and D Squadrons and Headquarters, proceeded to
Poona on July 5th and 6th, B Squadron under Captain G. J.
Silver, remaining at Allahabad, having moved to Neil Lines.
B Squadron rejoined at Poona on August 19th. The regiment
was in Elliot Lines, Ghorpuri.

Telegram received on July 19th to the effect that from
September 1st, the regiment would be converted to a Non-
Sillidar basis. During August all funds, with the exception of
the "Miscellaneous" were closed pending the visit of the
"Conversion Committee," and all men who refused to accept
Non-Sillidar conditions discharged.

During October, 50 Australian Remounts were received from
the Ahmednagar Remount Depot. A good level lot, of which
about half were partially trained, and were able to take their
place in the escort of H.R.H. the Prince of Wales, in November,
in Bombay. The remainder were quite raw—some unbacked.

The regiment, under the command of Lieut. Col. H. C. S. Ward, C.I.E., O.B.E., organised as three squadrons, total strength 5 B.O.'s, 12 I.O.'s and 268 other ranks, proceeded to Bombay, Marine Lines Camp, on November 11th, arriving on the 12th, to take part in the escort of H.R.H. the Prince of Wales on his arrival in Bombay on November 17th.

Captain L. D. W. Hearsey, M.C., who had been appointed an Honorary officer in the regiment and four other B.O.'s rejoined for this duty.

The regiment was formed up on November 17th outside the Taj Mahal Hotel and took part in the procession to Government House, the Prince seeing the Regiment rank past on arrival there, and congratulating the commanding officer on their smart appearance and turn out.

On November 17th, riots, engineered by Non-Co-operators, broke out in Bombay. The Regiment was continually called upon for duties in aid of the Civil Power, and rehearsals for the Trick-riding and Military Display were not found possible. On Monday, November 21st, the Grand Naval and Military Display took place, the trick-riding and the military and torch-light displays being much appreciated. The commanding officer was afterwards congratulated by H.R.H. on the excellent performances of the regiment.

The Depot 4th Cavalry arrived as a forerunner to amalgamation on December 3rd.

Captain E. W. D. Vaughan, M.C., was appointed Adjutant with effect from March 19th, 1921, vice Captain D. E. Whitworth, M.C., whose tenure had expired.

The amalgamation of the 2nd Lancers with the 4th Cavalry took place on the 1st April, 1922. The combined regiment was then known as the 2nd/4th Cavalry. In 1923 the amalgamated Indian cavalry regiments were renumbered, and the regiment was renamed 2nd Lancers (Gardner's Horse).

AN AFTERWORD

BY

Lieut.-General Sir G. de S. BARROW, K.C.B., K.C.M.G., A.D.C., G.O.C.-in-C., Eastern Command, India

In view of the fact that the 4th Cavalry was my military home for a quarter of a century (1886–1911) and that the (pre-war) 2nd Lancers were my Comrades-in-arms in France and Palestine during the Great War, I may claim to have an exceptional acquaintance with those two regiments which are now amalgamated and form the 2nd Lancers.

This is not the first time in the history of the British Empire that regiments have been amalgamated ; and rarely has the operation been carried out with the total absence of friction which has attended the union of the 4th Cavalry with the 2nd Lancers. Regimental customs and traditions are tenacious growths. It is well they are so. They do not, however, tend to simplify the process of amalgamation. We read, for instance, in a recent publication when referring to the introduction of Cardwell's Scheme that " As was natural, this revolutionary change which linked together, and made mutually supporting battalions which had not hitherto had any connection with each other, was highly unpopular in the British Army and led to much friction and heart burning, from the feeling that the old regimental individuality and *esprit de corps* would suffer in the process with results disastrous to military efficiency."

We may ask what was the reason that the 4th Cavalry and the 2nd Lancers were able, at once and without any apparent difficulty, to arrive at a state of coalescence which has, in similar instances, only been attained after much clashing and jarring and searchings of the heart. The answer lies in the similarity of ideas, and the spirit of comradeship which has for many years existed between the two regiments bound by ties of similar habits, customs and composition.

Although raised at different periods, the 2nd Lancers being the much older regiment, there has been for many years past a feeling of friendship beyond the ordinary. The Indian ranks of the two regiments have been drawn mostly from the same districts and villages, and Officers who have served in one regiment, in the junior ranks, have left their impression on the other when in a higher ·position. Two Commanding Officers of the 4th Cavalry had originally served in the 2nd Lancers ; one Commanding Officer of the 2nd Lancers came from the 4th Cavalry where he had served as Adjutant and Second-in-Command. One may add that both regiments had been noted for many years past for· their excellent horsemastership.

The two regiments were not together during the Great War. In France, the 4th Cavalry were employed as Divisional Cavalry and afterwards went to Mesopotamia. The 2nd Lancers went to France in the Mhow Cavalry Brigade of the Indian Cavalry Division, and afterwards formed part of the 4th Cavalry Division in Palestine. It was not my fortune to meet the 4th Cavalry during the war, but the 2nd Lancers served in my command both in France and Palestine, and I cannot let this opportunity go by of paying a tribute to their fine performances in the field. The vision of their achievements in the great cavalry manœuvre, which ended in the destruction of the Turkish armies in 1918, during which time they were constantly in the van, is often before me.

For many happy days in peace, and for the remembrance of confidence and comradeship in war, I am ever grateful to the lately constituted 2nd Lancers.

G. DE S. BARROW.

April 2nd, 1924.

APPENDIX I

November 30th.—10.35 a.m.—Brigade ordered to saddle up and concentrate at P.30.d. The Brigade were on their way to relieve the 72nd Infantry Brigade in the Centre Sector, 34th Divisional Front. Inniskillings returned to Ennemain and packed saddles, ready for mounted action. Lances and swords were sent up in waggons for 2nd Lancers and 38th C.I. Horse and issued later.

12.10 p.m.—Brigade, less 2nd Lancers, H.Q. and 8 guns 11th M.G. Squadron and advance parties from all units in the trenches concentrated in P.30.d.

2.20 p.m.—Brigade moved off under orders to proceed to camp between Longavesnes and Villers-Fauçon.

3.10 p.m.—Orders received to proceed as· fast as possible to camp S.W. of Saulcourt E.14b. (82.c.)

3.40 p.m.—Orders received to concentrate as quickly as possible in Square E.15. just north of St. Emilie.

4.15 p.m.—G.O.C. and Brigade Major reported at 4th Cavalry Division H.Q. E.22.b.5.0., Brigade moved on to E.18.

6.0 p.m.—2nd Lancers and H.Q., and 8 Guns 11th M.G. Squadron joined the Brigade north of St. Emilie.

6.40 p.m.—G.O.C. rejoined Brigade in E.18.

7.0 p.m.—Brigade Report Centre moved to E.24.c. Southern exit of St. Emilie.

7.45 p.m.—Intimation received that 55th Division preparing reserve line through Lempire-Malassise Fme-X.26-Vaucelette Fme. Mhow Cavalry Brigade detailed to reinforce line in case of attack. Brigade Major proceeded to Epéhy to get in touch with 166th Infantry Brigade holding centre of line. Returned 9.45 p.m.

9.5 p.m.—Order received to get in touch with 165th Infantry Brigade in St. Emilie.

11.30 p.m.—Intimation received that an attack on Lempire-Vaucelette Line is considered likely early on morning of 1st.

MAP ENLARGEMENT TO ILLUSTRATE

MHOW CAVALRY BRIGADE'S OPERATIONS

1ST DECEMBER 1917.

SQUARE X.   SHEET 57 C.

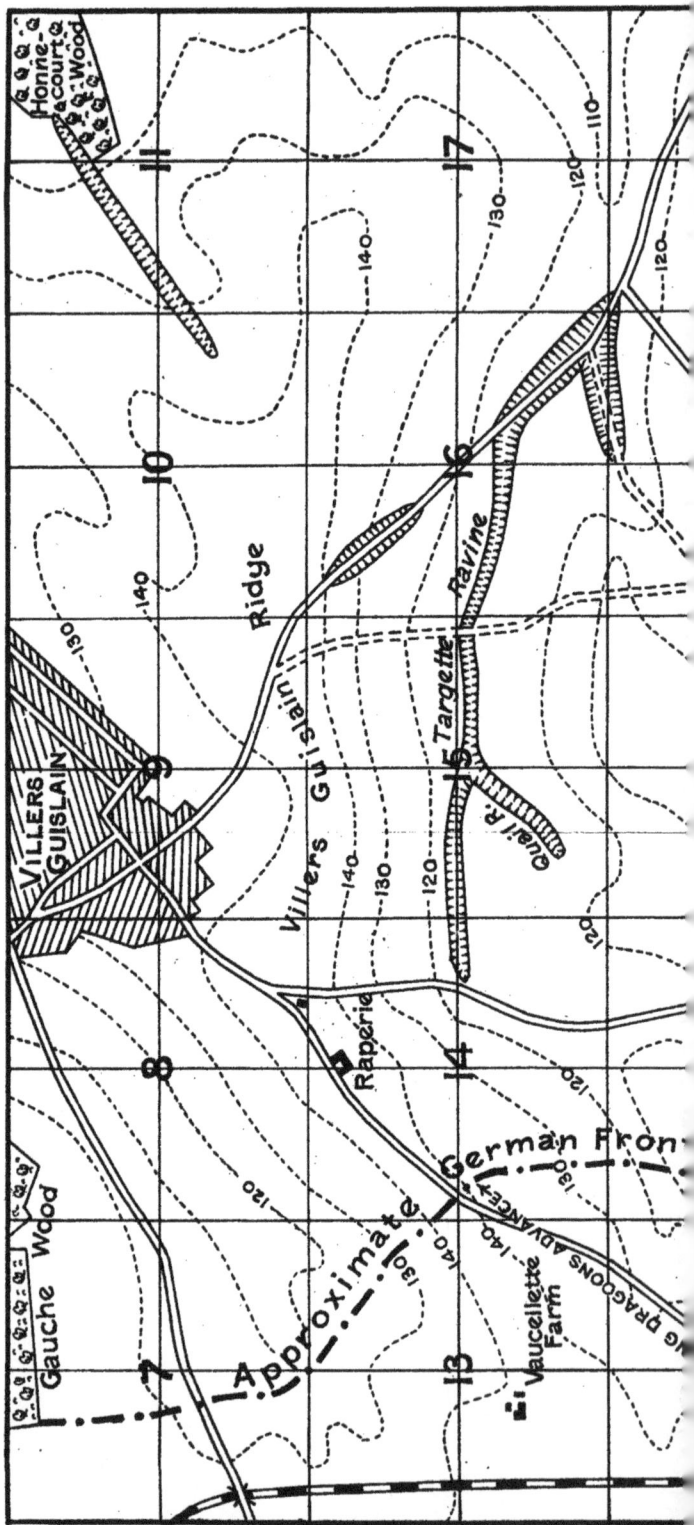

Honne- court Wood

11

17

140

130

120

110

120

10

16

Ridge

140

Targette Ravine

Quai. R.

130

120

120

Villers Guislain

140

130

120

VILLERS GUISLAIN

9

8

Gauche Wood

120

Raperie

4

120

German Front

MHOW DRAGOONS ADVANCE

130

130

140

Approximate

7

13

Vaucellette Farm

SQUARE F.   SHEET 62 C.

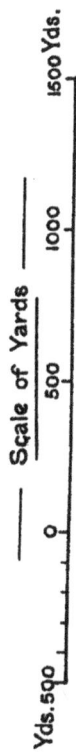

Scale of Yards

Yds. 500   0   500   1000   1500 Yds.

V.I. 10 Metres

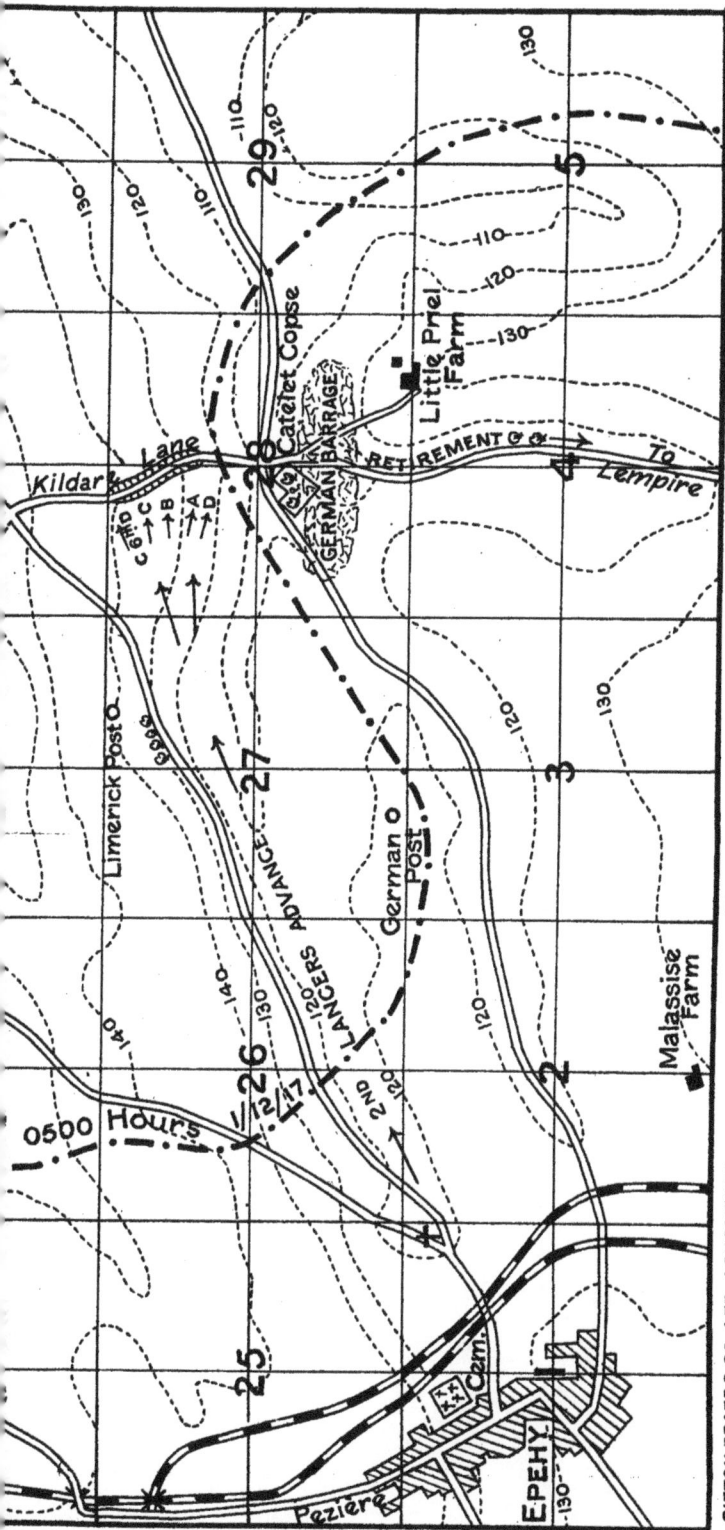

SIFTON PRAED & CO., LTD., LONDON S.W.

Mhow Cavalry Brigade ordered to be ready to move on receipt of order after 5.30 a.m.

December 1st.—1.45 a.m.—Warning received that Division, less Lucknow Brigade, and A Echelon, will be in position west of Peizière at 6.15 a.m. Mounted pack sections to join Brigade at rendezvous. All this to take place in event of Brigade not being required to reinforce Lempire-Vaucelette line at 5.30 a.m.

2.50 a.m.—4th Cavalry Division Order No. 22 received. 5th Cavalry Division, with Lucknow Brigade attached, to attack Villers Guislain and Gauche Wood at 6.30 a.m. Tanks co-operating. 4th Cavalry Division, less Lucknow Brigade, to assemble west of Peizière with object of taking advantage of the advance of the tanks and seizing Villers Guislain Ridge (X.10. Sheet 57.c.).

Mhow Brigade allotted 1 troop 4th Field Squadron. Mhow Brigade to reconnoitre crossings through a line of our wire just E. of Peizière and to keep close liaison with the tank attack.

As soon as a suitable opportunity presents itself, Mhow Brigade to move forward and seize and establish itself on the Villers Ridge about X.10, measures to be taken to watch the right flank.

4.0 a.m.—Mhow Brigade Order No. 22 issued on above.

5.30 a.m.—Brigade moved off to concentrate west of Peizière. G.O.C. and B.M. proceeded to meet Divisional Commander at E.4.d.8.

6.40 a.m.—G.O.C. rejoined Brigade west of Peizière. Brigade Report Centre established W.30.b.5.S. Situation and probable plan of action explained to Commanding Officers.

7.30 a.m.—Reports received from officers reconnoitring wire that there were exits by the Peizière-Villers-Guislain road and by 14 Willows road F.1.b.

8.10 a.m.—Reports received from Tank Liaison Officers that no tanks arrived at rendezvous and that consequently Lucknow Brigade were unable to attack but were supporting infantry in Vaucelette Fme.

8.15 a.m.—Order received from 4th Cavalry Division. " You are to endeavour to push forward towards your objective supported by the Artillery. . . . "

8.20 a.m.—Commanding officers arrived at Brigade H.Q. and situation explained. 2nd Lancers with two machine guns ordered to try and seize Targette, Quail and Pigeon ravines. Inniskilling Dragoons and four machine guns to follow as soon as 2nd Lancers were seen approaching their objective and endeavour to seize and hold the Villers Guislain Ridge about X.10.

8.38 a.m.—Division informed the Brigade was moving forward at once, and a request made that 5th Cavalry Division might co-operate and attack Villers Guislain. Artillery warned that Brigade was moving forward.

9.35 a.m.—2nd Lancers seen moving forward N.E. of the 14 Willows. At the same moment the leading squadron of the Inniskilling Dragoons moved off down the Peizière-Villers Guislain road, closely followed by two more squadrons (one squadron had accompanied 2nd Lancers).

9.40 a.m.—Headquarters and two squadrons Inniskilling Dragoons returned ; having come under very heavy machine gun fire. No one returned of the leading squadron.

10.10 a.m.—Following report sent to 4th Cavalry Division : " 2nd Lancers are believed to be in or about Pigeon Ravine, one squadron Inniskillings is with them. I am now sending two squadrons C.I.H. in support of them and am following with remaining two squadrons *via* road running through X.26.X.27,- X.22. Three machine guns will also accompany me."

10.15 a.m.—2 squadrons C.I.H. left their horses in Epéhy and proceeded forward dismounted ; they could only reach X.27 central when they were held up by machine gun fire.

10.20 a.m.—G.O.C. went to F.I.b.4.5, but nothing could be seen of the situation except led horses of the 2nd Lancers about X.27.b.9.9. Brigade Report Centre then moved to railway embankment near by.

10.50 a.m.—Following from 2nd Lancers received :— " 2nd Lancers and Capt. Moncrieff's squadron in fortified sunken road X.22.c., also four machine guns, lately held by one Company 418th Regiment.

(2) Herewith shoulder straps and papers of a prisoner (sent to 4th Cavalry Division).

(3) Enemy who retired from this position went north.

(4) Infantry in touch on our right.

(5) Enemy shelling Little Priel Fme. which is believed empty." Sent off 10.30 a.m.

11.0 a.m.—2nd Lancers asked if they were able to connect with infantry and hold out.

Informed that one squadron C.I.H. dismounted was being sent to their support, and also that Inniskillings had had to withdraw.

11.15 a.m.—Division informed that one squadron C.I.H. dismounted was being sent to assistance of 2nd Lancers ; that it was impossible to get through mounted. That 166th Infantry Brigade were arranging to advance at 1.0 p.m. and that C.I.H. had been asked to inform 2nd Lancers of this and to tell them to hold out until then. That one troop C.I.H. was being sent mounted by a more southerly route to try and get in touch with the 2nd Lancers.

11.30 a.m.—G.O.C. Mhow Cavalry Brigade conferred with G.O.C. 166th Infantry Brigade and arranged to lend him two dismounted squadrons C.I.H. to assist him in his attack on the Meath-Catelet line at 1 p.m.

11.45 a.m.—Officers Commanding these two squadrons went to confer with O.C. 1/5th King's Own.

11.55 a.m.—Following received from 2nd Lancers :— " Am connected with infantry on right about X.28.c.9.9. AAA Left flank about X.22.a.9.8. AAA Enemy machine gun 800 yards from left flank between us and you AAA Left flank in air and enemy attacking from left rear."

12 noon.—Message received from G.O.C. 166th which informed his infantry that the cavalry would only assist him to get his objectives : and that he must arrange to take over the whole of his new frontage and release the cavalry.

12.3 p.m.—Telephone conversation with 4th Cavalry Division informing them of arrangement co-operate with the infantry in their attack.

1.7 p.m.—Conversation confirmed.

1.45 p.m.—Message received from 2nd Lancers by lamp to effect that Colonel Turner had been killed or wounded in advance, and that machine gun reinforcements were required.

1.50 p.m.—O.C. 11th M.G. Squadron informed and a reinforcement of machine gunners sent up. They were unable to get through and remained with the squadron C.I.H. who had been sent to reinforce 2nd Lancers.

2.0 p.m.—Message received from above squadron C.I.H. that they were held up and unable to advance, the enemy were coming down on their left and they were going to fall back on the infantry strong post if necessary.

2.10 p.m.—Verbal message received to effect that attack in conjunction with infantry had failed with heavy loss and that the enemy were strongly entrenched and had many machine guns in position.

2.15 p.m.—Order received from 4th Cavalry Division giving enemy's apparent main line of resistance. Our artillery continuing to bombard Raperie till 3 p.m. At which hour Lucknow Brigade to attack Raperie from the west and Mhow Brigade to endeavour to obtain possession of some of their original objectives and Raperie from the south with the whole Brigade dismounted. One battery east of Epéhy to come under orders of Mhow Brigade. Sialkote Brigade to act as a mounted reserve and take advantage of any success obtained.

2.20 p.m.—G.O.C. Mhow Brigade informed O.C. 38th C.I.H. of the attack at 3 p.m. and directed that the two squadrons in advance about X.27 central should co-operate in this attack and would be supported by one squadron C.I.H. O.C. Inniskilling Dragoons was informed that in case of success of this attack his two squadrons would be required.

2.20 p.m.—Division informed of failure of attack in conjunction with infantry, and that total available force in hand of G.O.C. consisted of two weak squadrons Inniskilling Dragoons, 1 squadron C.I.H. and two machine guns. Further that the enemy had been found to be extremely strong in machine guns and that with the small force available he felt he was unable to attack his original objectives with any hope of success.

2.30 p.m.—Message received from machine gun reinforcement that he was about X.27 central with the leading dismounted squadron C.I.H.

3.0 p.m.—Message received from 2nd Lancers that their line ran X.28 central to X.22.c.9.8. German strong points at X.22.c.5.9 and X.21.c.8.0, Left flank very much in air, attack developing from left.

3.10 p.m.—166th Infantry Brigade were informed by G.O.C. 166th that two squadrons Cavalry were in posts about X.27 central. That he was being relieved by 110th Infantry Brigade that night and would ask this Brigade to relieve those cavalry posts and throw out a string of posts to join up with troops, believed Cavalry, in Kildare Post and near Adelphi. He also informed 166th that Mhow Brigade were unable to communicate with Cavalry in Kildare Post and Adelphi. That G.O.C. Mhow approved his suggestion and wished 166th inform troops in Kildare and Adelphi and told them to send their horses back to Epéhy.

3.10 p.m.—Officer Commanding the two squadrons that co-operated in the infantry attack at 1 p.m., was ordered to send back the machine gun reinforcement with him. And that he would remain in his present position until relieved by the infantry in the evening.

3.25 p.m.—Following received from 2nd Lancers :— " Squadron of C.I.H. not received AAA Some pressure on my left flank and left rear AAA Total strength 2nd Lancers and T.F. about 200, position as before." Sent off 3.10 p.m.

6.0 p.m.—Intimation received from 166th Infantry Brigade that 166th were dealing with situation at Kildare.

6.5 p.m.—Permission obtained from 166th Brigade to withdraw three advanced squadrons of 38th C.I.H.

7.0 p.m.—Three squadrons C.I.H. rejoined remainder of regiment in Square E. 6 (62.c).

8.40 p.m.—Orders received from Mhow Brigade to be withdrawn from the line after handing over positions to the infantry and then to bivouac in E.17 and be prepared to act as a reserve if required.

9.15 p.m.—Major Knowles, D.S.O., 2nd Lancers, reported at Brigade H.Q. that 2nd Lancers and one squadron Inniskilling Dragoons had been relieved and had moved into Camp in E.6.d.

December 2nd.—1.0 a.m.—Intimation received of expected heavy enemy attack on sector Gonnelieu-Vacquerie. Troops warned to be on the alert.

6.0 a.m.—Brigade Report Centre established at St. Emilie.

9.45 a.m.—Orders received to form Mhow Brigade into a Dismounted Battalion to act as a reserve to 4th Dismounted Brigade. In the event of its being required to proceed to southern exit of Epéhy and thence to railway cutting in X.25.a W.24.

10.15 p.m.—Intimation received that 1st Cavalry Division would relieve 4th and 5th Cavalry Division in the line that night.

11.10 p.m.—Orders received to move back to Athies next morning.

December 3rd.—9.0 a.m.—Brigade moved off.

1.0 p.m.—Arrived in billets.

APPENDIX II

Extract from the Cavalry Journal, Vol. X., No. 37, July,
1920. *" A Subaltern's letter to his old Squadron Leader."*

MILLBANK HOSPITAL,
WESTMINSTER.

February 14th, 1919.

MY DEAR COLONEL,

Many thanks for your letter and congratulations, which
I received yesterday when I went to the club for the first
time. I am getting about now, which, with my leg in a sort
of iron splint and a wing up, isn't too easy. I am well on the
road now, but it is going to be a long business, and I am
beginning to wonder if I shall ever play polo again, on account
of the arm, which isn't nearly so far advanced as the leg.
However, it was worth it. I have never enjoyed any time of
my life half as much as that week, and on the morning of the
20th (1918) after a charge outside Afule, having settled down to
a Bosche cigar and a bottle of ditto Hock, I would not have
changed places with President Wilson himself. In case you
would care to read about it, I will give you an impression of
the show as I saw it. It consisted chiefly in long marching,
which the horses stood wonderfully, which I think is a jolly
good chit for the men, who, very hard worked during the
summer in a most unpleasant climate, and always short
handed, never slacked off in the care of the horses. Also for
the farriers, as the number of shoes cast was ridiculously
small. For us the show started on the morning of September
the 19th, when we marched out (at 4.30 a.m.) of our camp
in the orange groves at Sarona, near Jaffa, moving up to our
position of readiness a few miles in rear of the front line.
About 9.30 a.m. we got the word to go, and moved up between
the 5th Cavalry Division and the hills (5th Cavalry Division
had their left on the coast), the Australian Cavalry Division
being in rear of us. Nothing worthy of note occurred till we
got to the point where the Musmus Pass crosses the hills to
the Plain of Esdraelon. We were not leading and the march

gave one the impression of a field day. We reached the entrance of the Pass about 8 p.m. We had done about 45 miles during the day, and then sat down to water and feed.

We then became leading Brigade, and I got orders to proceed as advanced squadron, with 3 armoured cars to help me. The inhabitants reported parties retreating up the Pass, and we fully expected to meet with some opposition. My orders were to proceed to a point which was nearly half-way up the Pass, where the Divisional Commander's orders were that we should halt for about four hours and put out outposts. We reached this point, having sent some 250 prisoners back, none of whom showed the slightest inclination to fight. I put out my squadron (D) as outposts, and as there were more stragglers close ahead, I asked Davison to get the Brigadier to consider the advisability of pushing straight on and scuppering the lot before they had time to rest and re-organise. At this point General Barrow arrived in a car, and having heard the situation, ordered the march to be resumed at once. C Squadron took on advanced guard and I fell in in the rear. Their experiences were much the same as ours and after collecting a few more stragglers, we crossed the Pass safely and arrived at Lejjun (or Megiddo) at the far end of the Pass, at about 4.30 a.m. on the 20th. Here I again put out outposts, while A, B and C watered and fed. We were then bumped into by the head of the Sialkot Brigade. The General Officer Commanding Sialkot Brigade then ordered the regiment to march on Afule, occupying the high ground on either flank. We started off from Lejjun with B (Whitworth) on the right, C (Turner, who fortunately had Mukand Singh to help him) on the track to Afule, in the centre, and A (King) on the left. I was in reserve with D. C had not gone more than a mile when they were held up by the infantry and machine guns in front of them, and had a few casualties. Then things started happening at a great pace. Davison galloped back and told me to gallop round the flank of the enemy and come in on their left. I started off at a trot, and very soon came under heavy fire and increased to a gallop. I then heard fire coming from two distinct points, one about 400 yards ahead of C Squadron, and one about 500 yards in rear of that lot. I then saw Whitworth, having gathered what was on, coming in

to help and moving on the outer circle to me. I left the rear
lot to him and went for the front lot, whom I hit about 30
seconds after he hit the rear crowd. I was moving in line of
troop column, and when within about 200 yards formed
squadron and charged, a bit opened out. Fire ceased when we
were within about 200 yards of them, and when we shouted,
the Jats put up a " View Holloa " as if all the foxes in Ireland
had been pushed out of cover at once. After that they saw
bright red, but they very soon stopped killing when they saw
that the Turks and Huns were petrified with fright. I pushed
my sword into one Turk, on about his left breast. I felt
rather an ass doing it, but as I say we were all seeing red.
While we were galloping round the armoured cars had come
into action and were doing good work on the Turk. They
stopped firing just at the right minute. Within about five
minutes from the time I got my orders from D.S.D., the place
was cleared and the prisoners were on their way back. The
total was, I think, five machine guns, 500 prisoners, about 60
killed or wounded with the lance and about 40 more from the
fire of the armoured cars. Not a man escaped. My casualties were—three horses hit, and Whitworth about the same.
The ground was flat and the going good with " Jowar " growing about knee-high. Time, about 6.30 a.m. B then went
back to their place on the right after rallying. Rallying was
the most difficult part of the show as everyone had gone
completely " Pagal." An aeroplane then dropped a message
just near me to say that the ground between us and Afule was
clear and that troops were leaving there as fast as 'buses and
trains could take them. So we advanced on Afule as quickly
as possible, but B and I got held up by bad ground, black
cotton, and had to slow up to a walk. Eventually I went in
sections along the road. We did not come under much fire.
A galloped behind the village, and shortly after I galloped
through, while Whitworth went for the aerodrome, collecting
three aeroplanes, and one later on which Daf. Chuni Lal made
some very good shooting for which he got an I.O.M. This was
about 8 a.m., and we did capture the place, despite what was
said in despatches. This is a rough plan. I am not good at
drawing maps at any time, but with one hand this will
probably be an awful effort. Several more prisoners were

o

captured at Afule.   We were in possession of Afule by 8 a.m.,
and were joined shortly afterwards by the rest of the Division.
We off-saddled, fed and watered, blew up the railway, and had
a bit of an easy till 1 p.m., when we came across a couple of
canteens, well stocked, which helped matters a great deal.
Shortly after 1 p.m., we started for Beisan, our objective, a
distance of sixteen miles from Afule.   We were still leading
Brigade and General Green trotted us the whole sixteen miles
in an endeavour to catch up a column which had been reported
ahead, but which as far as we could see, did not exist.   Any-
way, Beisan was entered without opposition about 5 p.m.
on the 20th.   This made over 80 miles in 32 hours.   We had
lost on the way, I think, 12 horses all told, including wounded
and exhausted.   At least six were wounded, while most
of the rest were remounts received the day before starting and
therefore soft.

As the regiment had done practically all the work, we hoped
to get a night's rest at Beisan, but instead got orders to take
a section of the outposts.   A and C found the pickets while
B and D were in support.   The next morning the regiment
went back into camp in the village and had an easy.   Prisoners
had begun to come in as the Turkish 7th and 8th armies had
begun to retire towards us.   The rest of our time was occupied
in escorting prisoners of whom some 50,000 passed through
Beisan.   The 29th and 36th, had a scrap south of Beisan in
which one of their I.O.'s. (29th) got a V.C.   B and D were
called out one night with the prospect of a scrap, but nothing
happened as the Turks walked in ; Gould and Tag rejoined at
Beisan.   On the 25th we got orders to proceed to Jisr Mujamie,
about 8 miles south of the Sea of Galilee (on the Jordan).
Here we linked up with the C.I.H. and the Dorsets were to
follow.   We started on the morning of the 26th with Deraa
our objective, the regiment leading again.   A strong party
of the enemy were reported at Irbid about 20 miles east of
the Jordan on the road to Deraa, and the 12th Turkish Army
were retreating along the Hedjaz Railway.   We linked up
with some of Lawrence's Arabs about five miles west of Irbid
and they confirmed the report about Irbid being held.   B were
leading when we got there and they were heavily fired on.
When we got to the top of the hill about a mile off, we were

fired on. Gould then ordered C to go round the right and attack the village from the south, myself to go from the north, and B to go round behind. There was a small village in the low ground in front of us, on the far side of which the ground sloped up to Irbid. I dropped my H.R.'s in this village to provide covering fire at about 800 yards.· As soon as I got out of the village I came under heavy fire which became heavier as I went on. The enemy were holding a high bank, commanding all the country round on the north side of the village, but it looked possible to gallop. From the row going on and the people I could see, I estimated the strength of the enemy at about two battalions with a dozen machine guns. When I got to within 200 yards of the bank I saw it was much steeper than I thought and with tired horses and bad ground in front we could not possibly get up with enough pace to do any good. So I swung the squadron right-handed into the village, hoping to get a footing there till the others got up. As I did so I felt a crack in my left knee and the horse I was riding (a chestnut called " Mony " that had once belonged to General Godwin) staggered a bit. He carried me about 200 yards till we got into the village and then laid down and died. I found that all we could muster was Kehri Singh and Basti, both dismounted and wounded, my orderly and about five men. I do not think we had an unwounded horse amongst us. I then looked round, and wherever I looked there seemed to be a machine gun. I could see no signs of B and C (I afterwards heard that they had both stopped about 600 yards outside Irbid). I did not consider my crowd of about half-a-dozen rifles enough to cope with the crowd we had to deal with, so decided to hop it, and gave orders accordingly ; telling anyone who got back to report the situation to headquarters. My knee was stiffening and I could not get along very well, and about 150 yards outside the village I caught it in the arm from a machine gun bullet, which broke the bone. I collected my arm and continued the movement, but 50 yards further on caught another in the left thigh which also broke the bone. That did it ; I could not move. However, Nand Singh turned up, slung me over his shoulder, and dragged me about 150 yards to a small dip in the ground. Here we were under cover from their fire which had been hottish all the time.

This was about 4 p.m.   I was making my exit south-west of
Irbid ; all our other wounded were north-west of the village.
I then lay and listened to a fire fight which went on till dark.
About 7 p.m., under· cover of dark, Nand Singh who had
refused to leave me, dragged me another 300 yards to where
the C.I.H. had put out outposts.   My broken bones had
stiffened and I had bled a good bit and this was hell.   The
C.I.H. got a stretcher and got me back.   I had a bad journey
down, taking ten days to get to Cairo, with two operations en
route and one when I got there and three since.   The enemy
left Irbid about 3 a.m. on the morning of the 27th and were
mopped up by the Dorsets and the C.I.H. at Er Remte, ten
miles east of Irbid.   They got 12 machine guns and 2,000
prisoners, so I was not far out.   I reckon I started 50 strong
(not counting the H.R.'s I had dropped), of which 30 became
casualties, fourteen were killed or died of wounds, amongst
whom was Raj Singh who had behaved most gallantly all
along.   The Turk treated our fellows shamefully, stripping
them all and aggravating a good many wounds, by pulling
them about to get their boots off.   My escape was entirely
due to Nand Singh, who got an I.D.S.M., but deserved an
I.O.M.   I think I was the last casualty the regiment had, for
they did not have any fighting after I left.   The Jats were
splendid.   They were in all the fighting there was and were
as keen as mustard the whole time.   A lot of the best N.C.O.'s
were away but it did not seem to make any difference.   We
lost a lot of good men, and for a month afterwards the squadron
was reduced to about 25 men all told.

I do not know whether you can gather what happened out
of this rather disjointed account, but it is rather hard to
write it.

Yours sincerely,

E.V.

APPENDIX III

NOTES ON THE HORSE

(By LIEUT.-COL. J. F. BENNETT.)

THE 2nd left Bombay a well mounted regiment. They only required, I think, seven horses to complete their mobilization strength. These were received from the 27th Cavalry on arrival at Bombay.

Approximately 75 per cent. of the horses were walers and the remainder country breds. Walers were bought in Calcutta at Rs. 475 a piece, country breds principally from the farm at Sargodha for a nominal Rs. 300. My figures are from memory. My reason for saying that the regiment was well mounted is that they were mounted on a level lot of sound horses, all good doers, ranging from 14.2 to 15.1 hands. There were no 16.3 blood horses supposed to be worth Rs. 3,000 apiece, nor were there any 13.2 ekka ponies worth Rs. 50 apiece. They were a level lot of well bred, not too well bred horses, of good ages throughout. This we owed to Colonels Davison and Commeline.

An attached Yeomanry officer once asked me why we were considered so well mounted. He was a good judge of a horse. He said " I can't see it ; you haven't a horse worth more than £30 at an auction." I said " Probably not, but we have very few that would fetch less." We had no " tail " ; all our horses were capable of carrying their weight and going on the next day. This made us a well mounted regiment. What is easy work for a well bred waler of 15.2 will kill a 13.3 Arab pony. The Arab pony will be game enough to stick to the horse for one day, perhaps two, but it will take him six months to recover from the effort. I have in my mind a beautiful little fleabitten grey Arab pony on which Farrier Major Maula Baksh was mounted. He was in A Squadron and was impressed with others on December 1st to carry a Sowar and his kit. He did it and came back, but he was a wreck for six months, though he recovered, and I played him against the

Desert Corps School at Richon le Zion in Palestine the following summer. I "zabardasti se" transferred him to the signal troop to carry a pack, which he did well. He was bound to have been evacuated from a squadron, and he was too good to lose. One learnt which horses to evacuate and which not.

SADDLERY

Our saddlery, as far as it went, was good, for it suited the man and the horse. The saddles had the perforated steel sideboards (Burton pattern) with numnah pannels. The only thing wrong with it was that it was not in every case in serviceable condition. It was good enough for parade and manœuvres, but knowing how hard it was for the sowar to make both ends meet, no squadron commander would insist on a serviceable standard.

On arrival in France our saddles were replaced much too quickly by English pattern saddles, few of which could be made to fit the backs of some of the smaller horses. On leaving France for Palestine the saddlery and equipment was as near perfect as it well could be, due to our three and a half years experience in fitting, and exchanging unserviceable equipment regardless of the expense. After our arrival in Palestine it could hardly have been worse. The saddlery and equipment of seven or eight regiments was despatched by the naval authorities in one ship to Egypt, and dumped in a heap at Alexandria to be scrambled for. We were the last regiment to reach Alexandria and got what was left. The loss to the Government was appalling, and to the regiment beyond remedy, even supposing that we had had time, which we had not. We embarked at Marseilles on April 12th and marched into Jericho on May 11th. Thus our beautifully fitted saddlery was lost to us.

Government saddles were good as far as they went, but they were heavier and not so adaptable as our own. In supplying native cavalry it somehow became ignored that there are three sizes of saddles, viz.: "L" (large); "M" (medium) and "S" (small). "L" are intended for heavy draught, "M" for horses over 15.2, and "S" for horses under 15.2. The letters denoting size are found under the front arch. This information is not in Cavalry Training. I obtained it from an A.S.C. handbook, from off which I disturbed a brooding Quartermaster.

Native Cavalry require only the " S " size of saddle. The following are some results of using the larger sizes :—

1.—Galls on the shoulder blades due to saddles being carried too far forward, and the shoulder muscles working under instead of in front of the saddle.

2.—Urgent orders on occasions of inspections to " Dismount and pull your saddles back before the Divisional Commander sees you."

3.—Childish advice from ordnance officers on the merits of stuffing large trees with bits of numnah to make them smaller, a temporary measure sure to result in trouble in the future.

SHOEING

On arrival in France, Indian shoes were found to be much too light and soft for the roads. Our spare shoes remained in the casino at Marseilles, until we were lucky enough to induce Government to take them over. They were replaced by heavier English ones which were much more suitable. As a result our naalbands who were cold shoers, and had only the tools necessary for fitting the light Indian shoes, were unable at first to deal with the heavier English pattern, which of course required hot shoeing. The difficulty was overcome by enlisting the aid of local French smiths, under whose instruction our naalbands very quickly became proficient in fitting shoes hot. In a short time it became an uncommon sight to see one of our horses having a shoe fitted on the line of march. In my own squadron Troop Commanders and naalbands were ordered to inspect shoes daily, and a lost shoe entailed an explanation from both.

A most useful regimental custom, due to Capt. Barton (known to all as " Cuthbert ") the Brigade Veterinary Officer, was that of removing all shoes every three weeks, thus keeping a week's wear in hand for emergencies.

Naalbands were very prone to go sick, and were very hard to replace. A shoeing school was started at Abbeville, but the men who were sent there were seldom volunteers, and were of little value when they returned. There were three good reasons for their inefficiency :

(*a*) The Sowar regards the profession of farrier as *infra dig.*

(*b*) There was no monetary recompense for the extra labour involved.

(*c*) They were not muscled up to the work by training in their youth.

The shortage of naalbands was probably the Squadron Commander's most insistent worry, and had by no means abated in 1920, despite much hearty growsing on the subject.[1]

CONDITION

The horses improved immediately on their arrival in France, due I should say, to the climate, the excellent oats and hay, and General Rimington's very sound orders on food, work, and exercise. We were exercising 18 kilometres a day and watering hot at pools on our way home, and I should imagine that very rarely, if ever before, has there been a Corps of Cavalry in the perfectly fit condition that the Indian Cavalry Corps was in 1915. We certainly never were again in France, nor in Palestine. It is impossible to overrate the fact that horses with backs and quarters on them can go farther, last longer, and kill the brutes that have only bellies, and that not allowing horses to trot for fear that " they will lose condition " is the surest way to getting them screwed when they have to be used. Cavalry horses want to be hard, hard and big if it can be got by good feeding and hard work, but hard first of all, and *they are better hard and fine through work than soft and big through want of it.* The big, soft horse will wear off whatever he has on him, and be weak, while the fine hard horse will keep what he has and go on on it.

[1] Note by W.K.B.—Scarcity of naalbands. This was a very serious matter. Naalbands received no extra pay ; they had much harder work than the ordinary sowar ; and it was still to some extent a question of caste. In peace time the naalband had only a sahib's pony to feed, and no horse to look after. On service he had to look after his horse and all horses were fed by Government. A great effort was made by Division and Corps H.Q. to get concessions for them ; but India was far away, and turned a deaf ear ; and naalbands were seldom sent as reinforcements. Hence the school at Abbeville was the best solution, and certainly did some good.

The French roadside was extraordinarily useful in supplementing short hay rations. One hour on the side of a French road, even in the depth of winter, whilst the horses grazed and the men smoked was well spent, and all helped towards condition.

CLIPPING

Clipping except the legs was a very good thing, and horses throve much better clipped than unclipped ; indirectly, so did clipping machines, for clipping legs breaks more teeth than clipping bodies. Horses throve better clipped with rugs than unclipped, even if they had occasionally to do without their rugs. It was quite easy to carry jhools " en banderole " round the horses' necks in cold weather on the march, and clipped horses, even in the snow, with their rugs were quite warm and comfortable. The reason why I lay stress on not clipping legs is that, apart from the saving of machines, horses with clipped legs picketed in mud and cold wind looked cold and uncomfortable, and on the principle that one's own legs are warmer with stockings than without, I am sure they were. The hair keeps a jacket of warm air round the legs in the same way that clothing does to men suddenly pitched into the sea, *vide* instructions to troops likely to be torpedoed.

Partial clipping, which usually means " trace high " or bellies and legs, I cannot see the slightest value in. It exposes the belly, which is a delicate part, and the legs to cold, and you cannot make it up with a rug. I much prefer the practice of whole clipping and the use of rugs whenever possible. I know that partial clipping facilitates cleaning, but to a horse outside in the cold, cleaning is of very little value. Mud caked on the hair, especially when it is dry, is warming and stops the wind reaching the skin. Horses picketed in the open always start to roll directly it gets cold, and I have always accepted this as Nature's instructions to put on a jacket of mud to keep the cold out.

HORSES

I think that there was very little difference between our walers and country breds. If anything the advantage lay with the latter, for he could do with less food, certainly with less hay, and did not mind the cold. The country bred thickened greatly in France and appeared to have much more substance than in India.   We were given a few American and Canadian horses in France.   They were indifferent, underbred, and nappy, and not in the same street as our walers.   There were very few English horses at first.

Remounts were generally very badly schooled.   The first batch of any size was one of 120, received at Athies to replace our December 1st losses.   They were principally from the North Irish Horse, a beautiful lot, well bred, and not too big. Horses were evacuated when necessary to Mobile Veterinary sections, and thence to the base.   Once lost it was almost impossible to get a horse back again.

MIRAUMONT, MARCH 19TH TO APRIL 13TH, 1917

The reputation of the 2nd Lancers for looking after their horses was fully maintained during the bitter weather at Miraumont.   Of the 400 horses lost by the 4th Cavalry Division during this period, only one was contributed by the regiment.   This belonged to the British batman of an I.A.R. officer, and was shot for weakness quite unwarrantably by an overzealous and youthful officer in charge of the transport on the line of march back to Orville.

The reasons to which I attribute our immunity from loss are :—

1.—The care taken to feed all hay from nets, preventing it being blown away or trampled in the mud, and ensuring it getting inside the horses.   I know that feeding hay from nets was a general order, but we *did it*, and from my personal observations, not everybody did so.

2.—The trouble troop leaders and men took to keep the mud scraped off the standings, thus giving the horses firm ground to stand on, at any rate for a time, and minimising the constant straining and changing of feet, which horses standing in mud keep up perpetually.

3.—We were careful to keep horses with " tails to the wind " and close together.

4.—The trouble we took with horses and mules to grow " full " tails, and counteract the senseless practice of the remount department in stripping all the hair out on the horses' tails and clipping it out of those of the mules.   I went round the lines early every morning whenever there had been rain or snow as part of my duty as 2nd-in-Command. On these occasions I found that every horse with a full tail had it jammed down tight. There was usually a lump of snow collected on the hairs at the root, and the inside of the thighs, his sheath, and his belly warm and dry, and the horse cheerful.

With remounts whose tails had not had time to grow it was exactly the reverse. The inside of the thighs, sheath, and belly were wet and the horse looked a picture of misery. The horse we lost was one of these.

Anything more senseless than taking the hair off a service horse's tail I cannot imagine. I do not mean shortening it to keep it out of the mud, but stripping it. It leaves tender skin exposed to the cold in a cold country, and to the scorching of the sun and the attacks of flies and mosquitoes in a hot one. I make this statement after seeing mules' tails swollen with cold in France, and with mosquito bites in Palestine. Why the average " Horsey " Englishman has to cut six inches off the dock, or pull all the hair out of the tail of a horse, in order to recognise him as such, beats me.

HEAVY DRAUGHT

Our experience of these was confined to the first winter. They seemed soft and unsatisfactory compared with the lighter horses which replaced them. At the same time this was probably attributable to the plasterer and glazier assistants masquerading as drivers, who did not know how to look after them,[1] and also to our disinclination at first to tell off an Indian N.C.O. to see that English drivers did their work. I found a great improvement in my horses as soon as I attached them to a section.

LIGHT DRAUGHT

Our light draught were good and did well principally because they were in charge of Indian R.H.A. drivers who were first class men ; but I think, on the whole, that there was nothing they did which mules could not have done better.

[1] One of these imperfect horsemasters was known as " Bluebeard ", a tonsorial allusion only. An infuriated vet. at Blessy was once heard to say to him " Your horse is crawling with lice, and what's more I believe he caught them from you ".

These drivers, by the way, left us when we left France, and we missed them badly. It was very trying to men and animals to have to start the march to Jericho with untrained men. What we did was to put the men who had been riding the A Echelon on to the B Echelon teams, and fresh men on to A Echelon. It naturally meant straggling and inferior march discipline ; however we got through, though a short opportunity to teach the fresh men, and get the others used to their mules would have made a lot of difference. I particularly remember the driving and distances being criticized adversely on a transport inspection. This was most unfair as all the men were fresh to the job, and the way the teams were turned out was superb. The turnout of the 2nd Lancers' transport was always very good, but on this particular occasion—at Deiran—it surpassed itself.[1]

MULES

The Indian mules were with us such a short time that it is hard to say much about them, but they did all they were asked to do, and the drabis did them well. I remember one particular drabi with a pair of small mules always in the pink of condition, and perfectly turned out, who made my life a burden whenever he thought that his mules had not got what he thought they ought to have. In the end he always got what he wanted.

The American mules, with our R.H.A. drivers, were all one could hope for as transport. They were kind, good tempered, and always triers. Of the whole lot there were not more than three which were in the least like the mule of fiction, and this I attribute to our men having ordinary " horse " or rather " mule sense," treating them well, and looking after them.

---

[1] Note by W.K.B.—One evil effect of the demand for eyewash, and frequent inspections by transport officers was that the transport men took to keeping one set of harness for inspections and one for work. The first was excellent, the other bad. When C Squadron paraded at Jenin to march to Roshpina in August 1920, with the prospect of the Nazareth hill before them they had very bad tackle on the mules, and the waggons were overloaded because they were carrying the good harness in them. I gave them an hour to cast the old stuff, and keep one set only.

LOADING TRANSPORT

This was merely a matter of practice, keeping the load low and broader at the bottom than at the top, also taking a pull at the loading ropes occasionally to keep them taut.

Overloading was not hard to check, always provided that the loading was supervised by an officer. The loading of sacks of coal on water carts, and the extravagant ideas of junior officers as to what constituted 30 pounds of kit were familiar instances.

GENERAL

I think that the time when the regiment was best mounted was when we left Marseilles for Palestine. I forget what the actual numbers were, but we had a percentage of spare horses. The actual number that we took on the S.S. *Maryland*, including a field ambulance, was about 800, every one of which we disembarked at Alexandria. This was about 70 more than had ever been loaded on the *Maryland* before. We were ordered not to use sidebars, and put as many on the ship as possible, so there was no object in not packing them in tight within reason. I think that they did just as well without sidebars as with, and I remember no horses getting down, or being badly knocked about. Anyhow we lost none.

There were only 100 2nd Lancers to look after the 800 horses. The remainder had been sent on ahead without horses. It was hard, as we were ordered to get all the men inoculated against enteric and, I think, plague, anyhow two inoculations per man. But for the able and willing (?) assistance rendered by the 300 other details, who included pay department clerks, S. & T. weighmen, and post office babus, things would have been much more difficult. They were allotted to each troop, and were most gallant in the way they assisted to clean horse decks and carry baskets of dung up to the bows to be hove overboard.[1]

A peculiar thing in this voyage was that all the horses in the best place and the most airy, *i.e.* the waist, developed colds

---

[1] As the indiscriminate throwing overboard of litter during the day would have made a splendid sort of paperchase track across the Mediterranean for the amusement of German submarines, it was accumulated during the day and flung overboard at night.

and fever, though, as far as I remember, only on one side, the port. The explanation arrived at for this—I give it for what it is worth—was that standing round a hatchway they never got fresh air, since the hatchway was constantly full of foul air coming up from the two horse decks below. The horses affected were principally officers' chargers, and other favourite horses which we wished to take particular care of, and for which we selected the best place. About 20 horses were affected, though my own and the horses standing exactly opposite and only about twenty feet away were not.

Two points struck me, one, that horses on the lowest horse deck did just as well, if not better, than those on either of the others, possibly because of the more equable temperature and the excellent ventilation, the other, that horses put on condition, due perhaps to the exercise they constantly got in keeping their balance, and accommodating themselves to the motion of the ship. There could be few things more nerve-racking than being in command of a horse ship between Marseilles and Alexandria at that time. We were extra-ordinarily lucky in our skipper, a Captain Evans, who was a really fine seaman. The *Maryland* had been torpedoed on a former voyage, and taken back into port going astern, as her fore part was stove in.

WITH A NEW DIVISION

I was once ordered to proceed for the purpose of instructing two territorial brigades of artillery in horsemastership, or the science of keeping their horses alive. It was interesting to me, and I think I was useful. There were eight batteries comprising the artillery of the —th Division, I have lost my notes, and forgotten the number of the batteries, and even of the division, which is perhaps just as well.

The men were all Lancashire factory hands, good men and keen, but hopelessly ignorant of horse knowledge. The value of the regular soldier for keeping horses fit enough to do their work was never better illustrated. Of the eight batteries, seven were appalling, and one in the pink of condition. After seeing the latter once I never went near it again, except for the purpose of cleaning my eye, and looking at fit horses. The Battery Sergeant-Major was an old " E " Battery R.H.A.

man. I have forgotten his name, but I served with him at
Meerut in 1905. His horses were big and round, and hard and
fit, and his men ran when he spoke to them. His lines were
clean as well as his men. I fancy a subaltern was occasionally sent down from the gun positions, but I do not remember
him. The remaining seven batteries were pitiable. They
suffered from excess of zeal, coupled with an absolute ignorance
of how to employ it. The horses were thin, starved, weak, and
lousy, and were eating their dung. They did stables for half-
an-hour at a time, four times a day, and they turned out for
exercise at a nominal 6 a.m., meaning half-past, with some of
the men carrying their saddles, and others lugging them through
the mud. The lines were a foot deep with mud. The main
reason for their condition was that all the guns were in the
lines, miles ahead. Practically all the N.C.O.'s were there,
and a subaltern at a time was sent back to the waggon lines
for a rest for a week.

All that needed doing was to lay down a routine, point out
the things which hit one in the face, suggest a remedy, and
keep on doing it.

Stable hours I reduced from four of half-an-hour to one of
one-and-a-half hours, not interfering with the time at which
the estaminets opened for the sale of beer, or the men's smoke
and sleep after dinner, and I gave them the routine of grooming
to carry out.

Harness cleaning as a parade I knocked off. It was done
from three to four, whilst the men smoked and chaffed each
other, instead of from two to four. The harness became
cleaner. I pointed out the advantages of feeding oats out
of nosebags instead of flinging them in the mud, likewise of
using haynets, and hanging them on the built up rope, also
that keeping the dung picked up, and not allowing oats to
get mixed up with it, was to some extent a check on the
awful habit of eating dung, which was almost universal, and
once learnt hard to stop. The horses were bad from bad
teeth, worms, lice, and want of care. Their food was wasted
and given dirty, principally because the men were not used
to horses, and the officers were not there, and not knowledge-
able when they were. The horses suffered from want of

exercise and want of rest through standing on muddy standings.

It is very hard to keep standings clean when horses are picketed on soft earth that has been used for some time ; but a great improvement can be made by having two lines, shifting the horses daily, and scraping the vacated ones and letting them dry. Horses do then get a certain amount of rest on a dry standing and the other one recovers in the meantime if it is scraped.

What I was up against was that no one saw anything that was wrong, or knew what was wrong when they saw it. On one occasion I had succeeded in getting green clover for one battery. It was being fed in nets from the built up rope, and I was going round the lines with the brigade commander, the captain in charge of the horse lines, a subaltern, and the battery sergeant-major. There was one net to two horses, and horses on each side of the rope. Horse No. 3 from the end on one side was a bad tempered brute and kicked at everything he could reach. He was tied up long and could reach three nets, and he kicked at every horse which tried to get near a net. The result was that one horse was getting the clover for six, and five were straining at their ropes to get away from him, and afraid to eat. Till I pointed it out, it did not seem to strike anyone that there was anything unusual, and that it was very easy to tie up the bad tempered horse by himself, and let the others eat in peace.

Watering was carried out five times a day. The weather was cold, and after standing in the mud all night the horses were not thirsty, and it was merely extra trouble to men and horses to turn out to water at 6.30 a.m. I cut water down to twice a day after exercise, as far as I could arrange it.

The death of Lieut.-Colonel J. F. Bennett not long after he wrote the foregoing notes was a great blow to his friends, who, in reading them, will recognize the cheery style of his speech and outlook on life. To young officers and N.C.O.'s of the regiment no better advice can be given than to try to model their supervision of horse management on his direct and common sense way of tackling that science, and to view problems sometimes from the horse's point of view.

APPENDIX IV

Silladar Cavalry

WHEN the Regiment returned to India after more than six years' absence from it, it found that the Silladar system, under which it had existed since about 1809, was doomed.

By the time that the Regimental History appears, the Silladar system will be a thing of the past ; and the glamour and interest which always surrounded it, will be becoming fading memories.

It is well to catch at a few of these and to record them while they are still fresh in the mind.

The following lines contain but a brief sketch of some of the features of the Silladar system, as it came down to us from more than a hundred years ago.

In its earliest days the Silladar was a man who placed his services, with his horse, arms and accoutrements, at the disposal of some Chief, Ruler, or Government. In return he received pay or its equivalent in loot. When his horse died, he supplied himself with another. It was a rough and ready irregular service, admirably suited to the conditions of the times. The little we know of the doings of Gardner's Horse in those far-off days, show that the relations of a Commandant to his regiment resembled those of a patriarch to his tribe.

The Mutiny saw further additions to these original Silladar Regiments, and it also saw the abolition of the Company's Regular Indian Cavalry regiments, with the exception of the four, later reduced to three, regiments of Madras Lancers.

The old simple Silladar system began to be modified to meet altered times and the requirements of service further afield.

A man on joining a regiment now no longer brought his horse with him. He received his horse from the regiment, and it was the regiment which fitted him out with arms, accoutrements, transport, tentage and all else, at a price. That price

P

was called the man's assami. In the 2nd Lancers, it was about
Rs. 350 to 400. In many other regiments much more.

It was seldom that a man joined with the whole of his
assami money. But the price of a horse he had to bring with
him and to pay cash down. The horse price was the minimum
cash sum that a regiment demanded before it would enlist
a sowar. It varied in different regiments, and, indeed in
different classes in the same regiment. In the 2nd Lancers
it was about 150 Rs.—less for some of the poorer classes. The
man owed the regiment and was charged interest on the rest
of his assami money. The regiment let him have on credit,
half a mule, a share of a tent, his saddlery, share
of mule's pack saddle and accessories, his uniform,
arms except the rifle which Government always supplied
and all other equipment and gear. The cost of all the
above was cut from the man's pay by instalments ; and
he was pretty hard up during the first years of his service.
He in fact received only enough pay to enable him to feed his
horse well, and himself often not too well.

When the sowar left the regiment, he received all or nearly
all his assami money back, and started life with a nice little sum
in hand. Every officer who has had to do it, will remember the
lengthy recital of every article and every strap in the retiring
sowar's equipment, together with its price, by the conscien-
tious pay sowar of the half squadron. The recruit enlisted
in the outgoing sowar's place, took over all the kit of this
latter, and was often enough supplied with old things at the
price of new ones. The recruit likewise received in theory the
retiring man's horse, but, in reality the worst horse in the
half squadron.

Nor did the sowar now have to find himself a new horse,
should his original horse die. He insured against horse loss
by a monthly subscription, which varied as time went on, but
which never exceeded Rs. 3 per month. For this, throughout
his service, he received a new horse in the event of the loss of
his former one. Similarly with his transport animal. In
some regiments, the sowar insured in the same way for the
replacement of saddlery, tentage, and other articles of equipment. But this was never done in the 2nd Lancers.

As time went on there were many other modifications of the old original Silladar system ; but in its essence it remained the same.   It was recruited still from the landed class, and its Indian officers were men of birth and standing.   A troop often consisted of its commander's own dependents, with whom his word was law.   Sometimes he owned the assamis of the whole troop.   The conditions of service were still easy.   No longer could a man, who wished to be at home for a year or two, furnish a substitute and include that substitute's service as service towards his own pension.   But leave was easily obtained, and the furlough was still for seven months.   In the 2nd Lancers, it always remained so, but in many regiments it was altered to two periods of $3\frac{1}{2}$ months.   Silladar regiments were always ready to lend money to the men, but these loans were invariably covered by the value of the debtor's assami and never exceeded the amount that the regiment was due to pay the man when he left the service.

The service was very popular, and appealed to " Izzat." No recruiting parties had to seek recruits.   Candidates for enlistment, after inspection at Durbar, were entered on the Ummedwar book, and, as vacancies occurred, were sent for and enlisted.   Crime was almost non-existent in a community where each member held so large a stake, and where the bonds of military discipline were so largely reinforced by those of the troop commander's personal influence, and that of innumerable bhaibands and fellow villagers in the squadron.

The Regimental Durbar, usually held weekly, was in some ways the meeting of the shareholders of a firm, at which was discussed every conceivable subject in which the firm was interested.   It opened with a recital of the minutes of the last meeting : interviewed various claimants for leave, loans, and compassionate allowances, discussed matters of equipment, took such disciplinary measures as were necessary, viewed Ummedwars and newly arrived recruits, heard the bunnias announce that they had been paid in full.   At Durbar all announcements of a public nature were made.   The Commanding officer was chairman, judge and arbitrator.   Anyone could come forward and speak, down to the lowest regimental sweeper.   The regiment followed the proceedings with wrapt interest and never seemed to find them too long.

When a man went on furlough, he rode into the village on his own horse, followed by an attendant on his baggage pony— and was looked on as a person of consequence.   When railways came in, this practice was less followed, but it was always kept up in the 2nd Lancers, the horses doing the long journey by rail to some central station whence they were within moderate distance of their owner's villages.   Woe to the man who brought his horse or transport animal back from furlough thin or poor.

In the lines, each man fed his horse by buying grain direct from the troop-bunnia.   The eight bunnias used to appear weekly at Durbar to state their weekly lie, namely that they had been paid in full (" Bhar-paya ").

The regiment was deeply in debt to its bunnias, who were finally done away with by Colonel Davison's exertions about 1905.   As nearly every man in the regiment owed them money, this was a difficult business.   They were a good riddance. Henceforward grain was bought under regimental arrangements and issued to the sowar by troop or half squadron commanders.

In 1882, when the regiment went on service to Egypt, it consisted of three squadrons and its baggage animals were ponies.

Between that year and 1889, the establishment of Silladar Cavalry regiments was raised to a four-squadron one, and from about 1890, the pony began to disappear and the mule to take his place as baggage animal throughout the Indian Cavalry. A Silladar regiment now furnished Government with an extraordinarily mobile body of over 600 horsemen, with half that number of baggage animals, and with complete camp equipment.   These could move anywhere and at any moment, except during the furlough season, when man and horse and baggage animal had to be recalled from distant districts.

On the march, the baggage animals each ridden by the syce, and travelling at the rate of not less than five miles an hour, dumped their loads in the new camp and immediately went off for the day's forage.   In those days grass could be cut anywhere it grew ; and the syce was much more the sowar's private servant than he.became later.

When regiments went on service, they were maintained in the field by the depots they left behind them. This served well enough for expeditions of short duration, or not far beyond the frontiers of India. But for service beyond the seas, the Silladar system never aimed at doing more than placing men and horses at the disposal of the Government, and these troops were maintained in the field partially as Silladars and partially by Government; that is, regiments still looked to their depots to maintain them partially, and the men still paid for the feed of their horses. Government supplemented to the extent demanded by circumstances.

It will be remembered that an attempt was made to carry on this system in France, but it was soon abandoned. Thenceforward the British trooper and the Indian were on the same footing, with this exception: the Indian trooper drew pay to feed his horse, which was now fed free for him by the Government. For the first time in the life of Indian Cavalry, the sowar was having it both ways.

During the last decade of the nineteenth century, began the speeding up and improvement of the military machine. This touched Silladar Cavalry pretty nearly, for it touched its pocket.

Greater efficiency was demanded, the work became harder. A man's kit wore out sooner, and his horse and mule required more food. And food both human and equine went up in price.

Greater demands were made on the personnel of a regiment to meet the requirements of grass farms and horse runs. Both were excellent things, but both took Indian officers and men away from the regiment. And both meant more office work, more finance work, and more ledgers and account books.

It will thus be seen how Silladar Cavalry, starting long ago as a slightly organized body of fighting men, had been gradually altering itself to move with the times.

It is rather a question whether with all its improvements the system was not now beginning to lose some of its original virtues; whether the system contained in itself sufficient stamina to bear the weight of those improvements ; whether David armed with a sling only was not a better man than David cumbered with Saul's armour.

A glance at the rôle which a Silladar Cavalry regiment fulfilled during the last half century of its existence and was fulfilling in 1914, may help to answer the above question. A regiment was now a dual concern, a fighting one and a business one. A Commanding Officer was responsible for the training and discipline of his regiment. But he was also the head of a firm which conducted a variety of businesses, which bought, bred, and trained horses and mules, and sold them : which farmed in a largish way : which bought whole-sale (amongst other commodities), grain, saddlery, boots, cloth, and retailed these things to the regiment. The firm was also a money lending one ; and a financier which dealt in lacs of rupees. And finally it was a firm of accountants, whose chief accountant—the Khizanchi—was often the only man with the leisure and brains really to understand the regimental accounts.

It may be questioned whether it was well to make a com-batant officer responsible for so much business. But it was so. The Commanding Officer was responsible for all the above. Is it to be wondered at that sometimes he gave too much time to the business aspect of his regiment, and too little to the training ?

True the Silladar system produced Indian officers and N.C.O.'s of the most wonderful abilities, integrity, and devotion, who conducted the various business enterprises of the regiment. But it was the Commanding Officer who had to stand the racket if anything went wrong.

As the business aspect of the regiment widened, and as there were new calls made on its personnel, to administer the grass farm, the regimental horse run, and so on, it would have been well had extra enlistments been permitted to do the extra work. But this was not allowed. There were therefore fewer men in the ranks, and more who were permanently absent on Administrative work of one kind or another.

When the call came in 1914 there stood ready for service thirty-six regiments of Silladar Cavalry, each able to place in the field five hundred trained men and horses, with half that number of transport animals. Behind each regiment stood its depot—in strength about one hundred men and horses, with transport.

More than half of these regiments were at once taken for service in France. But not with their transport ; and all, or very nearly all, the remainder saw service at one time or another in one or other theatre of war.

To make this statement is perhaps enough to prove that the Silladar system was equal to a great occasion. But no system can be pronounced wholly good, which while providing excellent troops for the field, is unable to maintain them there. In this the Silladar system failed ; but then the same may be said of the British Army system as a whole. The great body of Irregular Horsemen that went over seas possessed too little homogeneity, and too many peculiarities, for a Great War fought out at so great a distance from India, and India's usual maintenance-services. Some regiments landed in France admirably mounted and equipped ; others, and these were regiments with poor or bankrupt funds, brought horses and saddlery which were not serviceable. Each regiment, being a law unto itself as regards its patterns of equipment, there was a lack of standardization which soon came to be felt. There were too many departments puzzled by the Indian cavalry, and the Indian cavalry itself got tied up into knots in trying to maintain its accounts system at two spots some five thousand miles apart.

There were also many other difficulties, amongst them those of re-inforcements in British and Indian officers and other ranks. But these difficulties were not peculiar to the Silladar system, but were common to the British army as a whole.

Further during peace time manœuvres, Silladar cavalry regiments had often fallen foul of generals who knew little or nothing about the effect of hard work and long marches on the men's pockets. Some Commanding Officers (not the wisest of them) were too fond of emphasizing this, and in this way wrong impressions were given of the service as a whole.

It was also a sore temptation to the authorities to see so

many horses and such excellent transport available for all sorts of public purposes, such as mounting umpires, or for general usefulness at great State assemblages, and yet not be able to lay a hand on'such resources.

Further, military service, not necessarily active service only, so often now threw the Silladar system out of gear, and necessitated the system being in whole or in part annulled or supplemented, or tinkered with in some way or another, that its drawbacks were becoming unduly accentuated and its good points lost sight of.

APPENDIX V

Honours Awarded to the 2nd Lancers 1914–1920

Victoria Cross.

L. Daf. Gobind Singh (28th Cav.).

Companions of the Order of St. Michael and St George.

Brig.-General L. L. Maxwell.
Brig.-General G. Gwyn-Thomas.
Brig.-General A. G. Pritchard.

Lieut.-Colonel P. B. Sangster (for services while commanding 29th Lancers).

Companion of the Order of the Star of India.

Brig.-General M. E. Willoughby.

Companion of the Order of the Indian Empire.

Lieut.-Colonel H. C. S. Ward.

Companions of the Order of the British Empire.

Brevet Lieut.-Colonel W. K. Bourne.

Brevet Lieut.-Colonel H. C. S. Ward.

Bar to the Distinguished Service Order.

Major G. Knowles.

Companions of the Distinguished Service Order.

Major P. B. Sangster.
Major G. Gwyn-Thomas.
Major H. Y. Salkeld.

Major G. Gould.
Captain D. S. Davison.

Bar to Military Cross.

Captain D. E. Whitworth.

Military Cross.

Lieutenant L. J. Peck.
Captain D. E. Whitworth.
Lieutenant V. M. Smith.
Risaldar Mukand Singh Br.

Lieutenant L. D. W. Hearsey.
Captain E. W. D. Vaughan.
Lieutenant E. St. J. King.
Lieutenant R. P. L. Ranking.

Order of British India (2nd Class), with title of Bahadar.

Risaldar Major Ganga Datt.
Risaldar Mukand Singh.

Risaldar Suraj Singh.
Ressaidar Sohan Singh.

Indian Order of Merit (2nd Class).

2266 A.L.D. Udey Singh.
1417 A.L.D. Sahib Singh.
2136 A.L.D. Liakat Hussain.
Risaldar Suraj Singh

2366 Daf. Chuni Lal.
2283 Sr. Shezad Khan.
1725 L. Daf. Anokh Singh.

Bar to Indian Distinguished Service Medal.

2026 A.L.D. Sobha Singh.

Indian Distinguished Service Medal.

Ressaidar Abdul Latif Khan.
1329 K.D. Ram Pershad.
Risaldar Azim Ali (22nd Cavalry).
Jemadar Dhara Singh (32nd Lancers).
2318 Sr. Asa Singh.
1950 A.L.D. Gordhan.
1803 A.L.D. Karam Chand (28th Cavalry).
Ressaidar Het Ram.
Ressaidar Krishna Chandra Singh.
1515 K.D. Dharam Singh.
1861 Daf. Ram Singh.
1705 Sr. Mohan Singh.
2026 A.L.D. Sobha Singh.
2049 Sr. Amar Singh.

2152 Sr. Kehar Singh.
1917 Sr. Lahora Singh.
Ressaidar Jang Bahadar Singh.
A.L.D. Nun Singh (28th Cavalry).
2319 Sr. Bhagirath.
2247 Sr. Arjan Singh.
2252 Sr. Harnam Singh.
2065 Sr. Nand Singh.
1396 Daf. Jiwan Singh.
1595 Sr. Lal Singh.
1502 Daf. Mehbub Ali.
1564 Sr. Lachman Singh.
1584 Daf. Nihalu.
Risaldar Jiwan Singh.
Sr. Dalip Singh.
A.L.D. Rati Ram.

Indian Meritorious Service Medal.

1179 K.D. Udey Singh.
1298 K.D. Natha Singh.
1260 Daf. Ram Pershad Singh.
1090 Fr. Maj. Nizamuddin.
1313 Daf. Ahmed Ullah Khan.
1318 Daf. Abdul Rehman.
1336 Daf. Sham Singh.

1675 L.D. Bahal Singh.
1654 Sr. Jaggan Singh.
1711 K.D. Guranditta Mal.
1725 L.D. Anokh Singh.
1734 A.L.D. Mahomed Yasin.
1758 Sr. Gokal Singh.
1800 A.L.D. Sham Singh.

1409 Daf. Mahomed Zaman.
1521 Daf. Basti Singh.
 939 L.Daf. (Armr.) Bishem Singh
1443 Tr. Major Ganga Ram.
1608 Daf. Sargit Singh.
1609 K.D. Taj Mahomed.
1504 K.D. Kazim Ali.
1489 K.D. Manohar Singh.
1513 L.D. Hassan Baz.
1583 Daf. Wariam Singh.
1596 Daf. Phuman Singh.
1617 L.D. Dost Mahomed Khan.
1612 Daf. Sahib Dad Khan.
1643 K.D. Nihal Chand.
1694 Tr. Bairam.

1959 Tr. Nathu.
1969 L.D. Harphul.
1995 A.L.D. Bhaggat Singh.
2013 Sr. Kirpa Singh.
2035 Daf. Nand Ram.
2070 L.D. Sobha Ram.
2174 Sr. Jug Lal.
2268 Daf. Raganath Singh.
2295 Fr. Abdulla Khan.
2319 Sr. Bhagirath.
2352 Sr. Jog Raj.
1706 K.D. Molar.
1185 K.D. Bhagwan Dass.
1184 K.D. Ali Raza Khan.
1349 W.O. Lall Chand.

Mentioned in Despatches (Indian Ranks).

Risaldar Suraj Singh, Bahadur, I.O.M.

2185 L.D. Charan Dass.
2174 Sr. Jug Lal.

FOREIGN DECORATIONS.

Medaille Militaire (France).

1221 K.D. Sant Singh.

Order of the White Eagle (Serbia).

Lieut.-Colonel H. C. S. Ward.

Solidaridad (Panama Republic).

Captain E. W. D. Vaughan.

Croix de Guerre (Belgium).

2090 A. L. D. Bans Gopal Singh.

Order of St. Anne (Russia).

Brig.-General M. E. Willoughby.

Nominal Roll of Indian officers and other ranks nominated by the Officer Commanding the 2nd Lancers who have been selected for Jangi Inams under the Government of India's Special Reward Scheme for the Great War 1914–1919.

Regimental No.	Rank and Name.	Remarks.
1574	Lance-Dafadar Bishan Singh ..	Deceased.
1313	1st Grade Vety. Asst. Ahmedullah Khan.	Serving.
1951	Kot-Dafadar Tuhi Ram	Deceased.
1964	Dafadar Nihala	Deceased.
2421	Sowar Sher Singh	Deceased.
1936	Dafadar Hira	Deceased.
2256	Sowar Fakir Chand	Pensioned.
1472	Kot-Dafadar Dalla Ram	Pensioned.
1706	Kot-Dafadar Molar	Serving.
2400	Sowar Mumtaz Ali	Deceased.
1209	Farrier Ram Singh	Serving.
2138	Lance-Dafadar Sardara	Deceased.
2254	Lance-Dafadar Kalu Ram	Deceased.
2135	Lance-Dafadar Gaj Raj Singh ..	Deceased.
1489	Kot-Dafadar Monahar Singh ..	Pensioned
1184	Kot-Dafadar Ali Raza Khan ..	Pensioned.
2718	Dafadar Terbeni Singh	Pensioned.
1965	Lance Dafadar Hidayat Ali ..	Deceased.
1675	Lance Dafadar Bahal Singh ..	Serving.
2282	Sowar Bhikam Singh	Pensioned.
1873	Lance-Dafadar Hashim Beg ..	Deceased.
1690	Dafadar Bhola Singh	Deceased.
1584	Kot-Dafadar Nihalu, I.D.S.M. ..	Pensioned.
1603	Dafadar Bishan Singh	Pensioned.
	Awarded Jagir.	
	Risaldar-Major Hon. Lieut. Mukand Singh, Bahadur, M.C.	Pensioned.
	Risaldar Suraj Singh, Bahadur, I.O.M.	Pensioned.

Nominal roll of Indian officers and other ranks nominated by the Officer Commanding the 2nd Lancers who have been selected for Grant of Land under the Government of India's Special Reward Scheme for the Great War 1914–1919.

Regimental No.	Rank and Name.
	Risaldar Major Ganga Dat, Bahadur.
	Ressaidar Jiwan Singh.
	Ressaidar Het Ram, I.D.S.M.
	Ressaidar Bharpur Singh.
2339	Sowar Nathu.
1711	Kot-Dafadar Guranditta Mal.
1609	Kot-Dafadar Taj Mohammed.
2538	Sowar Mohan Lal.
1329	Kot-Dafadar Ram Parshad.
1515	Kot-Dafadar Dharm Singh.
1677	Kot-Dafadar Bishambar Singh.
1979	Lance Dafadar Pritam Dass.
2201	Sowar Ahmed Hussain.
1336	Dafadar Sham Singh.
	Risaldar Mohammed Raza Khan.
1298	Kot-Dafadar Natha Singh.
2207	Sowar Nur Mohammed.

APPENDIX VI

WAR SERVICES OF OFFICERS, 2ND LANCERS

(Dates in brackets indicate period served with regiment.)

Brig.-General M. E. Willoughby, C.B., C.M.G., C.S.I. (1914–15), Commandant 1913–17. Commanded 1914 to May, 1917. Liaison Officer Indian Cavalry Corps at G.H.Q. 1915 ; A.Q.M.G. Meerut Division (France and Mesopotamia) 1915–1916 ; Commanded 6th Cavalry Brigade, etc., in Mesopotamia 1916 ; D.A. & Q.M.G. 3rd Indian Corps, Mesopotamia, 1916–1919 ; D.A. & Q.M.G. North-West F.F. (3rd Afghan War) 1919. Five times mentioned in despatches. 2nd Class Order of St. Anne (Russia) with swords. C.B. 1918 ; C.S.I. 1920 ; 1914–15 Star.

Lieut.-Colonel H. H. F. Turner (1915–17). Commandant 1917 ; Commanded December 1915—December 1917 ; A.A. & Q.M.G., Indian Corps, 1914 ; A.A. & Q.M.G., 10th Division, 1915 ; Despatches, 1916. Killed, December 1st, 1917. 1914 Star (bar).

Brig.-General L. L. Maxwell, C.M.G. (1914–16). Commanded May, 1915, to December, 1915. Commanded Sialkote Cavalry Brigade, 1916–1918. C.M.G. Despatches. 1914–15 Star.

Brig.-General A. G. Pritchard, C.M.G. (1914–15). Commanded a mounted column Loos, 1915. Commanded 2nd R. Warwickshire Regiment, 1915–1917. Commanded 10th Infantry Brigade, April—December, 1917. Commanded a brigade in England, 1918. Commanded Lucknow Brigade, 1918. Four times mentioned in despatches. C.M.G. Brevet-Colonel. 1914–15 Star.

Brig.-General G. Gwynn-Thomas, C.M.G., D.S.O., p.s.c. (1914-18). Commandant, 1917–1920. Brigade-Major 122nd Infantry Brigade ; Commanded 26th Bn. Royal Fusiliers ; Commanded 115th Infantry Brigade ; Commanded 50th Infantry Brigade. Four times mentioned in despatches. C.M.G., D.S.O. 1914–15 Star.

Lieut.-Colonel J. F. Bennett (1914–18). Commanded, December, 1917, to September, 1918. 1914–15 Star.

Lieut.-Colonel G. Knowles, D.S.O. (1914–18). Commanded, November, 1918, to January, 1920. Twice mentioned in despatches. Bar to D.S.O. (Cambrai), 1918. Wounded Cambrai. 1914–15 Star.

Colonel P. B. Sangster, C.M.G., D.S.O. (1916). Brigade-Major, Ferozepore Infantry Brigade, 1914 ; D.A.A. & Q.M.G, Indian Cavalry Corps, 1915 ; Commanded 29th Lancers 1916 to 1920. C.M.G., D.S.O. Four times mentioned in despatches. Brevet Lieut.-Colonel. 1914 Star (bar).

Colonel W. K. Bourne, O.B.E. (1920). Commandant, 1920. D.A.A. & Q.M.G., Indian Cavalry Division, 1914 ; A.A. & Q.M.G., 1st Indian Cavalry Division, 1914–1917. Raised 2/35th Sikhs, 1917. Commanded 2/35th in Afghan War, 1919. A.A. & Q.M.G., Norforce, 1919. Four times mentioned in despatches. O.B.E. Brevet-Lieut.-Colonel. 1914 Star.

Lieut.-Colonel H. C. S. Ward, C.I.E., O.B.E. (1920). Staff Captain, I.S. Cavalry Brigade, 1914 ; G.S.O.2 in E.E.F., 1915–1916 ; G.S.O.1 2nd Mounted Division, Palestine, 1917 ; G.S.O.2 (I) 2nd Division, 1917–1919 (Afghan War) ; G.S.O.1 Khyber Area, 1920. Seven times mentioned in despatches. O.B.E., C.I.E., Serbian Order of White Eagle 4th Class with swords. Brevet Lieut.-Colonel. 1914–15 Star.

Major H. Y. Salkeld, D.S.O. (1914–18). Attached Secunderabad Cavalry Brigade, 1914. D.S.O. (Cambrai). 1914 Star (bar).

Major K. Robertson (1915–19). Attached 2nd Life Guards, 1914. Despatches. 1914 Star (bar).

Major G. Gould, D.S.O. (1914–15), (1918–19). Staff Captain and Brigade Major, Mhow Cavalry Brigade, 1915–18. Commanded 23rd September, 1918, to November, 1918. 1914–15 Star.

Captain D. S. Davison, D.S.O. (1915–19). Attached 4th Dragoon Guards, 1914. Wounded Messines, 1914. Adjutant, 1914–1917. Commanded September, 1918. Twice mentioned in despatches. D.S.O. (El Afuleh). 1914 Star (bar).

Captain D. E. Whitworth, M.C. (1915–20). On L. of C., France, 1914. M.G.O., 1915–17 ; Adjutant, 1917–20. Commanded January to April, 1920. M.C. (Cambrai). Despatches. Bar to M.C. (Beisan). 1914 Star.

Captain P. V. Blomfield (1914–16). Invalided out from injuries received in trenches, 1917. 1914–15 Star.

Captain E. W. D. Vaughan. M.C. (1914–18). M.C. (El Afuleh). Severely wounded, 1918 (Irbid). Solidaridad medal of Panamanian Republic (for Irbid). 1914–15 Star.

Lieut. N. H. Broadway (1916–17). Killed, December 1st, 1917 (Cambrai).

Captain H. Banister (1914–18). I.A.R.O. (Indian Education Dept.). Quartermaster, 1914–18. 1914–15 Star.

Captain O. A. Duke (1915–18), 22nd Cavalry F.F.(Attached). Regimental Bombing Officer, 1915–18. Commanded D Squadron at Cambrai. 1914–15 Star.

Captain V. Sherwood-Smith (1914–17). 32nd Lancers (Attached). Hotchkiss Officer, 1916–18. 1914–15 Star.

Lieut. B. Wilson (1915–16) (Planter). I.A.R.O. Invalided out, 1916. 1914–15 Star.

Lieut. A. Buck (1915). 1914–15 Star.

Captain G. Hearsey (1915–17). I.A.R.O. 1914–15 Star.

Lieutenant W. Dorling (1915–16). Indian Volunteer Officer (Planter). 1914–15 Star.

Captain H. G. Monks (1915–17). I.A.R.O. (Planter). Attached R.F.C., 1917. 1914–15 Star.

Captain L. J. Peck, M.C. (1915–20). I.A.R.O. (Indian Finance Dept.). D.R. in Indian Corps, 1915. M.C. (Cambrai) Offg. Adjutant, 1918. 1914–15 Star.

Captain J. A. Nash (1916–18). Res. of Officers (Imperial Bank of India, Calcutta). Served with a British Regiment, 1914. Commanded Indian Transit Camp, Suez, 1918–19. 1914 Star (bar).

Lieutenant J. Lyng (1916). Res. of Officers. Severely wounded, Neuville St. Vaast, 1916. 1914–15 Star.

Captain G. Murphy (1916–17). I.A.R.O. (Mining Engineer). 1914–15 Star.

Captain V. W. Smith, M.C. (1916–18), I.A.R.O. (Allahabad Bank, Calcutta). Signalling Officer, 1917–1918. M.C.

(Cambrai). Brigade Signalling Officer, Lucknow Cavalry Brigade, 1918–1919.

Captain F. Jackson (1916–18). Oudh and Rohilkand Rly. Vols. Attached Mysore Lancers, 1918–19.

Lieutenant F. T. Commeline (1916–19). German S.W. Africa, 1914. Signalling Officer, 1918–1919. 1914–15 Star.

Captain L. D. W. Hearsey, M.C. (1916–20). I.A.R.O. M.C. (Ghoraniyeh).

Captain B. C. Waller (1916–18). 36th Jacob's Horse.

Captain R. P. L. Ranking. M.C. (1916–19). Offg. Adjutant, 1918–1919. M.C. (Palestine).

Lieutenant C. D. Pritchard (1917–18).

Captain C. E. L. Harris (1917–20). Served in British Regiment, 1915, in France. Offg. Adjutant, 1919–1920. 1914–15 Star.

Lieut. G. Lawler (1917–20). A.D.C., 10th Cavalry Brigade, 1919. Killed, 1920 (Beisan).

Captain G. L. Silver (1917–20). Quartermaster, 1919–20.

Captain E. St. J. King, M.C. (1917–20). M.C. (El Afuleh). Signalling Officer, 1919–20.

Captain J. H. Wilkinson (1917–19). Quartermaster, 1918–19. A.D.C., 10th Cavalry Brigade, 1919.

Lieut. R. H. F. Turner (1917–19). Attached R.A.F., 1917.

Lieut. E. C. Johnson (1919–20). Attached 19th Lancers, 1918.

Captain G. Penn-Simkins (1919–20). Offg. Adjutant 1919–1920.

Lieutenant A. Brooke (1919–20). Attached 16th Cavalry, 1918.

Captain F. J. C. Bloomfield (1920). Brigade Signalling Officer in 5th Cavalry Division, 1919–20.

Lieutenant G. W. Bomford (1919–20). A.D.C., 10th Cavalry Brigade, 1920.

Lieutenant Studdy (1920). I.A.R.O. (Indian Police). Quartermaster, 1920. Served with Mysore Lancers, 1918. Despatches.

Lieutenant D. Raymond (1917–18). Westmorland and Cumberland Yeomanry. Served with own regiment in France, 1915–17. Despatches. Attached Mysore Lancers, 1918. Killed at Aleppo, 1918. 1914–15 Star.

Q

Lieut. H. Irwin (1918). I.C.S. (D.C. Saugor, 1913). A.P.M., 4th Cavalry Division, 1918.

Major J. H. Beer (1915). Sussex Yeomanry. Killed.

Lieutenant R. G. Seymour (1915). Royal North Devon Hussars.

Lieutenant L. A. Downey (1915). Sussex Yeomanry.

Lieutenant M. C. Hayter (1915). County of London Yeomanry. Killed.

Lieutenant A. B. Bullock-Webster (1917–18).

Lieutenant W. C. G. Norris (1917).

Lieut. G. L. Mallam (1917–18).

Hon. Lieutenant Ganga Dat, Bahadur (1914–18). Risaldar Major. O.B.I., 2nd Class. 1914–15 Star.

Hon. Lieutenant Mukand Singh, Bahadur, M.C. (1914–20). Wounded Cote Wood. O.B.I., 2nd Class. M.C. (Cambrai). Risaldar Major. 1914–15 Star.

Risaldar Major Mohammed Raza Khan (1914–16). 1914–15 Star.

Risaldar Bhajju Singh (1914–16). 1914–15 Star.

Risaldar Suraj Singh, Bahadur, I.O.M. (1914–20). Asst. A.P.M., Indian Cavalry Corps, 1914–15. I.O.M., 2nd Class. O.B.I., 2nd Class. 1914–15 Star.

Risaldar Mukh Ram (1914–19). 1914–15 Star.

Risaldar Jiwan Singh, I.D.S.M. (1914–20). I.D.S.M. (Beisan). 1914–15 Star.

Risaldar Diwan Chand (1914–18). 1914–15 Star.

Risaldar Abdul Latif Khan, I.D.S.M. (1914–20). I.D.S.M. (Authuille). 1914–15 Star.

Risaldar Krishan Chandra Singh, I.D.S.M. (1914–20). I.D.S.M. (Cambrai). 1914–15 Star.

Risaldar Imdad Khan (1914–20). Wounded. 1914–15 Star.

Risaldar Het Ram, I.D.S.M. (1914–20). I.D.S.M. (Cambrai). Wounded Cote Wood. 1914–15 Star.

Risaldar Bharpur Singh (1914–20). Wounded. 1914–15 Star.

Risaldar Devi Chand (1914–19). 1914–15 Star.

Risaldar Jang Bahadur Singh, I.D.S.M. (1914–20). I.D.S.M (El Afuleh). 1914–15 Star.

Risaldar Lehri Singh (1914–20). 1914–15 Star.

Risaldar Abdul Wahid Khan (1914–20). 1914–15 Star.
Risaldar Udey Singh (1914–20). 1914–15 Star.
Ressaidar Tek Singh (1914–17). 1914–15 Star.
Ressaidar Kehri Singh (1914–20). 1914–15 Star.
Ressaidar Habib-ul-Rahman Khan (1914–15). 1914–15 Star.
Ressaidar Molar (1914–17). 1914–15 Star.
Ressaidar Raj Singh (1914–18). Killed Irbid. 1914–15 Star.
Jemadar Guranditta (1914–18). 1914–15 Star.
Jemadar Mahommed Yusaf Khan (1914–20). Wounded. 1914–15 Star.
Jemadar Afzal Husain (1914–20). 1914–15 Star.
Jemadar Prag Singh (1914–18). Wounded and Prisoner of War (Cambrai). 1914–15 Star.
Jemadar Brij Lal (1914–20). 1914–15 Star.
Jemadar Teja Singh (1914–20). 1914–15 Star.
Jemadar Richha Ram (1914–20). 1914–15 Star.
Jemadar Ata Mahommed Khan (1914–20). Wounded and Prisoner of War (Jordan). 1914–15 Star.
Jemadar Sarjit Singh (1914–20). M.S.M. 1914–15 Star.
Jemadar Kanhiya Singh (1914–20). 1914–15 Star.
Jemadar Basti Singh (1914–19). M.S.M. Wounded. 1914–15 Star.
Jemadar Sanjam Singh (1914–20). Wounded. 1914–15 Star.
Jemadar Dalla Ram (1914–20). 1914–15 Star.
Jemadar Dharam Singh, I.D.S.M. (1914–20). I.D.S.M. (Cambrai). 1914–15 Star.
Jemadar Guranditta Mal (1914–20). M.S.M. 1914–15 Star.
Jemadar Taj Mahommed (1914–20). 1914–15 Star.
Jemadar Karam Singh (1917–19) 4th Cavalry. With own regiment 1914 (France). 1914 Star (bar).
Ressaidar Sheo Baksh Singh (1916–17). 5th Cavalry. Killed Cambrai.
Ressaidar Hazur Ahmed (1916–18). 5th Cavalry.
Ressaidar Jot Ram (1916–18). 5th Cavalry.
Jemadar Hari Singh (1916–18). 5th Cavalry.

Jemadar Sughar Singh (1916–18). 5th Cavalry.

Jemadar Kale Khan (1915–19). 8th Cavalry. 1914–15 Star.

Risaldar Azam Ali Khan, I.D.S.M. (1916–17). 22nd Cavalry F.F.

Jemadar Kesar Singh (1915–18). 22nd Cavalry F.F. 1914–15 Star.

Jemadar Gobind Singh, V.C. (1914–19). 28th Lt. Cavalry. V.C. (Cambrai). 1914–15 Star.

Jemadar Dhara Singh, I.D.S.M. (1914–17). 32nd Lancers. Wounded and I.D.S.M. (Cambrai). 1914–15 Star.

Jemadar Mohammed Ali (1914–16, 1920). 32nd Lancers. Served with Hedjaz forces, 1917 to 1919.

BRITISH OFFICERS WHO SERVED AT THE DEPOT BUT NOT WITH THE REGIMENT IN THE FIELD.

Major A. N. De V. Scott (Commanded Depot, 1914–1920).
Lieutenant G. E. Gateley, I.A.R.O.
Captain G. J. A. Macmullen, I.A.R.O.
Captain R. Ambler.
Lieutenant J. K. O'Moore-Farrell.
Lieutenant S. H. Johnson.
Lieutenant J. H. Clapp.
Lieutenant J. F. F. Barnes.
Lieutenant L. Lipscomb.
Lieutenant H. B. Dalrymple-Hay.
Lieutenant A. D. Macnamara.
Lieutenant H. V. Sutherland-Hawes.
Lieutenant S. Bremner.
Lieutenant G. E. R. Edgcombe.
Captain R. L. Duchesne.

www.ingramcontent.com/pod-product-compliance
Lightning Source LLC
Chambersburg PA
CBHW030406100426
42812CB00028B/2849/J